The Ultimate Guide

to

Offshore Tax

Havens

Samuel Blankson

ISBN: 1-4116-2384-3

Acknowledgements

I give full thanks to God (for filling my cup to overflowing and guiding me through the valley of the shadow of death), my wonderful wife Uju for making the journey fun and always being there for me, and my friends and family for their tireless belief.

Contents

Introduction

Let us now look offshore to the places you could move your business, family, and investments, to gain privacy, security, and a reduction or total elimination of your taxes.

Before you read any further, you need to decide if moving offshore is the right decision for you. You can regularly move between half a dozen high tax countries without incurring major taxes, as long as you do not generate any sources of income in these countries, or overstay the minimum period to become a taxable resident there. By the latter, I mean that you should never stay for longer than the 182 days[1] that normally entitles you to be considered a resident for tax purposes. For instance, if you spend less than 3 months a year in the US, UK, Australia, Canada, or in the many European and Asian developed countries, you would never qualify as a resident for tax purposes, yet you could enjoy the benefits of these countries whilst avoiding their associated tax headaches. To do this, you must first make sure that you are in a financial position to afford such a lifestyle.

One option would be to move yourself and your family around regularly. However, considerations such as schooling or friends for the children etc, would greatly limit you here, unless you were to take on all your family's assets through special offshore trusts, and a carefully drafted will. To avoid moving your family around, you could leave your family in one country, and support them with sufficient funds that would avoid attracting major taxes whilst you, the main tax liability, moved around to avoid attracting huge tax bills.

However, there are better ways than this complex and inconvenient lifestyle for cutting your taxes. You can relocate the whole family to an offshore tax haven. You can pick any of the many tens of locations that best suit you and your family. We will now explore this option by looking at the offshore options available to you worldwide.

Why Consider Moving Offshore

The benefit for doing anything offshore is normally related to tax avoidance and legal freedom. Many tax havens around the world offer financial security through government legislation, as well as privacy through their banking laws.

---

[1] This residency period is roughly 182 days a year on average for developed countries, the period differs from country to country. Even in the countries that allow 182 days, there are special rules if you stay more than 3 months a year over a set amount of years, e.g. you may become a resident if you stay for 3 months a year, for over 3 years.

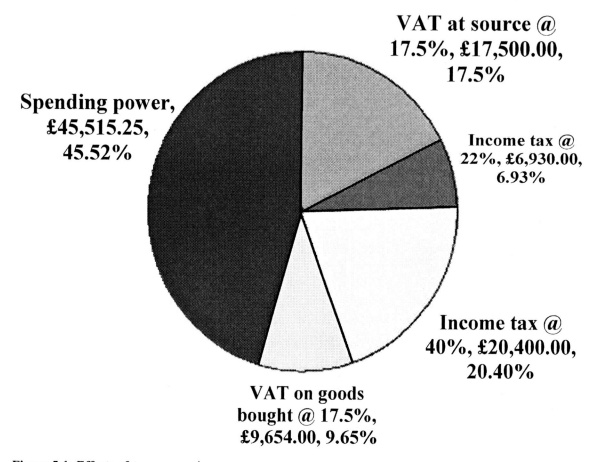

Figure 5-1: Effects of tax on your income

Many countries have restrictive tax laws that will erode your profits and often limit your spending power. In the UK, VAT is charged on most goods at a rate of 17.5%. Income tax is charged at a three-tiered rate depending on your income.

For example, if you generated £100,000 per annum, you would pay £17,500 before you received your gross income of £82,500. This £17,500 VAT would be kept by your employer, and paid back to Customs and Excise at the end of their business year. (If you were VAT registered and self-employed you would do the same). You would loose £6,930 from the remaining £82,500 to income tax at the lower rate (charged at 22% up to £31500), and £20,400 to income tax at the higher rate (charged at 40% after £31,500). You would be taxed a further 17.5% for VAT on all the goods and services you bought with the remaining £55,170. That would leave you with £45,516.00. See the chart in Figure 5-1 for a visual representation of the effects of these taxes on your income. This means that in total, you would loose 54.48%[2] of your generated income to taxes.

_____

[2] This value would be increased further because it does not include all the other taxes covered in the previous Onshore section, i.e. road tax, TV license, council tax etc. You may be able to offset some of these taxes as already mentioned in the Onshore section.

If however, you generated all this income offshore and you lived in a tax haven, you would earn £100,000 and keep £100,000. Do you think it is worth relocating offshore, to save 54.48% of your generated income?

See *http://www.lowtax.net* for a full listing of the offshore jurisdictions, and their detailed reports. Also, see Appendix 2 for a full listing.

Types Of Tax Havens

Not all tax havens are free from all taxes. Some of them offer a lower rate tax, or tax their businesses but not their citizens. Others tax their investors but not their locals, or visa versa. Because of this, you will need to be clear on exactly what you want to do offshore. Will you keep funds offshore, and invest from there internationally? Will you relocate there and become a resident? Will you start a business offshore and generate your income offshore? These options and many combinations of these options are available to you. By deciding which option to take, you will eliminate some of the countries from your list.

The geographical location of the country that you finally select will require great consideration. Do you want to live in a warm country or a cooler one? Do you want to live in a country with a culture that is similar to that of your current home? Alternatively, would you prefer to get away from it all? Do you need to be closer to Europe, America etc, or is the world your oyster?

The national language of the country will also play a part in your decision. Do you want French, English, Spanish, Portuguese, German, or another language to be the main language of the offshore jurisdiction?

The infrastructure of the country will also play a large part in your decision. Do you need the country to have modern communications, public transport, medical facilities, and utilities, or are you prepared to live somewhere without some of these amenities and facilities? Do you need a fax machine, internet, mobile phone etc to do business, and feel comfortable? If you do, you will have to avoid the under developed jurisdictions.

The cost of living in the chosen jurisdiction will determine whether you are financially able to afford the lifestyle in the offshore jurisdiction. In some offshore havens in Europe and the Caribbean, the cost of living is comparable to some western countries.

Security issues are perhaps the most important consideration. Is the country safe? Is there a military government? Are the government and policing forces corrupt? When last was the country involved in a civil war? Have they ever been involved in military action against their neighbours? Are there terrorists operating in the country? What is the crime rate? How are foreigners treated?

Finally, after you have eliminated all the jurisdictions that do not match your requirements, a handful will be left. The best way to finalise your decision is to travel to the jurisdictions and live there for a few months. This is sufficient time to decide whether you want to settle there or not.

Living in an offshore haven is perhaps the best way of accelerating the growth of your net worth. This is because you are saving money through spending less due to a lower cost of living, as well as eliminating loss of income through heavy taxes.

There are many more advantages to living in a tax haven, however for an investor, the privacy of banking, exemption from taxes, and a better quality of life, are often the most important.

For a list of offshore banks, visit *http://www.worldoffshorebanks.com.*

Offshore Havens

We will focus on three identified considerations when deciding on the offshore jurisdiction to select for relocation. These are:

Language
Geography
Religion

Language

Relocation is difficult enough without having to deal with a foreign language. For very few, moving to a country that speaks a different first language is desirable, as perhaps they want to learn that language, but the vast majority would like to move to a country which speaks the same language they are accustomed to. For this purpose, I have arranged the offshore havens linguistically. The main languages represented are:

English
French
Spanish
Italian
Portuguese
Russian
Indian
Chinese
Japanese
Swahili

Geography

As most of you have ties in your old country of residence, it will be favourable for the offshore locations you chose to be close to home. This will allow for regular visits to family and friends, and allow family and friends to visit you. Therefore, we will divide the world into nine sectors, to meet this geographic goal. These geographic divisions are:

North America and Canada.
South America.
Western Europe.

Eastern Europe and Russia.
Mediterranean, the Aegean, and North Africa.
Africa.
The Indian Ocean and the Middle East.
Asia and the Orient.
Australasia and Oceania.

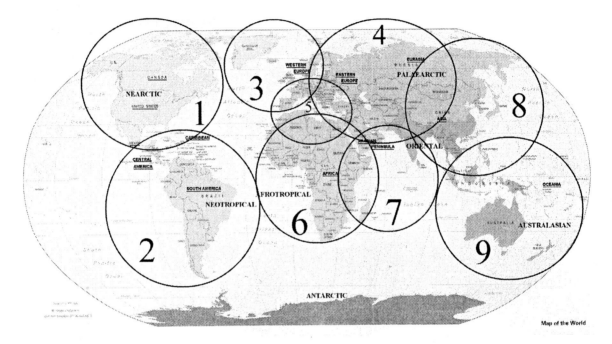

Figure 5-2: Geographic division for offshore selection

Religion

For some, religion is the most important factor to consider when moving offshore. For this purpose, I have included information on the religious representation in each offshore tax haven. These include the following:

Muslim.
Judaism and Christian.
Eastern (Hinduism, Taoism, Buddhism, Jainism, Sikhism etc).

See Appendix 3 for a list of states and their official religions.

Chapter 1

- *North America And Caanada*

North America And Canada

For Canadian and US citizens', choosing an offshore tax haven is easier because you have so much choice. Let us explore these choices further.

Some maps and data in this section are presented courtesy of the CIA World Factbook. You can find the fact book at the following website: *http://www.cia.gov/cia/publications/factbook.*

Canada

http://canada.gc.ca/main_e.html

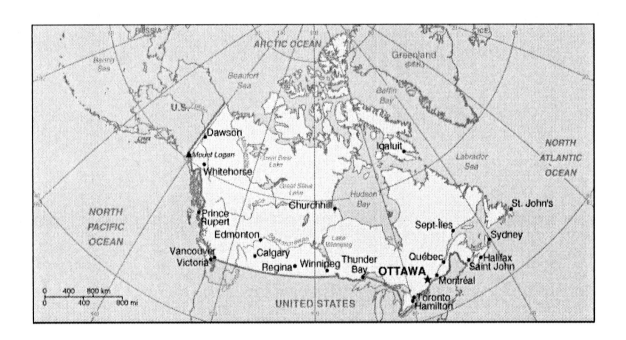

Associations:	N/A.
Banking:	See *http://muslim-investor.com, http://muslim-investor.com/news/ royal-bank-of-canada-islamic-investment .html* for Muslims and *http://www.aaadir.com/countries .jsp?ID=31.*

Business:	Canada does not tax you on your world income and assets within the first five years of trading in Canada. All Canadian derived income is taxed at high rates of 30% and above, although there are special concessions for film companies, and other types of companies. See *http://www.cra-arc.gc.ca/formspubs/t1general/ 2003/ menu-e.html* for more details.
Climate:	Varies from temperate in south to sub arctic and arctic in north.
Communications:	Excellent.
Corporate Tax:	0% of your offshore assets and incomes within the first five years stay in Canada. After five years, taxes are very high (over 55% in some cases).
Currency:	Dollar ($).
Entry and exit:	505 paved airports, and 852 unpaved airports.
GDP per capita:	$29,700 (2003 est.).
Language:	English 59.3% (official), French 23.2% (official), other 17.5%.
Location:	Northern North America, bordering the North Atlantic Ocean on the east, North Pacific Ocean on the west, and the Arctic Ocean on the north, north of the conterminous US.
Main industry:	Transportation equipment, chemicals, processed and unprocessed minerals, food products, wood and paper products, fish products, petroleum, and natural gas.
National disasters:	Continuous permafrost in north is a serious obstacle to development; cyclonic storms form east of the Rocky Mountains, (a result of the mixing of air masses from the Arctic, Pacific, and North American interior), and produce most of the country's rain and snow east of the mountains.
Non-resident stay:	183 days.
Personal Tax:	0%, if you stay less than 183 days in any tax year.
Religions:	Roman Catholic 46%, Protestant 36%, other 18%. Note: based on the 1991 census.
Stability:	Managed maritime boundary disputes with the US at Dixon Entrance, Beaufort Sea, Strait of Juan de Fuca, around the disputed Machias Seal Island and North Rock; and there is the uncontested dispute with Denmark over Hans Island sovereignty in the Kennedy Channel between Ellesmere Island and Greenland.

Muslim community information:
http://muslim-canada.org/

Jewish community information:
http://www.haruth.com /JewsCanada.html

Christian community information:
http://www.praize.ca/

Hindu community information:
www.hindu.org/temples-ashrams/#Canada

Sikh community information:
www.sikhwomen.com/community/Canada

Buddhist community information:
http://www.buddhismcanada.com

Jainism community information:
http://www.kutchi.com/JainTemples.html

Canada can be used as a stepping-stone to going totally offshore. It has been voted the best place to work and live in the world. The Canadian government has structured their tax laws in such a way as to allow new Canadian citizens or immigrants up to five years stay in Canada without taxing their non-Canadian based income or assets. These assets can be protected via a trust or corporation before moving to Canada.

This is great news for all world citizens who are investors, wealthy (can show a net worth over C$500,000, and can invest C$250,000 into Canada), business owners (with over C$750,000, and with a business plan in a qualifying trade that will provide employment to Canadians), or employed by a qualifying Canadian business in international financial centres like Montreal.

Canada will allow qualifying applicants to get citizenship. US citizens should seek acceptance through ancestry claims first. Your world assets will be untaxed by Canada for the first 5 years. Because of this, US citizens can move their assets offshore and protect them from capital gains (38%) and income tax (40%) with an offshore trust or offshore corporation before moving to Canada. Before the five-year period ends, control of these assets could be returned to the ex-US Canadian citizen. Find out more from *http://www.retirementhavens .com/residencehavens.*

Of course, Canada is no tax shelter after that initial five years have passed. You will have to move on before the five-year time limit runs out. Non- residents can stay in Canada and are allowed 183 days (see *http://www.cra-arc.gc.ca/tax/nonresidents/menu-e.html*) stay.

Canadians wishing to move from Canada's high income taxes can look to the US Nevada tax haven first before going totally offshore, see the next section.

See *http://www.lowtax.net/lowtax/html/offon/canada/canhom.asp* for further details.

USA

http://www.usa.gov

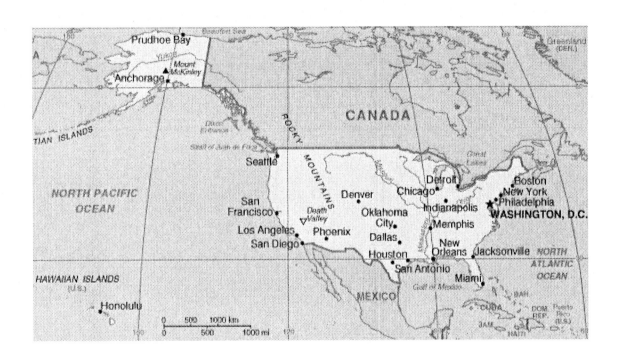

Associations:	N/A.
Banking:	*http://www.thecommunitybanker.com/bank_links/* (For further details, see *http://www.msa-natl.org/resources/Finance.html* and *http://islamic-finance.net/* for Muslims).
Business:	Offshore trusts, limited liability companies, and partnerships via Nevada tax haven.
Climate:	Mostly temperate, but tropical in Hawaii and Florida, arctic in Alaska, semiarid in the great plains west of the Mississippi River, and arid in the Great Basin of the southwest. Low winter temperatures in the northwest are ameliorated occasionally in January and February by warm Chinook winds from the eastern slopes of the Rocky Mountains.

Communications:	Excellent.
Corporate Tax:	0%, if you use Nevada tax haven companies and partnerships, as long as you do not have showrooms in U.S. (exports and imports), otherwise you will pay all the normal US taxes, which are high.
Currency:	Dollar ($).
Entry and exit:	5,128 paved airports, and 9,679 unpaved airports.
GDP per capita:	$37,800 (2003 est.).
Language:	English and Spanish (spoken by a sizable minority).
Location:	North America, bordering both the North Atlantic Ocean and the North Pacific Ocean, between Canada and Mexico.
Main industry:	Leading industrial power in the world, highly diversified and technologically advanced; petroleum, steel, motor vehicles, aerospace, telecommunications, chemicals, electronics, food processing, consumer goods, lumber, and mining.
National disasters:	Tsunamis, volcanoes, and earthquake activity around Pacific Basin; hurricanes along the Atlantic and Gulf of Mexico coasts; tornadoes in the Midwest and Southeast; mud slides in California; forest fires in the west; flooding; and permafrost in northern Alaska, a major impediment to development.
Non-resident stay:	153 days.
Personal Tax:	0%, if you stay less than 153 days in any tax year.
Religions:	Protestant 56%, Roman Catholic 28%, Jewish 2%, other 4%, and none 10% (1989).
Stability:	Prolonged drought, population growth, and outmoded practices and infrastructure in the border region has strained water-sharing arrangements with Mexico; undocumented nationals from Mexico and Central America continue to enter the United States illegally; 1990 Maritime Boundary Agreement in the Bering Sea still awaits Russian Duma ratification; managed maritime boundary disputes with Canada at Dixon Entrance, Beaufort Sea, Strait of Juan de Fuca, and around the disputed Machias Seal Island and North Rock; the Bahamas have not been able to agree on a maritime boundary; US Naval base at Guantanamo Bay is leased from Cuba and only mutual agreement or US abandonment of the area can terminate the lease; Haiti claims US-administered Navassa Island; US has made no territorial claim in Antarctica

(but has reserved the right to do so) and does not recognize the claims of any other state; Marshall Islands claims Wake Island. Currently at war with Iraq, Afghanistan and hostile towards, North Korea, Iran, Syria, Palestine, and Pakistan due to claimed harbouring of terrorists and support of terrorist activities harmful to the U.S.A.

Muslim community information:
http://www.alislam.org/contactus/

Jewish community information:
http://www.ujc.org/

Christian community information:
http://hirr.hartsem.edu/org/faith_denominations_ homepages.html

Hindu community information:
www.hindu.org/temples-ashrams/#Canada

Sikh community information:
http://allaboutsikhs.com/gurudwaras/gurud_55.htm

Buddhist community information:
http://www.buddhistinformation.com/

Jainism community information:
http://www.kutchi.com/Jainism.html

Although the U.S.A. has some of the highest taxes in the world, (especially estate and death tax), it also offers one of the best offshore tax havens. Business owners and investors from all over the world can make great use of the Nevada limited liability companies, partnerships, and trusts.

The Nevada based companies and partnerships are exempt from U.S. taxes for all of the following:

Income earned outside the U.S.
Gains from the sale of shares of corporate stock.
Non U.S. source interest and dividends.
U.S. bank interest.
Income from U.S. imports if no sales office is located in the U.S.
Income from U.S. exports to foreign countries if no sales office is located in the U.S.

In particular, the Nevada limited liability companies does not have to do the following:

File a U.S. tax return.
Pay U.S. income tax.

You can also use a U.S. trust to gain tax-exemption on:
Gains from the sale of shares of corporate stock.
Foreign source interest and dividends.
U.S. bank interest.

- Protecting you from being sued with a flee clause, allowing the trust to migrate offshore if a US court attempts jurisdiction over the trust.

For more information on income tax, treaties between the US and other countries, see *http://www.irs.gov/businesses/corporations/article/0,,id=96739, 00.html*.

Therefore, as you can see, the US Nevada tax haven may be able to help you. To live in the U.S. tax free, you will have to not over stay the 153 days (see *http://www.irs .gov/pub/irs-pdf/p519.pdf* for more information), unless you are a Canadian, in which case you could stay up to a year with a one-year extension.

See *http://www.lowtax.net/lowtax/html/offon/usa_new/usahom.asp* for more details. Also see *http://www.escapeartist.com/passports/passport_ facts5.html* for information on US citizens' correct procedures for severing the tax grip of U.S. government tax machine.

Bermuda

http://www.gov.bm/

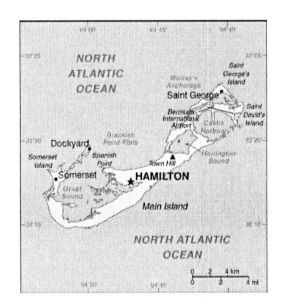

Associations:	United Kingdom.
Banking:	See *http://www.offshore-bank-list.com*.
Business:	Company incorporation and trusts. If you recruit locally, 12.75% payroll tax with 4.5% recoverable from employees wages. Social taxes levied against wages are currently $21.34 per week for the employee, and $21.34 per week for the employer (see *http://www. bermuda-online.org/employwp.htm* for work permit procedure).
Climate:	Subtropical, mild, humid, gales, and strong winds common in winter.
Communications:	Excellent.
Corporate Tax:	0%. Do not employ locally.
Currency:	Bermudian dollar (BMD).
Entry and exit:	One airport.

GDP per capita:	$36,000 (2003 est.).
Language:	English (official) and Portuguese.
Location:	North America, group of islands in the North Atlantic Ocean, east of South Carolina (US).
Main industry:	Tourism, international business, and light manufac-turing.
National disasters:	Hurricanes (June to November).
Non-resident stay:	You can apply for long-term residence. See *www.immigration .gov .bm.*
Personal Tax:	0% if your icome is not derived locally.
Religion:	Non Anglican Protestant 39%, Anglican 27%, Roman Catholic 15%, and other 19%. See *http://www. bermuda.com/categories /religion* for full contact list of all religions in Bermuda.
Stability:	Very stable.

Bermuda is very close to the US, and affords a high standard of living comparable to the US. It is a great place to carry out business and live, as long as your business does not recruit Bermudan staff. If you do recruit Bermudan staff, you will have to pay payroll and social taxes. Unless you marry a Bermudan for over 10 years and then apply, non-Bermudans cannot get citizenship. You can only buy houses if you pay 22% of the cost of the property to the government, and the property must have an Annual Rental Value (ARV) in excess of $43,800 (equivalent to a sale price of say $500,000). Expatriate long-term residency is limited to six years (see *http://www.bermuda. com/categories/relocating/ services.htm* for relocation help).

See *http://www.lowtax.net/lowtax/html/bermuda/jbrgat.html* and *http:// www.global-money.com/item.php?id=106* for further details.

Bahamas

http://www.bahamas.gov.bs

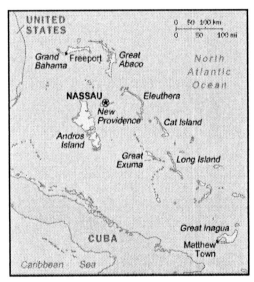

Associations:	UK Government.
Banking:	It has over 400 banks (see Appendix 4).
Business:	There are annual fees charged on businesses. Businesses are licensed and protected from the government.
Climate:	Tropical marine; moderated by warm waters of Gulf Stream.
Communications:	Excellent, with cellular, landline, and internet.
Corporate Tax:	0%.
Currency:	Bahamian dollar (BSD), pegged to the dollar $1=1BSD.
Entry and exit:	63 Airports (30 paved, and 33 unpaved).
GDP per capita:	$16,800 (2003 est.).
Language:	English (official), and Creole (among Haitian immigrants).
Location:	Caribbean, chain of islands in the North Atlantic Ocean, southeast of Florida, northeast of Cuba.

Main industry:	Tourism, banking, e-commerce, cement, oil refining and transhipment, salt, rum, aragonite, pharmaceuticals, and spiral-welded steel pipes.
National disasters:	Hurricanes and other tropical storms cause extensive floods and wind damage.
Non-resident stay:	You can get working permits as long as you do not compete for jobs with locals. To get permanent residence, you have to invest $500,000 or more into a home.
Personal Tax:	0%.
Religion:	Baptist 32%, Anglican 20%, Roman Catholic 19%, Methodist 6%, Church of God 6%, other Protestant 12%, none or unknown 3%, and other 2%.
Stability:	They have not been able to agree on a maritime boundary with the US. They are also concerned about refugees fleeing Haiti's deteriorated economic and political conditions.

Muslim community information:
http://www.islamicfinder.org/cityPrayer.php?Country =Bahamas

Jewish community information:
http://www.kosherdelight.com/Bahamas.htm

Christian community information:
http://www.whatsonbahamas.com/churches.lasso

The cost of living is low, but house prices are high for non-residents to buy in order to qualify for resident stay. Weather is fantastic and quality of life is excellent. There are no taxes if you just live there and do not work there or do business there, although you can do business there through an international company and still attract no taxes. Excellent location for ex-US residents, half an hours flight from Florida. Also close to Cuba, see map.

See *http://www.lowtax.net/lowtax/html/jbahom.html* for more details.

Chapter 2

- ***South America***

South America

The following tax havens can be used by both North and South American citizens. There are a broad range of languages (French (various including Canadian, Argentinean, and Brazilian), Spanish (various including Porto Rico), Portuguese (various including Brazil), and English (various including USA)). Moreover, although Christianity dominates this area, you will find Islam and Judaism, as well as some Hindu and Buddhist communities dotted within the list of Jurisdictions.

Cayman Islands

http://www.gov.ky

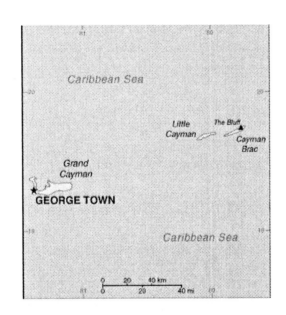

Associations:	United Kingdom.
Banking:	See *http://www.offshore-bank-list.com*.
Business:	A 50-year tax-exemption licence is offered for limited partnerships that do not carry out trade in the country. Incorporation fees for companies is less than CL$ 800, with annual fees not exceeding CL$600. For further details see *http://www.lowtax.net/lowtax/html/jcacos. html*.

Climate:	Tropical marine; warm, rainy summers (May to October) and cool, relatively dry winters (November to April).
Communications:	Good, with landline, cellular, and internet access.
Corporate Tax:	0%, with 7.5% stamp duty on transfer of property, and 1% for preparation of certain legal papers (securities, mutual funds, stock, and shares normally exempted).
Currency:	Caymanian dollar (KYD) $1 to 0.85 KYD.
Entry and exit:	2 paved airports, and 1 unpaved airport.
GDP per capita:	$35,000 (2002 est.).
Language:	English.
Location:	Caribbean, island group in Caribbean Sea, nearly one-half of the way from Cuba to Honduras.
Main industry:	Tourism, banking, insurance, finance, construction and construction materials, and furniture.
National disasters:	Hurricanes (June to November).
Non-resident stay:	Long-term residency will be granted to people willing to invest $180,000 into a property or local business. In addition, do not carry out any employment in the country. See *http://cayman .com.ky /reside.htm* for more details.
Personal Tax:	0% if you are not employed locally.
Religion:	United Church (Presbyterian and Congregational), Anglican, Baptist, Church of God, other Protestant, and Roman Catholic.
Stability:	Very stable.

The Cayman Islands are ideal for the Canadian, U.S., or other international individuals seeking to relocate. It has a very low crime rate and high standard of living. The best use of this island is to set up a trust or exempt limited partnership, and/or live there without seeking employment there.

Muslim community information:
http://www.tisci.org/

Jewish community information:
http://www.kosherdelight.com/Cayman.htm

Christian community information:
www.caymanvacations.com/indexmenu.htm?general/religion_churches. htm&2

St. Vincent and the Grenadines

http://www.svgtourism.com/

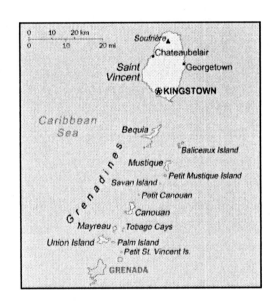

Associations:	UK Government.
Banking:	Four Major banks. For more information online, visit *http://www.aaadir.com/countri es.jsp?ID=263*.
Business:	Low annual fees on business. Offers banking licences, International Business Companies (IBCs), and high privacy and protection laws.
Climate:	Tropical; little seasonal temperature variation. Rainy season May to November.
Communications:	Very good, with cellular, landline, and internet supplied by Cable and Wireless.
Corporate Tax:	0% if you do not employ local staff.
Currency:	East Caribbean dollar (XCD). Pegged to US dollar at $1 to 2.7XCD.

Entry and exit:	6 airports (5 paved, and 1 unpaved). No direct flights out of the Caribbean.
GDP per capita:	$2,900 (2002 est.).
Language:	English and French Patois.
Location:	Caribbean, islands between the Caribbean Sea and North Atlantic Ocean, north of Trinidad and Tobago.
Main industry:	Food processing, cement, furniture, clothing, and starch.
National disasters:	Hurricanes; the Soufriere volcano on the island of Saint Vincent is a constant threat.
Non-resident stay:	You can get working permits as long as you do not compete for jobs with locals. To get permanent residence, you have to invest $500,000 or more into a home.
Personal Tax:	0% if you do not draw a local wage there.
Religion:	Anglican 47%, Methodist 28%, Roman Catholic 13%, Hindu, Seventh-Day Adventist, and Protestant.
Stability:	Very stable. Joins other Caribbean states to counter Venezuela's claim that Aves Island sustains human habitation, a criterion under UNCLOS, which permits Venezuela to extend its EEZ/continental shelf over a large portion of the Caribbean Sea. It has a low crime rate.

This is a beautiful yet very cheap place to live. It offers privacy and secrecy. No reporting required for IBCs. Low cost of offshore bank licence and IBC. It is 1500 miles from America. The only downside might be that you need to get connecting flights to reach it or depart from there. These however are numerous and frequent. It is a tropical paradise with low crime and a very obliging government.

Anguilla

http://www.gov.ai/

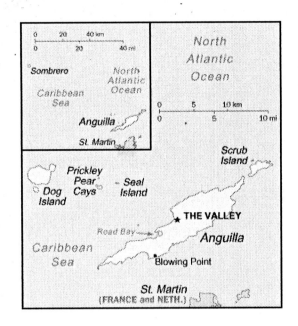

Associations:	French and Spanish Governments.
Banking:	See *http://www.anguillaoffshore.com/b_banks.htm*, and *http://www. offshore-bank-list.com/sitemap.html*.
Business:	Extremely flexible laws.
Climate:	Tropical: moderated by northeast trade winds.
Communications:	Modern telecoms infrastructure with internet connect-ivity available.
Corporate Tax:	0%.
Currency:	Eastern Caribbean Dollar (EC$) and United States Dollar (US$).
Entry and exit:	Direct flights to:

- Puerto Rico - British Airways and major American carriers, including American, Delta, and United.

- St Maarten - K.L.M., B.W.I.A., American Airlines, Air Canada, Continental, Air France, and United Airlines.
- Antigua - British Airways, Air Canada, American Airlines, and B.W.I.A.

LIAT, Tyden Air, and Winair also provide direct flights to Puerto Rico, St Maarten and Antigua.

GDP per capita:	$9,000 with no taxes.
Language:	English (official).
Location:	Caribbean, islands between the Caribbean Sea and North Atlantic Ocean, east of Puerto Rico.
Main industry:	Tourism (mainly high end) and financial services.
National disasters:	Frequent hurricanes and other tropical storms (July to October).
Non-resident stay:	Carry out business that recruits citizens and you will get a four-year working pas, easily renewable.
Personal Tax:	0%.
Religion:	Anglican 40%, Methodist 33%, Seventh-Day Adventist 7%, Baptist 5%, Roman Catholic 3%, other 12%.
Stability:	Has never had international dispute.

Advantages of Anguilla:

UK overseas territory.
Well-regulated financial services industry.
Common law legal system based on English law.
Well-developed professional infrastructure.
Same day company incorporation service.
World standard telecommunications system.
Easy air access to North America and Europe.
Neutral tax jurisdiction.
No foreign exchange restrictions.
Multi-year work permits available for professionals within the financial services industry.

Best place for non-UK expatriates seeking to set up a company or trust. You can get a four-year work permit to live in and work in this no tax, ultra low crime rate island, in the Caribbean Sea.

Aruba

http://www.aruba.com/home.htm

Associations:	Dutch Government.
Banking:	*http://www.offshore-bank-list.com/sitemap.html.*
Business:	Free trade zone.
Climate:	Tropical marine; little seasonal temperature variation.
Communications:	Very modern telecoms with internet, GSM, and land-lines.
Corporate Tax:	0%.
Currency:	Aruban guilder/florin (AWG) tied to $ and 1.79 AWG to $1.
Entry and exit:	One airport.
GDP per capita:	$30,000 has one of the highest standards of living in the West Indies.

Language:	Dutch (official), Papiamento (a Spanish, Portuguese, Dutch, and English dialect), English (widely spoken), and Spanish.
Location:	Caribbean, island in the Caribbean Sea, north of Venezuela.
Main industry:	Tourism, offshore banking, oil refinery, and storage.
National disasters:	None. Aruba is outside the Caribbean belt.
Non-resident stay:	90 dayd stay for non-Dutch. 180 days for Dutch. 14 days for visa holders. Visa not required for US, EU and Canadian nationals. For longer stays, you can get a temporary residence permit, but are restricted to not compete for jobs with Aruban nationals (you cannot work there whilst living there). No restrictions on real estate purchases.
Personal Tax:	0%.
Religion:	Roman Catholic 82%, Protestant 8%, Hindu, Muslim, Confucian, and Jewish.
Stability:	No international disputes.

With pleasant weather and locals, Aruba is ideal to do so much in. You can run a business and recruit locals, invest, and live there tax free. However, do not try to seek employment, either start your own business, or run your business elsewhere.

Muslim community information:
http://www.islamicfinder.org/getitWorld.php ?id=38050&lang=

Jewish community information:
http://www.ujcl.org/aruba/

Christian community information:
http://www.aruba-travelguide.com/churches/

Barbados

http://www.barbados.gov.bb/

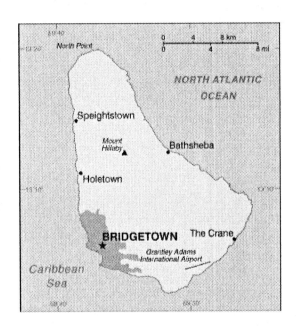

Associations:	United Kingdom.
Banking:	See *http://www.offshore-bank-list.com*.
Business:	High taxes (interest, dividend, withholding, rent, services, payment under settlement, royalties, management fees and more), land tax, stamp duty, and more. With very smart tax planning, you could operate a business there tax free. However, is it worth the hassle?
Climate:	Tropical. Rainy season (June to October).
Communications:	Good, with cellular, landline, and internet.
Corporate Tax:	High and complex. See *http://www.lowtax.net/lowtax/html/ jbsdctx.html*.
Currency:	Barbadian dollar (BBD).

Entry and exit:	One airport.
GDP per capita:	$16,200 (2003 est.).
Language:	English.
Location:	Caribbean, island in the North Atlantic Ocean, northeast of Venezuela.
Main industry:	Tourism, sugar, light manufacturing, and component assembly for export.
National disasters:	Infrequent hurricanes; periodic landslides.
Non-resident stay:	182 days per year. Aim for a non-resident status to avoid tax and VAT on all but your Barbados derived incomes, including income from an office or employment exercised there. World income is taxable for residents.
Personal Tax:	0% for non-residents.
Religion:	Protestant 67% (Anglican 40%, Pentecostal 8%, Methodist 7%, other 12%), Roman Catholic 4%, none 17%, and other 12%.
Stability:	Barbados intends to take its claim before UNCLOS arbitration that the northern limit of Trinidad and Tobago's maritime boundary with Venezuela extends into its waters; and joins other Caribbean states to counter Venezuela's claim that Aves Island sustains human habitation, a criterion under UNCLOS, which permits Venezuela to extend its EEZ/continental shelf over a large portion of the Caribbean Sea.

Although lovely, this country is only worth becoming a resident if you want to be constantly paying excessive fees to expert tax planners to help you avoid the high taxes. Businesses are subject to high taxes, but careful planning can virtually eliminate these.

Muslim community information:
http://www.islamicfinder.org/getitWorld.php?id=37806&lang=

Jewish community information:
http://www.kosherdelight.com/Barbados.htm

Christian community information:
www.caribbeanonlineyellowpages.com/listings_5/5_category_C_3747.html

United States Virgin Islands

http://www.senate.gov.vi/

http://www.gov.vi/

http://www.usvi.net/

http://www.usvitourism.vi/

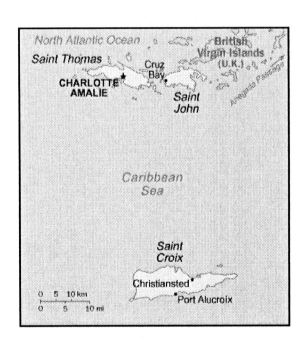

Associations:	United States of America.
Banking:	For further details see *http://www.see-caribbean.com /usvi/banks/* for details.
Business:	See *http://www.usvi.net/usvi/tax.html* for further details. You can utilise the US Virgin Islands for the following tax efficient offshore structures: Aircraft registration.

	Captive insurance.

Captive insurance.
Exempt companies.
Foreign sales corporations.
Inbound and outbound re-domiciliation of companies is permitted.

Climate:	Subtropical, tempered by easterly trade winds, relatively low humidity, little seasonal temperature variation; rainy season May to November.
Communications:	Very good.
Corporate Tax:	<ul><li>No sales taxes.</li><li>0% for exempt companies and foreign sales corporations. If you apply and are accepted for Industrial Development Program, you will be exempt from all taxes and only pay 1% customs duty.</li><li>Maximum graduated rate = 38.5% (this is compiled from a 10% surcharge and normal federal rates of the USA).</li><li>Real estate tax = 1.25% annually of 60% of actual property value.</li><li>Gross receipts tax = 4% for businesses with annual gross receipts of over $150,000. (These companies pay no tax on the first $5,000 of each month's gross receipts. After that they pay the 4% as usual).</li><li>Customs and Excise tax and duties = 4% with tourist items exempt from duties, and cigarettes and other goods charged at 6%. Alcohol is charged at a flat rate based on volume.</li></ul>
Currency:	US dollar (USD).
Entry and exit:	2 paved airports.
GDP per capita:	$19,000 (2001 est.).
Language:	English (official), Spanish, and Creole.
Location:	Caribbean, islands between the Caribbean Sea and the North Atlantic Ocean, east of Puerto Rico.
Main industry:	Tourism, petroleum refining, watch assembly, rum distilling, construction, pharmaceuticals, textiles, and electronics.
National disasters:	Several hurricanes in recent years; frequent and severe droughts and floods; and occasional earthquakes.
Non-resident stay:	A visa is required by non-US or non-Canadian citizens for up to 90 days stay. Do not over stay 90 days. Canadian and United

States citizens only need prove that they are citizens of the US or Canada.

Personal Tax:	0% for non-residents. See below for residents' taxes.
Religion:	Baptist 42%, Roman Catholic 34%, Episcopalian 17%, and other 7%.
Stability:	Very Stable.

These islands offer a brilliant way to keep your US or Canadian citizenship, whilst drastically cutting back on your taxes. Be aware you will loose your rights to vote in presidential elections if you become a citizen of the US Virgin Islands. For the rest of us, to avoid taxes, use the free zones offshore structures and avoid citizenship or permanent residency.

Saint Lucia

http://www.interknowledge.com/st-lucia

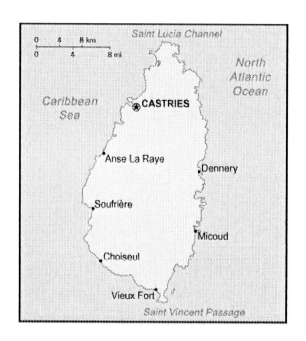

Associations:	United Kingdom.
Banking:	See Appendix 5.
Business:	For further details see *http://www.offshoreinvestment.com/survey/* and *http://www.stluciandc.com/*.
Climate:	Tropical, moderated by northeast trade winds; dry season from January to April, rainy season from May to August.
Communications:	Very good.
Corporate Tax:	0%.
Currency:	East Caribbean dollar (XCD). See *www.xe.com* for further details.

Entry and exit:	2 paved airports.
GDP per capita:	$5,400 (2002 est.).
Language:	English (official), and French Patois.
Location:	Caribbean, island between the Caribbean Sea and North Atlantic Ocean, north of Trinidad and Tobago.
Main industry:	Clothing, corrugated cardboard boxes, lime processing, beverages, tourism, assembly of electronic components, and coconut processing.
National disasters:	Hurricanes and volcanic activity.
Non-resident stay:	Invest in St Lucia through the purchase of a permanent residence, and live there continuously for five years. See *http://www.stluciacg.com/consulate/services_resi de nce.htm* for more information. You can become a citizen after a period of seven years residence. For further details, see *http://www.stluciacg.com*, and click the Citizenship link, or go to *www.stluciacg.com/consulate/ services_citizenship.htm* for further details.
Personal Tax:	0%. There are no income taxes or VAT levied in St Lucia. There is a 2% stamp duty on all property acquisitions. (See *http://www.rodney-bay.com/property_laws_regulations.shtml*).
Religion:	Roman Catholic 90%, Anglican 3%, Protestant and other 7%.
Stability:	Ultra stable - joins other Caribbean states to counter Venezuela's claim that Aves Island sustains human habitation, a criterion under UNCLOS, which permits Venezuela to extend its EEZ/continental shelf over a large portion of the Caribbean Sea.

This tax haven offers offshore company incorporation, citizenship, as well as the opportunity to buy freehold property. Situated in the Caribbean, it is ideal for those moving from high tax countries in the Americas or West Indian origin retirees.

Saint Pierre and Miquelon

http://www.st-pierre-et-miquelon.net

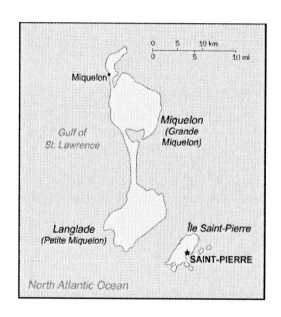

Associations:	France.
Business:	Consult *http://www.grandcolombier.com/sites.html*.
Climate:	Cold and wet, with much mist and fog; spring and autumn are windy.
Communications:	Poor.
Currency:	Euro (EUR).
Entry and exit:	2 paved airports.
GDP per capita:	$6,900 (2001 est.).
Language:	French (official).
Location:	Northern North America, islands in the North Atlantic Ocean,

south of Newfoundland (Canada).

Main industry:	Fish processing and supply base for fishing fleets; and tourism.
National disasters:	Persistent fog throughout the year, which can be a maritime hazard.
Non-resident stay:	A visa may be required if you are a non-EU, US, or Canadian citizen. 14-day travellers stay is standard, with 90 days permitted via application on arrival.
Religion:	Roman Catholic 99%.
Stability:	Very stable.

This cold and foggy North American member of the French republic is relatively close to Canada and the US. It is located about 15 miles south of Newfoundland: about 800 miles North-East from Boston, at the top of the Grand Banks of Newfoundland. Although it operates on French law, it has some special adaptations, which may be suited to those seeking lower taxes than the USA or Canada have to offer. It also gives you access to Europe through France.

Trinidad and Tobago

http://www.gov.tt/

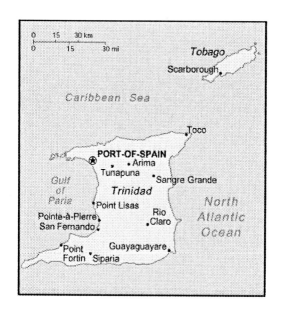

Climate:	Tropical; rainy season (June to December).
Currency:	Trinidad and Tobago dollar (TTD). See *www.xe.com* for current conversion rates.
Personal Tax:	0% for offshore companies, and companies operating in the free zone. Resident taxes are as follows: Income tax for residents is tiered up to 30%. Stamp duty and conveyance of real estate. Real estate taxes. Hotel room. Insurance premium tax. Road traffic licence. Vehicle transfer tax.

Betting, gaming, and lotteries tax.

Road improvement tax.

Double taxation treaties exist that could lower your residents taxes. See *http://www.tttax.com/* (T&T Investment Guide) for a full treatment of this topic.

Corporate Tax:

Withholding tax 20%.
Royalties are taxed at 20%.
Dividends 10% to 20%.
Corporation tax at 30% on chargeable profits.
Petroleum and petroleum companies at 35%.
Business levy at 2%.
Green fund levy at 0.10% on gross sales and receipts.

Petroleum taxes:
Petroleum profits tax at 50%.
Unemployment levy at 5%.

Supplemental Petroleum Tax (SPT):
Land operations at 5%.
Marine operations at 55%.
See *http://www.investtnt.com/Investguide/pdf/Investing%20in%20TnT%202003.pdf* for a full treatment of this subject.

Language:

English (official), Hindi, French, Spanish and Chinese.

Location:

Caribbean, islands between the Caribbean Sea and the North Atlantic Ocean, northeast of Venezuela.

Religion:

Roman Catholic 29.4%, Hindu 23.8%, Anglican 10.9%, Muslim 5.8%, Presbyterian 3.4%, and other 26.7%.

Stability:

Very Stable - Barbados will assert its claim before UNCLOS that the northern limit of Trinidad and Tobago's maritime boundary with Venezuela extends into its waters; Guyana has also expressed its intention to challenge this boundary as it may extend into its waters as well.

Communications:

Very good.

GDP per capita:

$9,600 (2003 est.).

Entry and exit:

6 airports (3 paved, and 3 unpaved).

Main industry:

Petroleum, chemicals, tourism, food processing, cement, beverage, and cotton textiles.

National disasters:	Usual path of hurricanes and other tropical storms.
Banking:	See *http://www.tntisland.com/ttbanks.html* for a full listing.
Business:	See *http://www.tidco.co.tt/* and *http://www.investtnt. com/* for further details. There are opportunities in the following sectors: Information technology. Food and beverage. Petrochemicals - chemicals, pharmaceuticals, and plastics. Metal processing. Printing and packaging. Leisure marine. Floriculture. Agriculture.
Non-resident stay:	Through investment, family, or skills that will benefit the islands. See *http://pubweb.fdbl.com/ihp8/global/media85.nsf/public-count ry-briefs/trinidadandtobago? opendocument* for full details.
Associations:	United Kingdom.

Conducting business in Trinidad and Tobago as a resident is not tax efficient, however, you can use the island's free trade zones and offshore structures to operate a 0% tax company. The islands are well connected to the USA and Europe, and offer an idyllic and stable residence. Beware of the double tax treaties with European and American countries.

Antigua & Barbuda

http://www.antigua-barbuda.com/

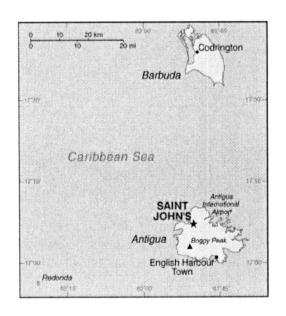

Associations:	United Kingdom.
Banking:	See *www.antiguaobserver.com/antigua/hcomerce.html* for further details.
Business:	Sole proprietorships. Partnerships. Branch of foreign corporations. Companies, public or private. See *http://www.antigua-barbuda.com/*.
Climate:	Tropical; little seasonal temperature variation.
Communications:	Very good.
Currency:	East Caribbean dollar (XCD). See *www.xe.com* for current conversion rates.

Entry and exit:	3 airports (2 paved, and 1 unpaved).
GDP per capita:	$11,000 (2002 est.).
Language:	English (official) and local dialects.
Location:	Caribbean, islands between the Caribbean Sea and the North Atlantic Ocean, east-southeast of Puerto Rico.
Main industry:	Tourism, construction and light manufacturing (clothing, alcohol, and household appliances).
National disasters:	Hurricanes and tropical storms (July to October); periodic droughts.
Non-resident stay:	For further details see *http://www.antigua-barbuda.com*.
Religion:	Christian, (predominantly Anglican, with some Protestant and some Roman Catholic).
Stability:	Ultra stable.

These paradise islands levy no personal taxes, and there are no export taxes except on lobsters, Sea Island cotton, sugar, molasses, and fish. Property owners pay a property tax based on the current construction value of the property, with a 0-20% surcharge depending on zoning regulations.

If you are thinking about setting up a commercial enterprise here, the islands levy a 40% corporation tax on incorporated companies, and 2% tax on unincorporated companies. However, the first $4,166 of your gross income in any calendar month is exempt from any corporation taxes. Commercial property owners pay three quarters of 1% of their taxable income, except hotels; they pay one fifth of 1% of their taxable value.

Montserrat

http://www.visitmontserrat.com/

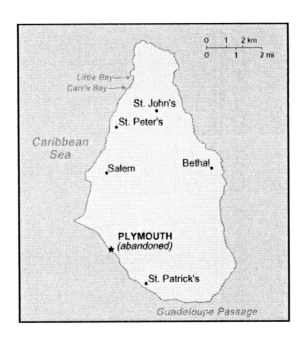

Associations:	United Kingdom.
Banking:	See *www.visitmontserrat.com/Business-Finance.htm* for details.
Business:	This offshore tax haven is good for setting up trusts, limited liablity companies, and for company manage-ment. Contact the following address for more information:

> International Financial Services
> PO Box 292
> Financial Service Centre
> Plymouth,
> Montserrat
> BWI

Tel: 00 1 664 4913057
Fax: 00 1 664 4912267
Or for more information, see *http://www.offshore-manual .com/taxhavens/Montserrat.html*

Climate:	Tropical; little daily or seasonal temperature variation.
Communications:	Very poor.
Currency:	East Caribbean dollar (XCD).
Entry and exit:	1 paved airport.
GDP per capita:	$3,400 (2002 est.).
Language:	English.
Location:	Caribbean, island in the Caribbean Sea, southeast of Puerto Rico.
Main industry:	Tourism, rum, textiles, and electronic appliances.
National disasters:	Severe hurricanes (June to November). In addition, volcanic eruptions. (Soufriere Hills volcano has erupted continuously since 1995. Much of this island was devastated and two-thirds of the population fled abroad because of the eruption of the Soufriere Hills Volcano that began on 18 July 1995).
Non-resident stay:	You must invest over $250,000 into property.
Religion:	Anglican, Methodist, Roman Catholic, Pentecostal, Seventh - day Adventist, and other Christian denominations.
Stability:	Ultra stable (however, see National Disasters note).

Montserrat is a paradise with a sinister side. Roughly, two thirds of the island is a no go zone due to volcanic activity. The Soufriere Hills volcano eruptions have all but destroyed the islands usefulness as a 2nd home. Many other Caribbean islands offer more safety. However, you could use the offshore structures in Montserrat without actually living there.

Guadeloupe

http://www.cr-guadeloupe.fr/

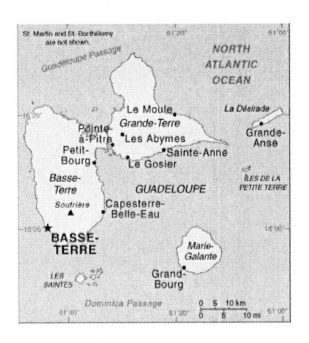

Associations:	France.
Banking:	For further details see *http://www.caribbean-direct.com/Guadeloupe-Direct/Helpful%20Info/GUAcurrency bankingF.html* and *http://caribbean-connection.com/ guadeloupe/ banking.html*.
Climate:	Subtropical tempered by trade winds; moderately high humidity.
Communications:	Very good.
Currency:	Euro (EUR) and French franc (FRF).
Entry and exit:	9 airports (8 paved, and 1 unpaved).
GDP per capita:	$8,000 (1997 est.).

Language:	French (official) 99% and Creole Patois.
Location:	Caribbean, islands between the Caribbean Sea and the North Atlantic Ocean, southeast of Puerto Rico.
Main industry:	Construction, cement, rum, sugar, and tourism.
National disasters:	Hurricanes (June to October); Soufriere de Guadeloupe is an active volcano.
Non-resident stay:	See *www.diplomatie.gouv.fr/venir/visas/documents/vdtc_001.html* for further details.
Religion:	Roman Catholic - 95%, Hindu and pagan African - 4%, and Protestant - 1%.
Stability:	Very stable.

These beautiful islands are subsidised by France and offer great vacationing potential. I would not advise setting up permanent residence there, as you would be subject to French tax laws, and exposed to the active volcano on the main island. Unemployment is very high, especially amongst the young. As the Caribbean offers better tax havens, I suggest you look elsewhere for a permanent residence.

St Martin / Sint Maarten

http://www.st-maarten.com/sxm/index.jsp

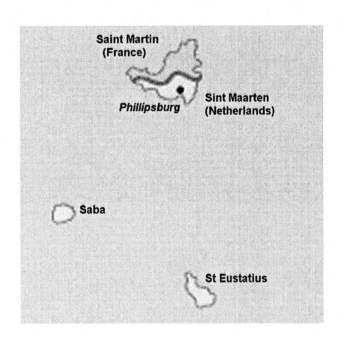

Associations:	France (Guadeloupe) and Netherlands (Netherlands Antilles).
Banking:	See *http://www.caribbean-direct.com/St-Martin-Direct/Helpful% 20Info/SMDcurrencybankingF.html* and *http:// www.caribbean-direct.com/St-Martin-Direct/Helpful%20Info/SMFcurrencybanki ngF.html* for details.
Business:	See *www.investinsxm.com/investor/reason_to_invest.htm* for further details.
Climate:	Tropical tempered by constant sea breezes, little seasonal temperature variation, and rainy season (May to November).
Communications:	Good.
Corporate Tax:	See *http://www.investinsxm.com/investor/taxation.htm* and *http://www.investinsxm.com/investor/incentives.htm* for details.

The following taxes exist in Sint Maarten for onshore companies:

- Profit tax (corporate income tax). There are credits and tax holidays offered as an incentive to stimulate investment in order to attract profit tax.
- Wage tax and income tax (a complex tabulation from 0.098% for incomes up to 10,000 Naf through to 57.2% on income above 117,000 Naf.

Social security

General Old Age insurance is 6% for employers and 5% for employees.

General Widows and Orphans insurance is 0.5% for employers and 0.5% for employees.

- Health insurance at 12% (employer contribution is 8.3% and employee contribution is 2.1%) and general insurance on special medical expenses at 2% (employer contribution is 0.5% and employee contribution is 1.5%).

Turnover tax. 1% on certain necessities and 3% on all other deliveries of goods and services, including catering establishments. This is an indirect tax with some exemptions.

Currency:	Netherlands Antilles Florin or Guilder (Naf). In French St. Martin, it is the Euro.
Entry and exit:	1 paved airport.
GDP per capita:	$11,400 (2003 est.).
Language:	French, Dutch, Spanish, and English.
Location:	Caribbean, islands in the Caribbean Sea, about one-third of the way from Puerto Rico to Trinidad and Tobago. North of St Kitts and Nevis.
Main industry:	Tourism.
National disasters:	Sint Maarten, Saba, and Sint Eustatius are subject to hurricanes from July to October.
Non-resident stay:	14 days with possible extension to 90 days.
Personal Tax:	See *http://www.investinsxm.com/investor/taxation.htm* for details.
Religion:	Roman Catholic, Protestant, Jewish, and Seventh - day Adventist.
Stability:	Very Stable.

This Island is one of a kind, with one side French and the other side Dutch. The top end tax rate is 57.2% on locally sourced income. The island gives you easy access and trade with Europe, and with double taxation treaties with France and the Netherlands, doing business here could prove tax efficient.

Dominica

http://www.dominica.dm/

http://www.ndcdominica.dm/index.php

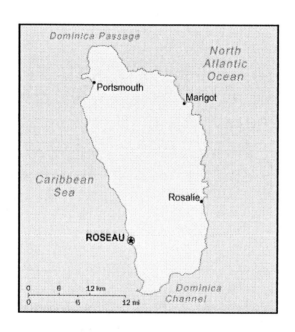

Climate:	Tropical; moderated by northeast trade winds and heavy rainfall.
Currency:	East Caribbean dollar (XCD).
Language:	English (official) and French Patois.
Location:	Caribbean, island between the Caribbean Sea and the North Atlantic Ocean, about one-half of the way from Puerto Rico to Trinidad and Tobago.
Religion:	Roman Catholic 77%, Protestant 15% (Methodist 5%, Pentecostal 3%, Seventh-Day Adventist 3%, Baptist 2% and other 2%), none 2%, and other 6%.
Stability:	Ultra Stable - joins other Caribbean states to counter Venezuela's

claim that Aves Island sustains human habitation, a criterion under UNCLOS, which permits Venezuela to extend its EEZ/continental shelf over a large portion of the Caribbean Sea.

Communications:	Very good.
GDP per capita:	$5,400 (2002 est.).
Entry and exit:	2 paved airports.
Main industry:	Soap, coconut oil, tourism, copra, furniture, cement blocks and shoes.
National disasters:	Flash floods are a constant threat; destructive hurricanes can be expected during the late summer months.
Banking:	See *http://www.buydominica.com/investor.htm* for further details.
Business:	Dominica offers many business investment opportuni-ties. It is well placed to access the European, Canadian, and American markets for imports and business investments into the following areas:

- Agricultural product and food processing.
- Agricultural product and preservation.
- Agricultural product and distribution.
- Aquaculture.
- Offshore banking.
- Tourism related business.
- Airline maintenance and service.
- Wine and distillery.
- Tobacco manufacturing.
- Exempt insurance.
- Offshore banking.
- Telecommunications.
- Manufacturing.
- Assembling.
- Service and distribution.
- Gambling (casino and online gambling licence).

Non-resident stay:	There is an economic citizenship program offered. By paying $50,000, you get citizenship for you, your spouse, and two children. Any extra children will cost $10,000 each.
Associations:	United Kingdom.

Dominica offers a tax free offshore bank account, and company formation that promises and maintains your secrecy. There are no reporting or filing requirements. For more information, see *http://dominica-taxhaven.com/ offshoreinfo.html.*

St Helena, Ascension, and Tristan Da Cunha (dependency of St. Helena)

http://website.lineone.net/~sthelena/tristaninfo.htm

http://www.sainthelena.gov.sh/

http://www.ascension-island.gov.ac

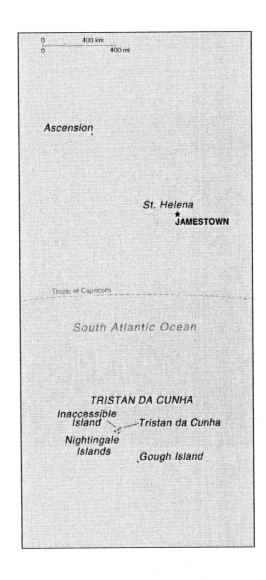

Associations:	United Kingdom.
Banking:	See *www.sainthelena.gov.sh/investment/currencyand banking.html* for further details.
Business:	Lobster fishing and fishing.
Climate:	Saint Helena - tropical; marine, mild, tempered by trade winds. Tristan da Cunha – temperate, marine, mild, tempered by trade winds (tends to be cooler than Saint Helena).
Communications:	Poor.
Currency:	Saint Helenian pound (SHP). See *www.xe.com* for current conversion rates.
Entry and exit:	One airport.
GDP per capita:	$2,500 (1998 est.).
Language:	English.
Location:	Islands in the South Atlantic Ocean, about midway between South America and Africa.
Main industry:	Construction, crafts (furniture, lacework, fancy woodwork), and fishing.
National disasters:	Active volcanism on Tristan da Cunha.
Non-resident stay:	Upon request to the island council.
Religion:	Anglican (majority), Baptist, Seventh - day Adventist, and Roman Catholic.
Stability:	Ultra stable.

These are some of the world's most remote locations. With less than 8,000 inhabitants, this is an extreme seclusion option for tax purposes. However, if that is what you are looking for, check out *http://www.sthelena.se/* and *http://website.lineone.net/~sthelena/tristaninfo.htm#Economy*.

Turks & Caicos

http://www.turksandcaicos.tc/Government

Associations:	United Kingdom.
Banking:	Visit *http://www.offshore-advisor.org/banking/turks-caicos-islands.htm* for a list of banks.
Business:	Import and stamp duty taxes. Import taxes do not exceed 2% or $550. The government will be applying withholding taxes from January 2005 to fall in line with the European Union's Savings Tax Directive. Many types of companies and trusts can be set up here.
Climate:	Tropical; marine, moderated by trade winds, sunny and relatively dry.

Communications:	Good, with landline and internet.
Corporate Tax:	0%. Employees and employers contribute 3% of their salary each to an approved superannuation scheme, usually the Vanuatu National Provident Fund.
Currency:	US dollar (USD).
Entry and exit:	8 airports (6 paved, and 2 unpaved).
GDP per capita:	$9,600 (2000 est.).
Language:	English (official).
Location:	Caribbean, two island groups in the North Atlantic Ocean, southeast of The Bahamas, north of Haiti.
Main industry:	Tourism and offshore financial services.
National disasters:	Frequent hurricanes.
Non-resident stay:	$250,000 in a home, $125,000 into an enterprise on any island other than the capital, $250,000 investment into an enterprise on the main island, or $50,000 invested in a government approved project. All enterprises and projects must help the economy or provide employment to locals. Fees vary from $250 for a labourer living there for over 10 years, to $10,000 for a self-employed business owner.
Personal Tax:	0%.
Religion:	Baptist 40%, Methodist 16%, Anglican 18%, Church of God 12%, and other 14% (1990). See *http://www.turksandcaicos.tc/ Churches*.
Stability:	Very stable - they have received Haitians fleeing economic collapse and civil unrest.

The others ...

There are other tax havens near the Americas that North Americans, Canadians, and South Americans, will find closest to their old home countries and can utilise. Some offer easy permanent status qualification procedures, whilst others still request the investment of over $250,000 into a private property. The one thing that is true about all of them is that they are all in, or near the equatorial belt, and thus have pleasant weather and a visually pleasing environment and scenery. Their political status is less stable, and thus I have not given them full status. You can find out more about these tax havens at *http://www.lowtax.net*.
For a language and religion breakdown of these countries see:

http://www.cia.gov/cia/publications/factbook/fields/2098.html and
http://www.cia.gov/cia/publications/factbook/fields/2122.html

Panama

http://www.presidencia.gob.pa

You can stay there for 180 days tax free. If you want to settle there, you can get a lifetime residency pass if you can show that you receive $500 per month or more pensions from abroad.

http://www.henleyglobal.com/panama-pension.htm

Belize

http://www.belize.gov.bz

This Belize permanent residence charges are as follows:

Central Americans
Salvadorans Nicaraguans and Hondurans: $525.00
Guatemalans and Mexicans: $250.00
Caricom nationals: $600.00

Other commonwealth nationals: $1,000.00
All other nationals: $1,250.00
Nationals of the Peoples' Republic of China: $3,000.00
Permanent residence card: $125.00
Permanent residence replacement card: $50.00

http://www.ambergriscaye.com/pages/town/immigrationpolicy.html

Costa Rica

http://www.costaricaweb.com/govenm

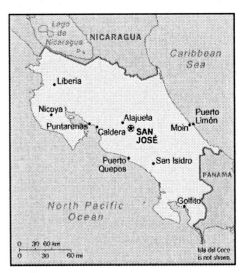

Permanent residence will cost you less than $500, and you can do it from the comfort of your home country.

http://www.costarica.com/Home/Travel/Things_to_Kn ow/Relocation_Information/Permanent_Residency/Ov erview

British Virgin Islands

http://www.loc.gov

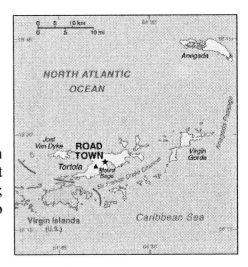

Marriage with a local citizen, or investing a large sum of money ($250,000 into a local property), will get you permanent residence. Do not stay past six months; otherwise, your world income will be subject to British Virgin Island taxes.

Netherlands Antilles

http://www.gov.an

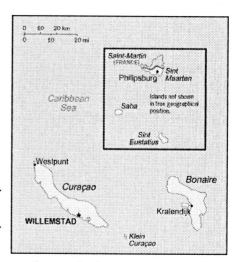

Do not stay over 90 days. If you want to stay longer, you will need to apply for permanent residency. Part of the process requires you to declare an amount sufficiently big enough to sustain you for the rest of your stay there. Once you have declared this sum, you will be taxed on all income derived from this sum. This tax haven levies taxes your whole world income.

http://www.netherlands-embassy.org/article.asp?articleref=AR00000400EN

St kitts and nevis

http://www.stkittsnevis.net

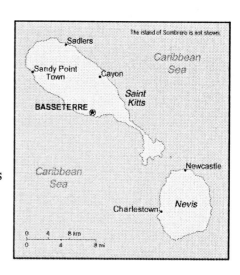

The investment of $250,000 in local property guarantees permanent residency in St Kitts and Nevis.

http://www.henleyglobal.com/stkittsnevis2.htm

Chapter 3

- *Western Europe*

Western Europe

Europe is within close range of some of the best tax havens in the world. With a wide mixture of religions and cultures, as well as languages to choose from, you are bound to find what you are looking for there. Although the weather may not always be like the tropical paradises we have just left in the Americas, you can find sunnier regions further south in the Mediterranean and Aegean area. See Appendix 6 for a complete map of Europe. We will now explore Europe in more detail.

UK

http://www.direct.gov.uk

Associations:	EU.
Banking:	See Appendix 7 for a list.
Business:	See the VCT section in The Practical Guide to Total Financial Freedom: Volume 1 on Tax Avoidance for information on VCTs, or go to *www.bvca.co.uk*. Film partnerships offer some tax shielding to investors, go to *http://www.lowtax.net/lowtax/html/offon/uk/ukfilm .html* for more

information.

A resident non-domicile's foreign income is tax free.

A reporting requirement on businesses that collects money for, or on behalf of foreigners, will affect the following businesses:

Building societies, banks, and other deposit-takers.

Registrars, custodians, and nominees; authorised unit trusts and open-ended investment companies; lawyers and stockbrokers; or any other person who makes savings income payments in the course of their business or profession.

Climate:	Temperate; moderated by prevailing southwest winds over the North Atlantic Current, more than one-half of the days are overcast.
Communications:	Excellent.
Corporate Tax:	See the Onshore section of Chapter 5.
Currency:	British pound (GBP). See *www.xe.com*.
Entry and exit:	471 airports (334 paved, and 137 unpaved).
GDP per capita:	$27,700 (2003 est.).
Language:	English, Welsh (about 26% of the population of Wales) and a Scottish form of Gaelic (about 60,000 in Scotland).
Location:	Western Europe, islands including the northern one-sixth of the island of Ireland, between the North Atlantic Ocean and the North Sea, northwest of France.
Main industry:	Machine tools, electric power equipment, automation equipment, railroad equipment, shipbuilding, aircraft, motor vehicles and parts, electronics and communications equipment, metals, chemicals, coal, petroleum, paper and paper products, food processing, textiles, clothing, and other consumer goods.
National disasters:	Winter windstorms; floods.
Non-resident stay:	UK residents have to declare and pay tax on their world income (see *http://www.netaccountants.com/nonuk.html)*, so do not over stay your tax free welcome.
Personal Tax:	0%, unless you are deemed a resident. Residency here is defined by:

- More than 182 days stay in any tax year.
- Exceeding 91 days per tax year for four consecutive tax years. In this case you will be resident in your fifth year or from the beginning of the four years prior.

- If you visit regularly and these visits are not accidental or due to an occasion.

Non-residents are only liable to UK income tax on income derived from:

- Property in the UK.
- Trade or profession undertaken through a UK branch or agency
- Employment, whose duties are performed in the UK.

Religion: Anglican and Roman Catholic 40 million, Muslim 1.5 million, Presbyterian 800,000, Methodist 760,000, Sikh 500,000, Hindu 500,000, and Jewish 350,000.

Stability: Currently the largest ally of the U.S. in the Iraq and Afghanistan conflicts. Since Gibraltar residents voted overwhelmingly by referendum in 2003 against a total shared sovereignty arrangement, talks between the UK and Spain over the fate of the 300-year old UK colony have stalled. Spain disapproves of UK plans to grant Gibraltar greater autonomy. Mauritius and Seychelles claim the Chagos archipelago (British Indian Ocean Territory), and its former inhabitants since their eviction in 1965; most reside chiefly in Mauritius, and in 2001 were granted UK citizenship and the right to repatriation. The UK continues to reject sovereignty talks requested by Argentina, which still claims the Falkland Islands (Islas Malvinas), South Georgia, and the South Sandwich Islands. The Rockall continental shelf dispute involving Denmark and Iceland remains dormant. Territorial claim in Antarctica (British Antarctic Territory) overlaps Argentine claim and partially overlaps Chilean claim. The UK are also involved in disputes with Iceland, Denmark, and Ireland over the Faroe Islands continental shelf boundary, outside 200 NM[3].

Muslim community information:
http://www.ukim.org/DesktopDefault.aspx

Jewish community information:
http://www.somethingjewish.co.uk/

Christian community information:
http://uk.praize.com/

---

[3] Nautical miles.

Hindu community information:
http://www.shopumust.com/temple_uk.html

Sikh community information: *http://www.geocities.com/gurdwaraworld/gurd3.html*

Buddhist community information:
http://buddhanet.net/euro_dir/eur_uki1.htm

Jainism community information:
Shree MahavirSwami Digamber Jin Mandir
1 The Broadway (via Montrose Road)
Wealdstone
Harrow
MIDDLESEX
HA3 7EH
UK

Tel: +44 (0) 20 8440 8994 (Dr Dinker Shah),
+44(0)20-8863 3974 (Chandrakant Shah)
Fax: +44 (0) 20 8440 8994

Chandrakant Shah (Email: *cmrshah@hotmail.com*)
Dr Dinker Shah (Email: *dinker_shah@yahoo.co.uk*)

Ireland

http://www.irlgov.ie/departments/default.asp

Associations:	United Kingdom.
Banking:	See *http://www.ibf.ie/about/members.shtml* for full list.
Business:	Please note that Irish residents can use a Nevada limited liability company and trust to carry out import and export operations with the UK directly from the USA. Check with a tax and offshore specialist about specifics. See *http://www.trustusa.co.uk*.
Climate:	Temperate maritime; modified by North Atlantic Current, mild winters, cool summers, consistently humid, overcast about half the time.
Communications:	Excellent.
Corporate Tax:	Financial companies can apply for a 10% corporation tax without even incorporating in Ireland. They just need provide jobs

through their enterprise. A business management company can be used to manage the operations in Ireland without an office being setup.

Currency:	Euro (EUR) and Irish Pounds (IR£).
Entry and exit:	36 airports (16 paved, and 20 unpaved).
GDP per capita:	$29,800 (2003 est.).
Language:	English is the language generally used; Irish (Gaelic) is spoken mainly in areas located along the western seaboard.
Location:	Western Europe, occupying five-sixths of the island of Ireland in the North Atlantic Ocean, west of Great Britain.
Main industry:	Food products, brewing, textiles, clothing, chemicals, pharmaceuticals, machinery, transportation equipment, glass, crystal, and software.
National disasters:	None.
Non-resident stay:	Do not stay over six months in any year or 240 days over any two consecutive year period, unless you want to be considered a resident and have your world assets taxed.
Personal Tax:	Non-residents pay income taxes on Irish income, VAT on Irish purchases, as well as stamp duty.

Income tax:

First IR£17,000	22%
Over IR£17,000	44%

There are personal allowances of IR£4,700 per person, or IR£9,400 for couples. Non-director employees receive an extra IR£1,000. Mortgage interest and pension contributions are also deductible. Capital acquisition tax is deductible at 20% on all gifts onshore or offshore with any resident's involvement (if the giver or receiver is Irish). Exemption is granted from IR£15,000 to IR£300,000, depending on the relation of the receiver to the giver i.e. children, relations, friends etc. Inter-spouse transfers are exempted. VAT is levied at 21%. Exit from investment funds is taxed at 23%. Stamp duties apply to the transfer of most property.

Religion:	Roman Catholic 91.6%, Church of Ireland 2.5%, and other 5.9% (1998).
Stability:	There are disputes with Iceland, Denmark, and the UK, over the

Faroe Islands continental shelf boundary outside 200 NM.

Muslim community information:
http://www.iol.ie/~afifi/BIC/guide.htm,
http://www.csc.tcd.ie/~muslim/

Jewish community information:
http://www.jewishireland.com/

Christian community information:
http://www.ifesireland.org/

Hindu community information:
http://www.irelandvinayakatemple.org,
http://www.iskcon.org.uk/govindadwipa/

Buddhist community information:
http://www.dublinbuddhistcentre.org/

With a high standard of living and very good quality of life, Ireland has a lot to offer the non-resident seeking to stay there within the non-resident time limits. I would not advise you becoming a residence there unless tax avoidance is not high on your agenda.

Isle Of Man

http://www.gov.im

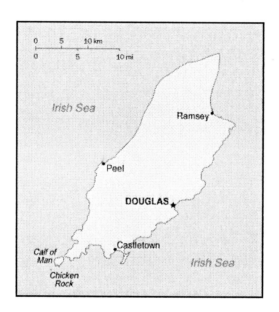

Associations:	United Kingdom.
Banking:	See *http://www.escapeartist.com/Isle_of_Man/Isle_of_Man2.html* for more details.
Business:	• Exempt companies.
	• International businesses.
	• International limited partnerships.
	• Limited liability companies.
	• Trusts.
Climate:	Temperate; cool summers and mild winters, and overcast about one-third of the time.
Communications:	Very good.
Corporate Tax:	Currently income tax is 10% for income under £10,000, and 18%

for all income over. The government has a reduction program aimed at reducing it to 0% for all but banks and financial companies by 2006. VAT is levied at 17.5%.

Currency:	British pound (GBP). Note - there is also a Manx pound. See *www.xe.com*.
Entry and exit:	One airport.
GDP per capita:	$21,000 (2001 est.).
Language:	English and Manx Gaelic.
Location:	Western Europe, island in the Irish Sea, between Great Britain and Ireland.
Main industry:	Financial services, light manufacturing, and tourism.
National disasters:	None.

Non-resident stay: Residency is defined by:
- More than 182 days stay in any tax year.
- Exceeding 91 days per tax year for four consecutive tax years. If this happens, you will be resident in your fifth year, and from the beginning of the four years prior.
- If you visit regularly and these visits are not accidental, or due to an occasion.
- Even as a resident, you only pay VAT. You do not pay tax on your offshore interests. If you work or own a business onshore, you will pay the appropriate income taxes and social taxes too.

Personal Tax: There are no taxes other than VAT for non-residents.
Most interest originating from onshore and paid to non-residents does not attract tax. VAT is levied at of 8% on fuel, and 5% on holiday accommodations.
Social security contributions are as follows:

Description of contributions	Rate
Employer's contribution	6.3%
Employee's contribution	6.3%
Self-employed contribution	11.6%
Employer's contribution: Redundancy Fund	1.2%
Employer's contribution: Industrial Training Fund	0.5%

Religion: Anglican, Roman Catholic, Methodist, Baptist, Presbyterian, and Society of Friends.

Stability: Very stable.

Muslim community information:
http://www.islamicfinder.org/cityPrayer.php?Country =Isle_Of_Man

Jewish community information:
http://www.jewishgen.org/JCR-UK/community/iom/

Christian community information:
http://www.church-iom.org.im/

This tax haven is one of the best options for UK and Western Europeans. Situated within less than half an hours flight from the UK mainland, the Isle of Man offers much to the individual wishing to move offshore to avoid tax, yet be close enough to the UK for the occasional tax free visits. The only drawback is mainly for the French and German speakers of Western Europe. The main language in the Isle of Man is English. For this purpose, we shall next explore havens that bridge this gap.

Jersey

http://www.gov.je

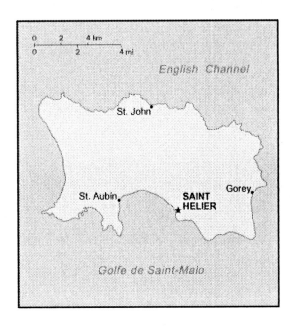

Associations:	United Kingdom.
Banking:	Over 60 banks. See *http://www.iom.localwebguide.co.uk/direc tory/disp_company.shtml?category=finance* and *http://www.quali steam.com/Offshore/Isle_of_Man* for more information.
Business:	Isle of Man authorities actively discourage new businesses from exploiting the limited resources of the island. The companies available from the island are:

- Private company limited by shares.
- Exempt private companies.
- Public company limited by shares.
- Branches of overseas companies.
- International business companies.
- General partnerships.

- Foreign partnerships.
- Limited partnerships.
- Trusts
- Local trusts.
- Unit trusts.

For further explanation, see *http://www.gov.je/onestop*.

Climate:	Temperate; mild winters, and cool summers.
Communications:	Excellent.
Corporate Tax:	Companies are treated as individuals, so the same residence rules and taxation applies as you read for personal tax. This is true for all but the international company, which is taxed at 30%. Trusts of non-residents attract tax.
Currency:	British pound (GBP). Note - there is also a Jersey pound. See *www.xe.com*.
Entry and exit:	One airport.
GDP per capita:	$24,800 (1999 est.).
Language:	English (official), French (official), and Norman-French dialect spoken in country districts.
Location:	Western Europe, island in the English Channel, northwest of France.
Main industry:	Tourism, banking and finance, and dairy.
National disasters:	None.
Non-resident stay:	Residency is defined by:

- More than 182 days stay in any tax year.
- Exceeding 91 days per tax year for four consecutive tax years. In this case you will be resident in your fifth year, or from the beginning of the four years prior.
- If you visit regularly, and these visits are not accidental or due to an occasion.

Even as a resident, you only pay VAT and no tax on your onshore interest. If you work or own a business onshore, you will pay the appropriate income taxes and social taxes too.

Personal Tax:	0% for offshore income sources, apart from income tax at 20%, and social security contributions are payable too. Property owners and occupiers may be liable for small parish taxes. Stamp duty from 0.5%, increasing from £50,000 purchases by 0.5% increments, to a maximum of 2%. There is also a perks tax for

any non-monetary gifts given to employees. Non-residents are taxed on Jersey income only, apart from bank interest and residents who are taxed on world income interest.

Religion: Anglican, Roman Catholic, Baptist, Congregational New Church, Methodist, and Presbyterian.

Stability: Extremely stable.

Christian and Jewish community information:
http://www.jersey.co.uk/jsyinfo/ churches.html

This French and English speaking islands offer French speakers a tax haven close to France and the UK. As long as you do not do business or earn a wage there, you can literally live there free. With pleasant weather and an easygoing lifestyle, you will not want for much.

Guernsey

http://www3.gov.gg

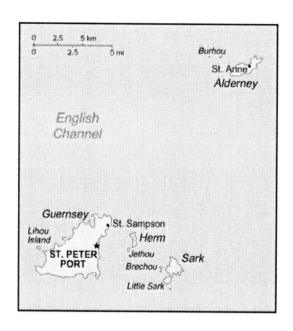

Associations:	Great Britain.
Banking:	See *http://freespace.virgin.net/bank.help/Facts/documen ts /10912.html* for further details.
Business:	The company types are:

- Life insurance and assurance companies.
- Private companies limited by shares.
- Companies limited by guarantee.
- Exempt private companies.
- Exempt investment schemes.
- Exempt insurance companies.
- International companies.
- Branches of overseas companies.
- General partnership.
- Limited partnership.

- Trusts, international trusts (allows the exportation of a Guernsey trust by replacing the resident trustees).
- Unit trusts.

Climate:	Temperate with mild winters and cool summers; about 50% of days are overcast.
Communications:	Excellent.
Corporate Tax:	30% for international companies, £600 per annum for exempt companies, and 20% for all other company type incomes. Trusts owned by non-residents with no resident association are exempt from tax, as are unit trusts.
Currency:	British pound (GBP). Note - there is also a Guernsey pound. See *www.xe.com*.
Entry and exit:	Two airports.
GDP per capita:	$20,000 (1999 est.).
Language:	English, French, and Norman-French dialect spoken in country districts.
Location:	Western Europe, islands in the English Channel, northwest of France.
Main industry:	Tourism and banking.
National disasters:	None.
Non-resident stay:	182 days in the year, or up to 31st July of the year.
Personal Tax:	0% for non-residents apart from income tax at 20% (Guernsey source income). Social security contributions, property owners, and occupiers may be liable for small parish taxes. Be careful in Guernsey, owning a property may make you a resident. Residents pay 20% income tax on worldwide income. See *http://www.tax.gov.gg/law/* for more details.
Religion:	Anglican, Roman Catholic, Presbyterian, Baptist, Congregational, and Methodist.
Stability:	Extremely stable.

Christian Community information:
http://www.islandlife.org/churches_gsy.htm

Similar to Jersey tax laws, Guernsey will tax you 20% on your world income if you won property there, spend over 182 days a year there, or 20% on your onshore income if you do not. Its advantages to French speakers are its closeness to France, and its residents speaking French and English.

France

http://www.premier-ministre.gouv.fr

Associations:	EU.
Banking:	See *http://www.escapeartist.com/banks4/banks4.htm* for more information.
Business:	Special tax concessions for the following enterprises:

- Patent holding companies.
- Energy conservation Enterprises.
- Small Medium-sized Enterprises (SMEs).
- Tax free zones.
- Local investment funds.
- Mineral extraction companies.

- Oil and gas companies.
- Media publications.
- Daily newspapers.
- Innovation financing companies.
- Investment tax credit for staff training.
- Scientific and technical research.

See *http://www.lowtax.net/lowtax/html/offon/france/fras pec.html* for more details.

Climate:	Generally, cool winters and mild summers, but mild winters and hot summers along the Mediterranean. Occasional strong, cold, dry, north-to-north westerly wind known as mistral.
Communications:	Excellent.
Corporate Tax:	Business tax from 0% to 4% (complex calculation) on head businesses, and all branches 33.33% with 2% surcharge. France accommodates large multinational corporations who operate stocking, labelling, packaging, distribution, and control & co-ordination of administrative and logistic activities in France, with a 6% to 10% fixed tax (depending on operational structure of the corporation). See *http://www.msi-network.com/content/doing_business_in_france_taxsystem.asp* for more details.
Currency:	Euro (EUR). See *www.xe.com*.
Entry and exit:	477 airports (281 paved, and 196 unpaved).
GDP per capita:	$27,500 (2003 est.).
Language:	French 100%, with rapidly declining regional dialects and languages (Provencal, Breton, Alsatian, Corsican, Catalan, Basque, Flemish).
Location:	Western Europe, bordering the Bay of Biscay and English Channel, between Belgium and Spain, southeast of the UK; bordering the Mediterranean Sea, between Italy and Spain.
Main industry:	Machinery, chemicals, automobiles, metallurgy, aircraft, electronics, textiles, food processing, and tourism.
National disasters:	Flooding, avalanches, midwinter windstorms, drought, and forest fires in south near the Mediterranean.
Non-resident stay:	You are deemed a tax-resident if you qualify for any of the following options: You stay over 183 days.

You have a home in France.
France is the place of your principal abode.
France is the place where you perform your principal professional activities.
France is the centre of your economic interests.
See *http://riviera.angloinfo.com/information/1/cds.asp* for more information.

Personal Tax:
Varies from 0% to 52.75% with property and housing taxes, and VAT at 19.6% with lower rates for certain products and services (lower rates of 5.5% for food, some agricultural products, medicine at 5.5% or 2.5%, books, hotels, public transport, newspapers and magazines at 5.5% or 2.1%, and some types of entertainment). Taxes are levied on French based income. For French citizens considering moving offshore, first switch assets to capital appreciation assets offshore before moving.

Religion:
Roman Catholic 83%-88%, Protestant 2%, Jewish 1%, Muslim 5%-10%, and unaffiliated 4%.

Stability:
Stable - Madagascar claims Bassas da India, Europa Island, Glorioso Islands, and Juan de Nova Island. Comoros claims Mayotte. Mauritius claims Tromelin Island. There is a territorial dispute between Suriname and French Guiana. There is a territorial claim in Antarctica (Adelie Land). Also, Matthew and Hunter Islands, east of New Caledonia, are claimed by France and Vanuatu.

Muslim community information:
http://www.islamicfinder.org/cityPrayer.php?country =France

Jewish community information:
http://www.kosherdelight.com/FranceJewishLinks.htm

Hindu community information:
http://perso.wanadoo.fr/temple.hindou/

Buddhist community information:
http://www.buddhanet.net/euro_dir/ eur_fr/eur_frag.htm

France is no tax haven unless you are a large multinational, or operate a business that gives you special tax concessions. I advise for tax saving purposes that you visit, enjoy, and leave the country before 183 days. Do not buy a villa unless you can remove yourself from the ownership with an offshore trust. Although France has not actively been going after tax avoiders, they are slowly waking up, and the future may be worse for residents with large offshore incomes.

Monaco

http://www.monaco.gouv.mc

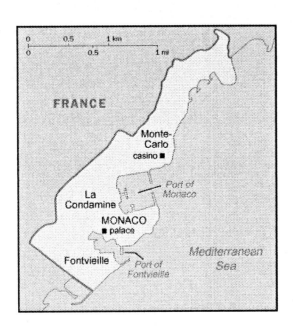

Associations:	France.
Banking:	See *http://www.offshore-advisor.org/banking/monaco .htm*, *www.Qualisteam.com/Banks/Europe/Monaco* for more information.
Business:	The corporate entities that exist in this principality are:

- Societe Anonyme Monegasque.
- Branch, Societe En Nom Collectif.
- Societe En Commandite Simple.
- Trusts.
- Foundations.

For an explanation and definition of these entities, visit *http://www.lowtax.net/lowtax/html/jmccos.html*.

Climate:	Mediterranean with mild, wet winters, and dry hot summers.
Communications:	Excellent.
Corporate Tax:	There is an employer's contribution, which is 28% to 40% (averaging 35%), and the employee pays 10%-14% (averaging 13%). If you hire staff, you pay nearly 50% of their salary towards social insurance. Stamp duty and capital transfers apply for property registration transac-tions, and are as follows:

- 7.5% on the registered value of a business sold.
- 7.5% of the registered value of real estate sold (which includes other associated fees).
- 3.65% of the value of a registered mortgage (which includes other associated fees).
- 2% of the value of a civil judgment registered.
- 5% on the sale of personal assets, unless they are sold by auction, in which case the tax is reduced to 2%.
- 1% on the registered value of a short-term lease, which value is determined according to set formulas.
- 6.5% on the registered value of a long-term lease, which value is determined according to set formulas.

Residents also pay inheritance taxes as follows:
Direct line spouses (wife, parents, and children) – nil.
Brothers and sisters - 8%.
Uncles, aunts, nieces, and nephews - 10%.
Other relatives - 13%.
Unrelated persons - 16%.

VAT is levied at 19.6% except on water, food products, medicines, books, special equipment for handicapped people, hotel accommodation, public transport services, and public entertainment services (5.5%).

Currency:	Euro (EUR). (See *www.xe.com*).
Entry and exit:	No airports; linked to the airport at Nice, and France by helicopter service.
GDP per capita:	$27,000 (1999 est.).
Language:	French (official), English, Italian, and Monegasque.
Location:	Western Europe, bordering the Mediterranean Sea, on the southern coast of France. Near the border with Italy.
Main industry:	Light manufacturing; banking and financial services; shipping

and trade; research and development in biotechnology and marine environments; and tourism.

National disasters:	None.
Non-resident stay:	See Personal Tax section above.
Personal Tax:	0%, unless you are a French national. Exemptions exist for French nationals who are either of the following:

Have not been habitually resident in Monaco for five years on 13th of October 1962, and you do not hold dual French and Monegasque nationality.

You are not attached to the Prince's household.

You are not the French spouse of a foreigner residing in Monaco, and the marriage did not take place before the 1st January 1986.

Religion:	95% Roman Catholic.
Stability:	Extremely stable.

Christian community information:
See *http://www.catholic-hierarchy.org/diocese/dmona.html* for detail on Archdiocese of Monaco.

There are no mosques or synagogues in the principality. This principality may not be ideal for non-Christians/Catholics who need a local place of worship.

This is an ideal place for non-French, national French, or Italian speakers, with a lot of money. To avoid paying any taxes, do not carry out business or employ staff there. It is on the French and Italian Riviera, and benefits from the Mediterranean weather. To come and go from there, you will need to drive, take the train, bus, or fly via helicopter to Nice. If you cannot afford to enter France regularly in order to leave via Nice, you may be inconvenienced. However, you could always travel by Yacht!

We have now covered English, French, and Italian speaking tax havens for Europeans, but what about the German speakers? We will next look at some of the options for Northern Europeans.

Germany

http://www.deutschland.de

Associations:	European Union.
Banking:	See *http://www.germanbanks.org/* for further details.
Business:	Provision for insurance fluctuation:

- Contributions to a fund for a 15 to 30 year cover of liabilities insurance can be offset against current profits. The fund can only cover liabilities with historical unpredictability.

Shipping tax:

- German shipping companies can opt to be taxed under a tonnage system.

Tax free investment grants in West Berlin & former East Germany:

- Grants are available to German manufacturers of movable goods subject to wear and tear, as long as they are made in Germany and stay there for three years after manufacture. The grant is currently 10% to 20%.

Real estate capital gains roll-over relief:

- If the property or land is held for over six years.
- Sale of property and capital gains from such property is tax free. The tax may be rolled over for four years as a tax free reserve.

For other business reasons to invest in Germany, see *http://www. lowtax.net/lowtax/html/offon/germany/gerhom.html*.

Climate:	Temperate and marine. Cool, cloudy, wet winters. Summers are occasional, and there is warm mountain (foehn) wind.
Communications:	Excellent.
Corporate Tax:	The corporate tax rate is 25%. In the case of individuals and partnerships, the general income tax rates are lowered in accordance with the single taxpayer's rates. See single taxpayer's table in the Personal Tax section.

In addition to this tax reduction, the German trade tax is taken into consideration in determining the income tax. Income tax is charged on to following:

- Income from an agricultural or forestry business, which the taxpayer maintains in Germany.
- Income from a permanent business establishment or permanent agent in Germany, including gains from the sale of assets by that entity, as well as gains from the sale of substantial stakes in a resident company (at least 10%).
- Income from independent personal services performed or utilized in Germany.
- Employment income if the employment was or is either performed or utilized in Germany.

Income from certain capital investments, in particular:

- Income from dividends and similar investment instruments, e.g. profit-bearing bonds, as well as income from participation in a business as a silent partner, or through a profit-participating loan if the borrowing company has its domicile, place of management, or seat in Germany.
- Interest on mortgage loans; generally, speaking, other kinds of interest do not constitute taxable income.

- Income from royalties and from granting the use of movable property within Germany.
- Income from German real estate.
- Gains from the sale of German real estate owned for less than ten years.

The German VAT (Mehrwertsteuer) is levied at 16%. A reduced rate of 7% applies to certain products, including food and printed material. Medical and insurance services are generally exempt, as are exports of goods abroad, and services rendered abroad. In Germany, fuel, alcoholic beverages, tobacco products, tea, and coffee, carry sales taxes in addition to the Mehrwertsteuer. There is also a church tax (Kirchensteuer), of 8% to 9% of the Einkommensteuer/Lohnsteuer. But you are not required to pay the tax unless you wish to be officially affiliated with one of Germany's established churches, usually Catholic or Protestant (Evangelisch).
See *http://www.worldwide-tax.com/germany/indexger many.asp* for more information.

Currency:	Euro (EUR).
Entry and exit:	550 airports (331 paved, and 219 unpaved).
GDP per capita:	$27,600 (2003 est.).
Language:	German.
Location:	Central Europe, bordering the Baltic Sea and the North Sea, between the Netherlands and Poland, south of Denmark.
Main industry:	Among the world's largest and most technologically advanced producers of iron, steel, coal, cement, chemicals, machinery, vehicles, machine tools, electronics, food and beverages, shipbuilding and textiles.
National disasters:	Flooding.
Non-resident stay:	Do not stay over 183 days in any 12-month period, buy a house, or rent a house where the lease is over 3 months. Non-residents are taxed only on their German based income, whilst German residents are taxed on their worldwide income.
Personal Tax:	Do not work in Germany or carry out business there if you can. You are allowed 183 days in every 12-month period.

Single Taxpayers:

Income	Tax rate
€0 to € 7,664	0%
€ 7,664 and € 52.152	16% to 45%
Over € 52.152	45%

Married Taxpayers:

Income	Tax rate
€0 to € 15.328	0%
€ 15.328 and € 104.304	16% to 45%
Over € 104.304	45%

Religion: Protestant 34%, Roman Catholic 34%, Muslim 3.7%, unaffiliated or other 28.3%.

Stability: Stable – there are some far right Nazi militants. There are regular anti-semitic attacks across the country by far right militants.

Jewish community information:
http://www.zentralratdjuden.de/
http://www.berlin-judentum.de/
http://www.uni-potsdam.de/u/juedstud/

Muslim Community information:
http://www.islaminstitut.de/index.php

Christian community information:
http://www.christiantopsites.com/search/ Church_Sites/Germany/

Hindu community information:
http://siddhanta.shaivam.org/toi_germany.htm

Sikh community information:
http://www.sikh-religion.de/html/gurdwara-adressen.html

Buddhist community information:
http://www.dharma.de/dbu/frameset.php

Do not do business or buy or rent property (over a three-month lease) in Germany, or else you will be subject to some heavy taxes on your worldwide income and assets. You can visit and enjoy Germany for no more than 183 days within any 12-month period.

Switzerland

http://www.gov.ch

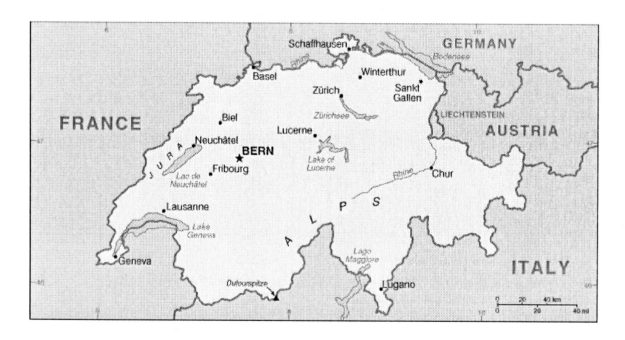

Associations:	EU.
Banking:	See Appendix 8 for a list.
Business:	Switzerland is excellent for the following structures:

Stock corporations.
Holding companies.
Domiciliary companies.
Auxiliary companies.
Service companies.
Mixed companies.
Branches.
See *http://www.lowtax.net/lowtax/html/jswcos.html* for further explanations.

Climate:	Temperate, but varies with altitude; cold, cloudy, rainy/snowy winters, cool to warm, cloudy, humid summers with occasional showers.
Communications:	Excellent.
Corporate Tax:	There are capital gains taxes of 18% (average), and capital transfer taxes of 4% (average); these taxes are widely varied among the Swiss Cantons.

Stamp duty is levied as follows:

- 1% on the issue of shares where the value of the shares is over SFr 250,000 (Swiss branches of foreign companies are exempt), where:
    - Shares are issued at a premium.
    - A loan is made by a shareholder to a company without any consideration.
    - The nominal value of shares when a majority shareholding is transferred as a consequence of a liquidation (even if the shares are worthless).
    - A rate of 0.15% on the transfer value of shares in Swiss resident companies.
    - 0.3% on the transfer value of shares in non-resident companies if the transfer is carried out by a bank, stockbroker, investment fund manager, other financial institutions including any company that owns securities with a value in excess of SFr10m, and all its intermediaries. In this case, the tax is split between the buyer and the seller, and is automatically deducted by the dealer.
    - 0.12% per annum on bonds issue.
    - 0.06% per annum on bank-issued medium term bonds, and on the issue of financial paper.
    - 5% on non-life insurance premiums.
    - 2.5% on a life insurance premium paid in one contribution.
    - Inheritance tax is levied by the Canton passed away in, and is calculated on the estate of the deceased.

Currency:	Swiss franc (CHF). See *www.xe.com.*

Entry and exit:	65 airports (42 paved, and 23 unpaved).
GDP per capita:	$32,800 (2003 est.).
Language:	German (official) 63.7%, French (official) 19.2%, Italian (official) 7.6%, Romansch (official) 0.6%, and other 8.9%.
Location:	Central Europe, east of France, north of Italy.
Main industry:	Machinery, chemicals, watches, textiles, and precision instruments.
National disasters:	Avalanches, landslides, and flash floods.
Non-resident stay:	Over 180 days in the country per 12-month period, or over 90 days in the same home.
Personal Tax:	To work in Switzerland, you need a work permit that is granted for up to 120 days at a time. The grant of a work permit will also attract income taxes to your wages.
	Fiscal Deal: under this deal a wealthy resident showing a net worth of over SFr 2,000,000 will be granted residence, and taxed only on the income they declared (SFr 2,000,000). Non-Fiscal deal residents are taxed up to 30% on their world income, as long as it does not arise from offshore enterprises or real estate located out of Switzerland.
	Personal taxes are charged up to 11.5% at federal level and approximately 23% at cantonal level. Hidden profits (excessive bonuses or interest on loans) are charged at 35%. VAT is levied at 7.6% or 2.4% on personal consumption goods, and 3.5% on hotels.
	Inheritance tax
	Non-residents only pay inheritance tax on Swiss based real estate. A resident's worldwide estate, excluding real estate not situated in Switzerland, is subject to inheritance tax. This tax is progressive and varies from canton to canton. Only one out of the 25 cantons does not levy gift tax.
	VAT
	In addition, every company subject to VAT can deduct VAT paid at earlier stages in the economic process.
	For a list of the cantons and their tax details, go to *http://directory.google.com/Top/Regional/Europe/Switzerland/ Cantons/*.
Religion:	Roman Catholic 46.1%, Protestant 40%, other 5%, and none 8.9% (1990).
Stability:	Ultra safe and stable.

Muslim community information:
http://switzerland.isyours.com/e/guide/religion/ islam.contacts.html

Christian community information:
*http://search.looksmart.com/p/browse/us1/us317837/us317918/us576440/us161208/us9695
71/us10095580/*

Jewish community information:
http://www.amyisrael.co.il/europe/switzerland/

Hindu community information:
http://siddhanta.shaivam.org/toi_swiss.htm

Sikh community information:
http://allaboutsikhs.com/gurudwaras/gurud_49.htm

Buddhist community information:
http://www.sbu.net/index.html

Switzerland is one of the most accommodating European countries. Not only does it offer total freedom of religious expression with no prejudices, it also offers some of the lowest taxes in Europe. For non-resident German, French, or Italian speakers, this may be the haven for you.

Campione

http://www.campioneitalia.com/

http://www.campione-consulting.com/

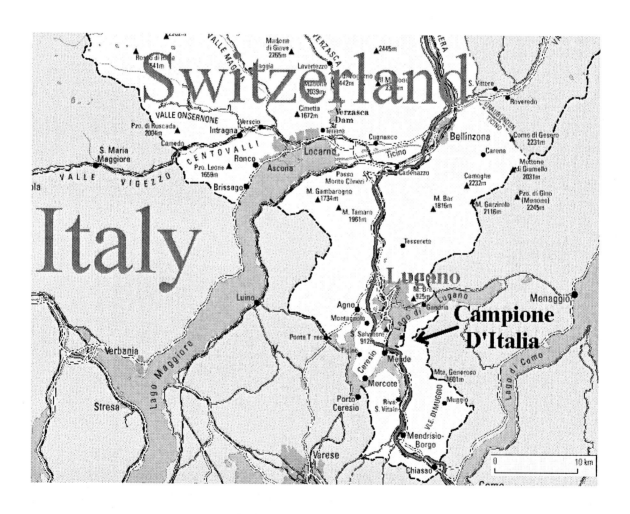

Associations: Italy and Switzerland

Banking:	You will have to use Swiss banks. Try those in Lugano.
Business:	It is possible to incorporate in Italy in one of the forms below.

A public limited liability company (with the suffix SPA):

- There must be at least two shareholders (individuals or bodies).
- The company must have a minimum share capital of EUR 120,000.
- At least 30% of the capital must be deposited in a bank.
- The company may offer shares to the public.
- The company must keep a register of shareholders.
- The company may issue shares of different classes that confer different rights on the shareholders.

A private limited liability company (with the suffix SRL.):

- The share capital is presented in quotas.
- The company keeps a shares register in which the names of the owners appear.
- The company may not offer shares to the public.
- The minimum registered share capital - EUR 10,000.
- One single shareholder suffices.

There are three forms of partnership:

- An unlimited partnership - the partners are liable for the transactions carried out by the partnership, without any limit in amount. All or some of the partners may serve as managers of the partnership.
- A limited partnership - this is made up of general partners who have unlimited liability and limited partners, whose liability is limited to the amount they invested as capital in the partnership. Only a general partner may serve as a manager of the partnership.
- Partnerships limited by shares - in principle, this is similar to a limited partnership. The main difference is the share of partners in a limited partnership. It is represented by share capital, as distinct from a limited partnership in which the partners hold quotas and not shares.

Climate:	Campione's climate is much like that of Switzerland's: generally temperate (except on the highest elevations). The average annual average temperature is about 50 degrees F (10 degrees C), and yearly rainfall is moderate, and mostly in the winter in the form

	of snow.
Communications:	Excellent.
Corporate Tax:	Business operations are tax free as long as they are not in Italy. If you do want to operate in Italy as well, use a Swiss or Liechtenstein company for those transactions. Corporation tax is 33% with non-domicile companies paying 4.25% to 8.5%.
Currency:	Swiss franc (CHF) or euro (€). See *www.xe.com*
Entry and exit:	One Airport.
GDP per capita:	Highest in the world.
Language:	Italian.
Location:	Campione is located in the Swiss Canton Ticino on the lakeside of the lake Lugano, about 10 driving minutes from Lugano and 45 highway minutes from Milan. Campione is an Italian enclave in Swiss national and economical territory. It is entirely surrounded by Switzerland. There are no border controls, so there is complete freedom to pass in and out of Campione.
Main industry:	Gambling.
National disasters:	None.
Non-resident stay:	No restrictions. Property prices are on par with Tokyo.
Personal Tax:	You are taxed only on income sourced in Campione. Same income tax rates as Italy, but for the first CHF 200,000, the tax is paid in Lira at a fixed rate of 237 Italian Lira to 1 CHF (the current official rate is 1200 Lira to 1 CHF). Income tax is 45% over CHF 200,000, but there are more ways around this than there are roads into Campione. There is no VAT at all. There are no personal income taxes on non-Italian or Campione source income, and no municipal taxes at all in Campione, as all Campione's income is derived from the Casino. Banks cannot be established in Campione (according to a Swiss/Italian treaty), so you will have to use Swiss banks, preferably in Lugano. Campione residents (in contrast with foreigners in Switzerland) are not subject to Switzerland's double taxation agreements with the USA, Canada, and most of Western Europe. Profits from bank deposits, shares, bonds, real estate and other transactions from a Swiss or international source are not registered for tax purposes for Campione residents, as long as they pass through Swiss banks. The cost of living is very high.

Religion:	It is roman Catholic due to links with Italy, but its residents are from all beliefs.
Stability:	Ultra stable.

For further information, see *http://www.escapeartist.com/campione/ campione.htm*.

This is the best place for high net worth individuals in Europe, or the world for that matter. You will have to eventually learn Italian, but you will enjoy all the benefits of Switzerland without paying any taxes. Do not do business in Italy or stay over 183 days in Italy. With good tax planning, you should be able to live in Campione and pay no taxes, or pay very little. Consult a specialised tax advisor in this matter, (try *http://www.henley-partner .com/campione.htm*). Beware of blowing all your money in the Casino if you are prone to gambling.

As a resident of Campione, you are not subject to Switzerland's double taxation agreements with the USA, Canada, and most of Western Europe. Profits from bank deposits, shares, bonds, real estate, and other transactions from a Swiss or international source, are not registered for tax purposes for you the Campione resident, as long as they pass through Swiss banks.

The Netherlands

http://www.government.nl

Associations:	European Union.
Banking:	See *http://www.escapeartist.com/banks27/banks27.htm* for further details.
Business:	Holland is a great location for a holding company as it has more tax treaties (100, 10 less than the UK) than Denmark. Also, note that Aruba and the Dutch Antilles hold tax treaties, allowing withholding tax on outgoing dividends to be a mere 8.3%. See *http://lowtax.com /lowtax/html/offon/netherlands/nethold.html* for more information. You may also want to locate your interest and royalty conduit companies in the Netherland, as withholding taxes are not levied on interest payments, and their tax authorities will accept very low loan differential margins. This is true also

for royalty conduit companies.

Climate:	Temperate; marine, cool summers, and mild winters.
Communications:	Excellent.
Corporate Tax:	All other sources of Netherland's sourced income are taxed. There are special tax rates for ex-pats (approximately 36.4% of an expatriate's income is taxable for up to four years). There exists a 30% exemption from social taxes, income tax, and children's schooling fees exemption, from tax for expatriates. Your employer has to prove that he cannot get a Dutch national to do the job before you are allowed to stay from four to ten years.
Currency:	Euro (EUR). See *www.xe.com*.
Entry and exit:	27 airports (20 paved, and 7 unpaved).
GDP per capita:	$28,600 (2003 est.).
Language:	Dutch (official language) and Frisian (official language).
Location:	Western Europe, bordering the North Sea, between Belgium and Germany.
Main industry:	Agro industries, metal and engineering products, electrical machinery and equipment, chemicals, petroleum, construction, microelectronics, and fishing.
National disasters:	Flooding.
Non-resident stay:	It is based on durable ties, rather than on time. This apparently means how close you are to a place.
Personal Tax:	Non-residents are not taxed on real estate, interest on a loan secured on dutch real estate, or on sale of shares. Note that there are special terms with each of these, so investigate further before diving in. Try *http://lowtax.com/lowtax/html/offon/netherlands/nettax.html* for more information.
Religion:	Roman Catholic 31%, Protestant 21%, Muslim 4.4%, other 3.6%, and unaffiliated 40% (1998).
Stability:	Very stable.

Jewish community information:
http://www.nik.nl/
http://www.esnoga.com/

Muslim community information:
http://www.isim.nl/
http://www.islamicuniversity.nl/

Christian community information:
http://www.doopsgezind.nl/
http://www.pkn.nl/
http://www.nak.org/home-nl.html
http://www.katholieknederland.nl/

Buddhist community information:
http://www.boeddhisme.nl/
http://www.zen-deshimaru.nl/
http://www.geocities.com/sakya_nl/

Japanese community information:
http://www.shinto.nl/

Hindu community information:
http://www.hindoeraad.nl/

More religions in Netherlands:
http://www.rnw.nl/rninfo/html/spirituallife.html.

This is a great place to stay for as long as you like, as your world incomes are not taxed. Just do not work there or run a business there. Business owners who are looking to offset their taxes from trading, should consider the royalty or dividend conduit company benefits, and possibly a Dutch holding company.

The Netherlands also offers benefits through Aruba and the Dutch Antilles. As Dutch Antilles companies can impose corporate income taxes, the effective tax can be reduced when dealing with Holland through your Dutch Antilles company. By levying a corporate income tax, you will benefit from the double taxation treaty between Holland and these offshore islands. (You will own the offshore company of course).

Denmark

http://www.denmark.dk

Associations:	None.
Banking:	See *http://www.escapeartist.com/banks24/banks24.htm* for more information.
Business:	Holding companies.
Climate:	Temperate; humid and overcast, mild, windy winters, and cool summers.
Communications:	Excellent.
Corporate Tax:	See table below.
Currency:	Danish krone (DKK). See *www.xe.com*.
Entry and exit:	99 airports (28 paved, and 71 unpaved).

GDP per capita:	$31,200 (2003 est.).
Language:	Danish, Faroese, Greenlandic (an Inuit dialect), and German (small minority). Note: English is the predominant second language.
Location:	Northern Europe, bordering the Baltic Sea and the North Sea, on a peninsula north of Germany (Jutland); also includes two major islands (Sjaelland and Fyn).
Main industry:	Food processing, machinery and equipment, textiles and clothing, chemical products, electronics, construction, furniture and other wood products, shipbuilding, and windmills
National disasters:	Flooding is a threat in some areas of the country (e.g., parts of Jutland, along the southern coast of the island of Lolland) that are protected from the sea by a system of dikes.
Non-resident stay:	Only as an expatriate with a work permit, or as spouse and family of expatriate with a non-work permit. Those seeking work permits must be people with special qualifications like researchers, artists, managers, certain consultants and instructors, specialists (engineers, doctors, nurses, athletes/coaches, and architects), as well as persons establishing new businesses in Denmark.
Personal Tax:	Tax Rates for 2004:

Sources	Year 2004
Labour market contribution	8%
Special pension savings	1%
Personal relief (18 yrs +)	DKK 36,800
Personal relief (under 18 yrs)	DKK 27,300
Bottom-bracket tax	5.5%
Middle-bracket tax	6%
Bottom limit for middle-bracket tax	DKK 216,800
Top-bracket tax	15%
Bottom limit for top-braket tax	DKK 304,800
Tax ceiling	59%
Graduated limit for share income	DKK 42,400
Share income below limit	28%
Share income above limit	43%
Value of free (company) car	25/20%
Trifle limit for certain fringe benefits	DKK 4,900
Bottom limit for anniversary bonuses	DKK 8,000
Upper limit for capital pension relief	DKK 40,100
Bottom limit for certain earned income deductions	DKK 4,900
Graduated limit for imputed rent value /property value tax	DKK 3,040,000
Municipal property value tax (property value up to DKK 3,040,000)	1.0%
Municipal property value tax (property value above DKK 3,040,000)	3.0%
Income limit for 25% additional commuting relief	DKK 218,400
Commuting relief (home to work/work to home)	
- first 24 kilometres	no deduction
- 25 - 100 kilometres	DKK 1.62/km
- over 100 kilometres	DKK 0.81/km
Occupational mileage allowance	
- mileage up to 20.000 km/yr.	DKK 2.98/km
- mileage beyond 20.000 km/yr.	DKK 1.62/km
Upper limit for tax free gifts to close relatives	DKK 49,900
Upper limit for tax free gifts to sons-in-law and daughters-in-law	DKK 17,500

For residents there is also church tax (if you want to be affiliated with the The Danish National Evangelical Lutheran Church).

Religion: Evangelical Lutheran 95%, Protestant and Roman Catholic 3%, and Muslim 2%.

Stability: Very stable - the Rockall continental shelf dispute involving Denmark, Iceland, and the UK remains dormant (Ireland and the UK have signed a boundary agreement in the Rockall area). There is a dispute with Iceland over the Faroe Islands fisheries median line boundary within 200 NM. There is a dispute with Iceland, the UK, and Ireland, over the Faroe Islands continental shelf boundary outside 200 NM. Faroese continues to study proposals for full independence. There is an uncontested dispute with Canada over Hans Island sovereignty in the Kennedy Channel between Ellesmere Island and Greenland.

Christian community information:
http://www.interchurch.dk/LutheranChurch/

Jewish community information:
http://www.kosherdelight.com/Denmark.htm

Muslim community information:
http://www.islam.dk/

Hindu community information:
http://siddhanta.shaivam.org/toi_denmark.htm

Buddhist community information:
http://home5.inet.tele.dk/suddhi/en_page.html

Sikh community information:
http://www.sikh.dk/contactusenglish.htm

If you want to move to this cold (in winter), tax heavy country, you are reading the wrong book. It is primarily good only for setting up holding companies. Denmark should be avoided for anything else, as the tax burden, not to mention the difficulty in acquiring residency without specialised education and skill, is greatly limited. What Denmark offers for its citizens however, is a fantastic social security package upon retirement.

Luxembourg

http://www.gouvernement.lu

Associations:	European Union.
Banking:	For more information see *www.business.com/directory /financial_services/banking/banking_institutions/commercial_ba nks/luxembourg/* information.
Business:	Luxembourg can be used to set up the following:

* Societe anonyme (joint stock company).

Societee a responsabilite limite (limited liability company).

General partnership.

Limited partnership.

Branch of overseas company.

Holding company.

See *http://www.offshoresimple.com/luxembourg.htm* for further information.

The offshore structures best suited to Luxemboug are as follows:

International holding companies:
- o Holding the stakes of a multinational in its international subsidiaries. This allows an international holding company to accumulate dividends (from its subsidiaries) in a tax-efficient way. This structure leaves the controlling company exempt from withholding tax when it pays out its own dividends to its international multinational company.
- o Lending money to all members of a group in which it has invested at least 10% of its capital. It can then receive interest or other types of payment in a tax-efficient way, and can pay them onto its owners without taxation.

Licensing, royalties and franchising
The legislation was drafted mainly for patents, and is great for that. It has been used for licensing and franchising with some limitations.

Investment fund management
Three types of funds are provided:
- o A mutual fund (unit trust) or fond commun de placement, which does not have separate legal identity, but which has a set of legally-defined relationships between fund, manager, and custodian.
- o Societe d'investissement a capital variable (SICAV) is an open-ended vehicle having a variable capital, which is always equal to the net asset value of the fund.
- o SICAF (Societe d'investissement a capital fixte) is a closed-end fund, normally used for private placements.

Luxembourg is increasingly becoming the choice of US mutual funds.

Offshore banking unit
These offer:
Multi-currency lending and loan syndication.
Issuance and listing of securities, particularly eurobonds.
Custodial and depositary services.

Fiduciary business, which is the local equivalent of the trust.
Project and international financing vehicles.
Equity and financial derivatives issuance and trading.
Foreign exchange trading.
Trade finance.
Gold trading (settled through CEDEL[4])

Financial Services Company
This allows financial institutions to offer fiduciary products to their clients without the being seen as the owner of the product.

Insurance
Pension providers can sell and operate their schemes in multiple EU countries.

Ship management and maritime operations
Companies that run from Luxembourg receive favourable tax advantages.
10% tax for non-resident crew, rollover of capital gains on liquidated vessels within two years for the purchase of a new vessel, thus avoiding tax on the sale, exemption from municipal business tax, tax credits and accelerated depreciation allowances.

Climate:	Modified continental with mild winters, cool summers.
Communications:	Excellent.
Corporate Tax:	Withholding tax is deductible from dividends (25%), profit shares (variable), royalties (10% to 12%), directors' remuneration (20%), management fees (28.2%), and auditors' fees (39.7%).

Impot sur le Revenu or IR (income tax) is charged on:
- Income from trade or business - business income.
- Professional income.
- Agricultural and forestry income.
- Self-employment income.
- Employment income.
- Pensions and annuities.
- Investment income.
- Income from letting and leasing.
- Other income (including capital gains).

---

[4] A centralized clearing system for eurobonds.

The top tax rate is 47.15%. (After the current government reforms, this may drop to 38% with the minimum income before taxes apply, rising from LUF 270,000 to LUF 393,314).

Sole proprietors and partnerships turning over LUF 900,000 will also pay municipal business tax. There is a fortune tax which taxes world wide net worth.. This is mainly on agricultural property businesses and real estate. Liabilities and debts are deductible after 0.5% is levied for wealth tax.

Currency:	Euro (EUR). Luxembourg Franc (LUF) is now obsolete. (US$1.00 is equivalent to LUF 33.5342).
Entry and exit:	One airport.
GDP per capita:	$55,100 (2003 est.).
Language:	Luxembourgish (national language), German (adminis-trative language), and French (administrative language).
Location:	Western Europe, between France and Germany.
Main industry:	Banking, iron and steel, food processing, chemicals, metal products, engineering, tires, glass, and aluminium.
National disasters:	None.
Non-resident stay:	Six months stay. Tax is levied against your worldwide income.
Personal Tax:	It ranges from 20% to over 47%.
Religion:	87% Roman Catholic, 13% Protestants, Jews, and Muslims (2000).
Stability:	Ultra safe and stable.

Muslim community information:
http://www.islamicfinder.org/getitWorld.php?id =25628&lang=

Jewish community information:
http://www.maven.co.il/synagogues/synagogues-search.asp?C=409

Buddhist community informatio:
http://www.buddhanet.net/euro_dir/eur_bell .htm#luxembourg

Christian community information:
http://www.reformiert-online.net/weltweit/85_eng.php

The horrendously large taxes on high net worth assets and incomes make this country one to miss concerning residency. However, if you are running a company and require minimising your exposure to taxes by utilising one of the business structures offered though the offshore business sector, then Luxembourg may be the place for you. Incorporation is easy and simple and with the help of an astute financial and offshore advisor, you will be able to fully utilise these structures, and cut your withholding and income taxes to a minimum.

Liechtenstein

http://www.liechtenstein.li

Associations:	Switzerland.
Banking:	There are four main banks in Liechtenstein. See *http://www.swconsult.ch/cgi-bin/banklie.pl* for more details.
Business:	The offshore structures offered in Liechtenstein are: Company limited by shares. Limited liability companie.

- The Establishment (Anstalt). Be careful when using this. As a non-resident, avoid using an Anstalt to invest in property or securities in your home country, otherwise you run the risk that you will be taxed personally on its income, and even worse, that the Anstalt's stock in your country and real estate will be taxable property in your home country for estate tax purposes upon your death.

The foundation (Stiftung).
The trust enterprise.
Trusts.

There are some taxes associated with these structures that you will be able to reduce to a single figure percentage tax liability in the set-up year, and less than 1% tax in subsequent years with advice from a good trust lawyer and tax advisor (these are abundant in Liechtenstein). For a secret ultra low tax holding company, have a look at this tax haven.

Climate:	Continental; cold, cloudy winters with frequent snow or rain, cool to moderately warm, cloudy, and humid summers.
Communications:	Excellent.
Corporate Tax:	Income tax, net worth tax, gift tax, estate tax, and the property profits tax. VAT applies to most goods and services. Avoid these and only incorporate there. A Liechtenstein trust attracts taxes.
Currency:	Swiss franc (CHF).
Entry and exit:	No airports. Use road to Switzerland's Zurich airport (one hour drive).
GDP per capita:	$25,000 (1999 est.).
Language:	German (official) and Alemannic dialect.
Location:	Central Europe, between Austria and Switzerland.
Main industry:	Electronics, metal manufacturing, dental products, ceramics, pharmaceuticals, food products, precision instruments, tourism, and optical instruments.
National disasters:	None.
Non-resident stay:	Do not maintain a home, work, or run a business there.
Personal Tax:	0% if you do not own a home or work there (draw a wage). Residents are taxed on world net worth and income.
Religion:	Roman Catholic 76.2%, Protestant 7%, unknown 10.6%, and other 6.2% (June 2002)
Stability:	Ultra stable - Liechtenstein's royal family claims restitution for 1,600 Sq KM of land in the Czech Republic, confiscated in 1918.

This german-speaking tax haven in the middle of Switzerland and Austria offers ultra low tax asset protection. Whilst not being the best-connected place to live, basing a trust or incorporating your company there will provide you with security, protection, secrecy, and very low taxes.

Austria

http://www.austria.gv.at/,

http://www.parliament.gv.at/

Associations:	EU, German, Slovene, Croatian, and Hungarian governments.
Banking:	Private, secure, and tax free for non-residents. See *http://www .internationalist.com/service/banks/austria.html*.
Business:	Resident corporations are subject to tax on their worldwide income. Non-resident corporations are taxed on income attributable to an Austrian permanent establishment, deposits with Austrian banks, immovable property located in Austria, income from silent partnerships in Austria, income from leasing or renting certain property in Austria, income from commercial or industrial consulting, or income from providing labour for domestic use.
Climate:	Temperate; continental, cloudy, cold winters with frequent rain,

	some snow in lowlands, snow in mountains, and moderate summers with occasional showers.	
Communications:	Excellent.	
Corporate Tax:	Corporate tax rate is 34%.	

Corporate tax rate is 34%.

Capital gains are generally taxed at regular corporate income tax rates. Capital gains on the disposal of qualifying shareholdings in other companies under affiliation privilege are exempt from tax.

Losses can be carried forward for a period of seven years. Losses may not be carried back.

There is a 15% allowance for export receivables.

Withholding tax on dividends and interest varies from 0% to 25%. Withholding tax on royalties varies from 0% to 20%.

VAT is at 20%. There is a reduced VAT rate of 10% (in basic goods like food, renting, or leasing real property).

Employee social security contributions are 21%.

Inheritance tax is levied on contributions of capital to Austrian corporations.

Tax of 1% to 2.5% is levied on the issue of stock, on any increase of capital stock, or other capital holding in a corporation.

Currency: Euro (EUR).

Entry and exit: 31 Airports.

GDP per capita: $30,000 (2003 est.). The cost of living is very high.

Language: German (official nationwide), Slovene (official in Carinthia), Croatian (official in Burgenland), and Hungarian (official in Burgenland).

Location: Central Europe, north of Italy and Slovenia.

Main industry: Construction, machinery, vehicles and parts, food, chemicals, lumber and wood processing, paper and paperboard, communications equipment, and tourism.

National disasters: Landslides, avalanches and earthquakes

Non-resident stay: EU citizens do not need a visa or permit to take up residence in Austria. In Austria, registration of an address (Meldepflicht), within three days of entry is mandatory for all.

Personal Tax: Non-residents are required to pay tax on Austria source income:

Income Rate	(%)
Up to 50,000	10
Next 100,000	22

Next 150,000	32
Next 400,000	42
Over 700,000	50

Employee social security contributions are18%
Acquisition tax on real estate varies from 2% to 3.5%.

Religion: Roman Catholic 74%, Protestant 5%, Muslim 4%, and other 17%.

Stability: Very stable - minor disputes with the Czech Republic over the Temelin Nuclear Power Plant.

This is a high tax and high living expenses zone, which should be avoided. You may consider setting up an Austrian holding company (currently second only to Denmark for holding company formation), private foundations, and venture capital funds. There are advantages to other high tax countries in the form of grants, loans, allowances, roll over relief etc. For our purpose of avoiding tax, Austria should not be considered.

Andorra

http://www.andorra.ad/

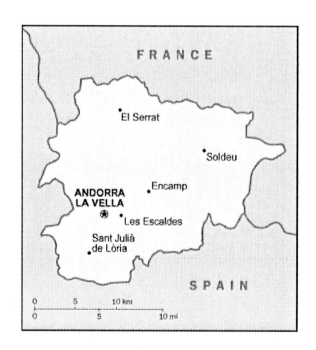

Associations:	French and Spanish governments.
Banking:	Numbered accounts offered. Secrecy and privacy well established. See *http://www.offshore-bank-list.com/ sitemap.html*.
Business:	Foreigners can only own a third of any enterprise trading in Andorra. The other two thirds have to be owned by citizens.
Climate:	Temperate; snowy, cold winters, and warm, dry summers.
Communications:	40% of population are internet users with cell phones.
Corporate Tax:	0%.
Currency:	Euro (EUR).
Entry and exit:	No Airport, access by road from France or Spain.

GDP per capita:	$20,000 with no taxes.
Language:	Catalan (official), French, Castilian, and Portuguese.
Location:	Southwestern Europe, between France and Spain.
Main industry:	Tourism (mainly skiing).
National disasters:	Avalanches.
Non-resident stay:	183 days or less per year. You will need a Passive Residence Permit (PRP) or a work permit.
Personal Tax:	0%.
Religion:	Roman Catholic (predominant).
Stability:	Has never had international dispute.

To gain nationality without carrying out business in Andorra, you need to get a Passive Residence Permit (PRP). To qualify, you need to satisfy the following criteria:

- Have annual income of €24,000 for the head of the family, and €6,000 for each dependent family member.
- Prove that you were a good citizen in your previous domicile.
- Show that you have health insurance and a pension plan.
- Buy or rent a house or apartment in Andorra.
- Pay €24,000 and €6,000 per dependent to the government. This amount will earn no interest but is refundable upon your departure of Andorra.

If you are European and want somewhere close to home, but tax free to live, Andorra is it. However, do not carry out businesses there (manufacture and hire staff etc). There are better places for that elsewhere.

Chapter 4

- ***Eastern Europe And Russia***

Eastern Europe And Russia

See Appendix 6 for a complete map of Europe. We shall now look at havens in the former eastern Europe and Russia.

Lydhveldidh Island (republic of Iceland)

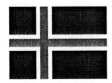

http://www.government.is/

http://brunnur.stjr.is/interpro/stjr/stjr.nsf/pages/english-index

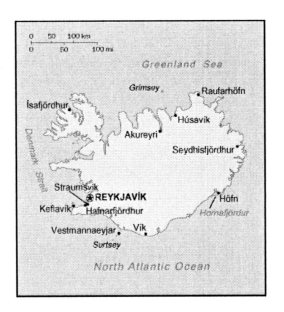

Associations:	US and Denmark.
Banking:	See *http://www.lais.is* for further details.
Business:	See *http://eng.idnadarraduneyti.is/* for further details.
Climate:	Temperate, and moderated by North Atlantic current; mild, windy winters, damp, and with cool summers.
Communications:	Excellent.
Currency:	Icelandic krona (ISK). See *www.xe.com* for current conversion

	rates.
Entry and exit:	100 airports (5 paved, and 95 unpaved).
GDP per capita:	$30,900 (2003 est.).
Language:	Icelandic, English, Nordic languages, and German widely spoken.
Location:	Northern Europe, island between the Greenland Sea and the North Atlantic Ocean, northwest of the UK.
Main industry:	Fish processing, aluminium smelting, ferrosilicon production, geothermal power, and tourism.
National disasters:	Earthquakes and volcanic activity.
Non-resident stay:	See *http://www.mfa.is/consular-information/* for further details.
Religion:	Evangelical Lutheran 87.1%, other Protestant 4.1%, Roman Catholic 1.7%, and other 7.1% (2002).
Stability:	Ultra stable - the Rockall continental shelf dispute involving Denmark, Iceland, and the UK (Ireland and the UK have signed a boundary agreement in the Rockall area) remains dormant. There is a dispute with Denmark over the Faroe islands fisheries median line boundary within 200 NM. There are disputes with Denmark, the UK, and Ireland over the Faroe Islands continental shelf boundary outside 200 NM.

Iceland is attractive to foreign corporations, as it levies no taxes on received dividends, and has an attractive 18% corporation tax on net income. Repatriated profits from branches are also tax-exempt. When no double tax treaties exist, Iceland offers foreign tax credits to aid the avoidance of double taxation. In addition to this, to top it off, exported goods and services are VAT free. See *http://www.itc.is/Iceland/corporation_taxes.htm* for further details.

Alderney

Sark

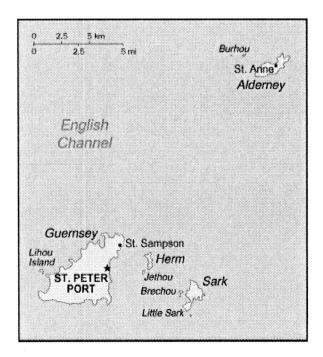

http://www.alderney.gov.gg/
http://www.gov.gg/aa-gov-about-index.htm

Alderney is 15 minutes from the UK by airplane, and offers the same benefits as Guernsey. You will note Sark, Herm, Jethrou, Little Sark, and Brechou are alternatives for this region, although Guernsey, Alderney, and Sark are the most developed with modern amenities. These islands are great tax havens due to their proximity to the UK and France. See *http://www.alderney.gov.gg/* for more information about these beautiful Islands. Also, see the section on Guernsey in this chapter.

Spain - Llivia and Os De Civis

http://home.no.net/enklaver/www.llivia.com
http://www.llivia.com/

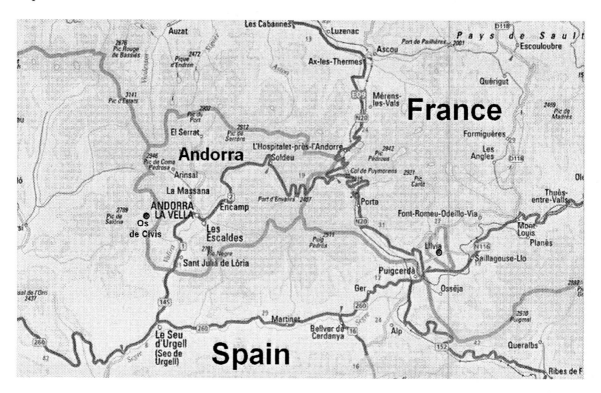

Llivia is east of Andorra and accessible through Andorra, whilst Os de Civis is west of Andorra. These Spain and Fraunce enclaves offer lower property prices than Andorra, and are great for ex-northern European residents (Sweden, Denmark, Germany, Norway etc). They offer special tax treatment from Spain and France, and levy no VAT. A short visit to these town enclaves will reveal the answers to all your tax questions concerning them.

Åland Islands - Finland

http://www.aland.fi/virtual/eng/frame.html

http://www.aland.fi

http://www.markovits.com/nordic/aaland.shtml

Associations:	Finland.
Banking:	See *http://www.qualisteam.com/Banks/Europe/Finland/* for further details.

Business:	Captive insurance and internet gambling. The traditional industries of fishing, shipping, and tourism are also an option.
Climate:	Cold temperate; potentially sub arctic but comparatively mild because of moderating influence of the North Atlantic current, Baltic Sea, and more than 60,000 lakes.
Communications:	Good.
Corporate Tax:	Åland Islands stand outside the European Tax Union. Corporation tax is 29%. A special corporation tax rate is charged for certain types of companies, and companies carrying out businesses in certain sectors. Social services contribution by employer is 25.6% of the employee's salary.

Ferries, ships, and flights to the Åland Islands sell duty free goods.

Other Taxes	Rate
Dividend	29%
Royalties	29%
	29%
Interest	(For residents, as non-residents are exempt from deductions at source).
Non-Resident Salary	35%
Sportsperson or Artist Payment	15% (To non-residents, for a personal exhibition or appearance in Finland)

Currency:	Euro (EUR).
Entry and exit:	1 paved airport. Ferry from Finland and Sweden.
GDP per capita:	€34,000 euro.
Language:	Swedish.
Location:	Northern Europe, in between the Baltic Sea, Gulf of Bothnia, and Gulf of Finland, between Sweden, Finland and Estonia.
Main industry:	Shipping, agriculture, fishing, and tourism.
National disasters:	None.
Non-resident stay:	Resident status is gained after a six-month stay. Live in Åland for five years and you will be able to apply for regional citizenship. If you moved there after your 12th birthday, you may be drafted by Finland for military service.
Personal Tax:	Income tax:

Tax Rate	Tax Base (EUR)
0%	1 - 11,599
12%	11,600 - 14,400
16%	14,401 - 20,000
22%	20,001 - 31,200
28%	31,201 - 55,200
35%	55,201 and over.

Tax is levied against world income.

Your citizenship expires after three years leave of absence.

Tax credit is allowed for tax deducted outside the islands.

There is advance tax submission for self employed.

Church tax is voluntary.

Municipal tax fluctuates between 15.5% - 19.75%, depending on the municipal authority.

Capital gains tax is 29%. Capital losses can be offset against tax.

The tax year ends December 31st

Employee contribution to sickness insurance is 1.5% and 4.8% for pension and unemployment insurance.

Religion: Evangelical Lutheran 89%, Russian Orthodox 1%, none 9%, and other 1%.

Stability: Ultra stable.

This group of islands offers a slightly lower tax than the mainland Finland, but like Finland, they tax your world income. If Swedish speaking is a definite requirement for your tax haven residence and you want to stay close to Sweden and Finland, you may want to consider Åland, but I would not as the tax savings are not great. Its isolation requires you to have an independent source of income. I suggest you look elsewhere for lower taxes.

Kaliningrad Oblast - Russia

http://www.gov.kaliningrad.ru

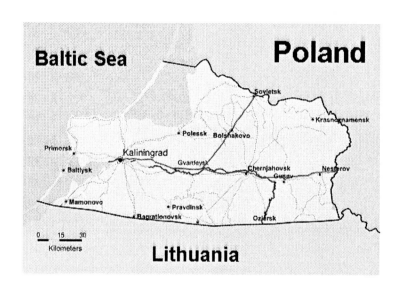

Associations:	Russia.
Banking:	See *http://www.mavicanet.ru/directory/eng/23472.html* and *http://www.klgd.ru/en/city/economy/finance.php* for more details.
Business:	The main advantage of Kaliningrad is the Special Economic Zone (SEZ). The SEZ allows manufacturing companies to produce, import and export goods and products duty free, as long as they hire locals, and bring some economic prosperity to the area. See *http://www.klgd.ru/en/city/economy/zone.php*, *www.klgd.ru/en/city/economy/ip.rar*, *http://www.klgd.ru/en/city/economy/buisness.php*, and *http://www.klgd.ru/en/city /economy/zone.php* for more details. Kaliningrad has the only ice free port in the Baltic Sea coast.
Climate:	Transitional; between maritime and continental, wet, moderate

winters, and summers.

Communications:	Good.
Corporate Tax:	0% if you operate in SEZ.
Currency:	Russian ruble (RUR). See *www.xe.com* for current conversion rates.
Entry and exit:	One paved airport. International flights to Copenhagen and Hamburg. See *http://www.klgd.ru/en/city/economy /trans.php* for details.
GDP per capita:	$8,900 (2003 est.).
Language:	Russian, and others.
Location:	Northern Asia (that part west of the Urals is included with Europe), bordering the Arctic Ocean, between Europe and the North Pacific Ocean.
Main industry:	See *http://www.klgd.ru/en/city/economy/industry.php* for details. The main industries are as follows: Fishing industry. Machinery building. Pulp and paper industry. Food industry. <ul><li>Coke production.</li><li>Extraction of natural resources (oil, amber, peat, and coal).</li></ul>
National disasters:	Spring floods and summer/autumn forest fires throughout Siberia and parts of European Russia.
Non-resident stay:	72-hour visa for $35 or 14 days visa for $150.
Personal Tax:	Same as Russia unless you have non-resident status.
Religion:	Russian Orthodox, Muslim, and other.
Stability:	Stable.

Whilst Kaliningrad may be a tax efficient location for conducting importation and manufacturing businesses, Kaliningrad may not be your ideal tax haven for permanent domiciliation. I advice you live elsewhere and do business there. For those interested in manufacturing and shipping goods to Russia, Germany, Holland, and the rest of Western Europe, consider Kaliningrad. The SEZ will reduce your production costs and increase your profits.

Baarle-Nassau and Baarle-Hertog - Netherland or Belgium

http://www.baarle-hertog.be/
http://www.baarle-nassau.nl/

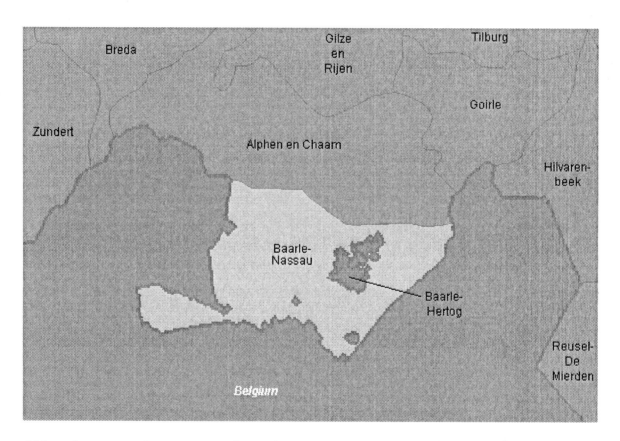

Although not a tax haven per se, the enclave towns of Baarle-Hertog (a group of 22 Belgian enclaves) is situated within the Netherlands. The Dutch municipality of Baarle-Nassau, (a group of three enclaves) is situated within Belgian soil, furthermore, Baarle-Nassau has a small enclave inside one of the Belgian enclaves. Depending on your preference of tax payments, you could move to either one of these municipalities for a better tax position. Houses on the boarder need only move their front doors over the dividing line in order to qualify as residents of that country.

Helgoland, Schleswig-Holstein, Germany

http://www.helgoland.de/

Associations:	Germany.
Banking:	See Germany.
Business:	Import/export, tourism, and health spas.
Climate:	Mild maritime weather, favoured by the Gulf stream. This gives Helgoland warm and bright summers, and mild winters.
Communications:	Very good.
Corporate Tax:	No EU VAT. All other are taxes are levied just as in Germany.
Currency:	Euro (EUR).

Entry and exit:	1 paved airport.
GDP per capita:	$27,600 (2003 est.).
Language:	High German, Low Saxon, Danish, and Frisian.
Location:	Located 70 km from the German coast line.
Main industry:	Tourism.
National disasters:	None.
Non-resident stay:	Up to 90 days before you will require a permanent resident permit.
Personal Tax:	The tax rates are same as Germany, but there are no EU VAT duties levied. The island administration does levy their own VAT on certain imports and exports.
Religion:	Protestant 34%, Roman Catholic 34%, Muslim 3.7%, and unaffiliated or other 28.3%.
Stability :	Ultra stable.

This island levies 13% customs duties, and thus tourists flock there for low tax shopping, as well as the health aspects of the clean air islands. If you want to conduct business in Germany, and being 50 KM off the coast of Germany does not affect your business, consider Helgoland. Your health will benefit from the stay. The other tax considerations are the same as for Germany, and are thus too high for my liking.

Büsingen Am Hochrhein - Germany

http://www.buesingen.de

This small German enclave in the canton of Schaffhausen, northern Switzerland, offers the best of Swiss tax laws with German language and government. See the *http://www.buesingen.de* website under Politik - Steuerregelung. Their VAT (7.6%) and taxes are as follows:

Single:	30% after €10,225 euro
Married:	30% after €20,450 euro
Child:	30% after €5,113 euro

There are also special business benefits related with VAT and income.

Germans wanting to reduce taxes but still live near Germany could consider moving there. Buesingen lies near the following lovely Swiss/German boarder towns:

http://www.stadtschaffhausen.ch
http://www.neuhausen.ch
http://www.doerflingen.ch
http://www.feuerthalen.ch
http://www.diessenhofen.ch
http://www.steinamrhein.ch
http://www.gailingen.de
http://www.singen.de

Germany also has a group of five enclaves created by a railway track between the towns of Rötgen and Monschau (south of Aachen) that were granted Belgian sovereignty. Please be aware that conscription into the German army is possible in this region.

Livigno

http://www.livigno.it/

http://www.aptlivigno.it

Associations:	Italy
Banking:	See *www.livigno.com/en/cultura/scoprire/strutture_ pubbliche/ finanziarie.htm* for further details.
Business:	Mainly tourism related ski resorts and hotels.
Climate:	Cold and dry, mostly alpine.
Communications:	Good.
Currency:	Euro (EUR).
Entry and exit:	Only accessible by road and rail. See *http://www.livigno.com /en/cultura/conoscere/notizie_generali/collegamenti3.htm* for a

	list of nearby airports in Milan, Zurich, and other towns.
GDP per capita:	$27,000.
Language:	Italian, English, German, and French.
Location:	Livigno is situated in Valtellina, Northern Italy, just south of Switzerland, Liechtenstein, and Austria.
Main industry:	Tourism.
National disasters:	Avalanches.
Non-resident stay:	Same as Italy, see *http://www.italyemb.org/Visti.htm* for details. Up to 90 days stay without a visa.
Personal Tax:	0%. Livigno is tax free.
Religion:	Roman Catholic (see *http://www.livigno.com/en/club /chi_abita/parrocchia* or *http://www.livigno.com/en/cultura/ scoprire/chiese /index.htm* for further details).
Stability:	Ultra Stable.

This northern Italian town situated near the Alps and the Swiss border is a 0% tax haven. However, it is cut off from the rest of Italy during the winters, and is only accessible through a three-mile tunnel starting in Switzerland. This is a fantastic place to live if you are Italian or Swiss.

Chapter 5

- ***Mediterranean, The Aegean And North Africa***

Mediterranean, The Aegean And North Africa

The Mediterranean area is full of beautiful countries and islands that offer sun, sea, and low tax. We shall now explore the region that serves southern Europe, northern Africa, southwest Asia, the USSR, and the Middle East. See Appendix 6 for a complete map of Europe.

San Marino

http://inthenet.sm/

http://www.interni.segreteria.sm/

http://www.sanmarinosite.com

Associations:	Italy.
Banking:	See *http://www.carisp.sm/*, *http://www.bsm.sm/*, *http://www.omniway.sm/carispsm/*, and *http://www.bac.sm/* for further details.
Business:	No VAT. There are tax incentives for non-tourism businesses.

	Check with local government offices.
Climate:	Mediterranean; mild to cool winters, warm and sunny summers.
Communications:	Excellent.
Currency:	Euro (EUR).
Entry and exit:	Can only be accessed by rail and road.
GDP per capita:	$34,600 (2001 est.).
Language:	Italian.
Location:	Southern Europe, an enclave in central Italy.
Main industry:	Tourism, banking, textiles, electronics, ceramics, cement, and wine.
National disasters:	None.
Non-resident stay:	Most western countries are allowed 30 days without the need for a visa. Longer stays will require permission and a visa.
Religion:	Roman Catholic.
Stability:	Ultra stable.

This small but unforgettable country has a booming tourism industry and a thriving financial centre. Taxes are low, and non-resident investments are tax free. Even if you do not settle here, San Marino is a great place to visit.

Mount Athos

http://www.ouranoupoli.com/athos/athos.html

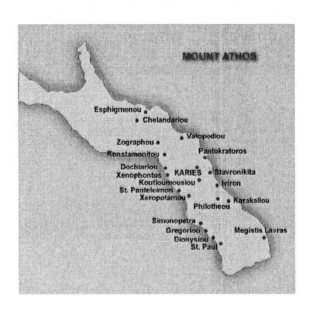

Associations:	Greece
Banking:	None. Use Greek banks.
Business:	None. This is a religious place dedicated to monastic living. See *http://abacus.bates.edu/~rallison/friends* for more details.
Climate:	Dry Mediterranean summers. The winters are mild with little snow, and temperatures that seldom reach under -2 degrees celsius.
Communications:	Very poor.
Corporate Tax:	No business activities permitted.
Currency:	Euro (EUR).

Entry and exit:	Only accessible by boat.
GDP per capita:	Exceedingly low. Heavily subsidised by Greek government and Greek Orthodox Church.
Language:	Greek 99% (official), English, and French.
Location:	Situated in the entire third eastern peninsula of Halkidiki, called the peninsula of Athos, in the Aegean Sea.
Main industry:	None (religious pilgrimages are closest industry).
National disasters:	None.
Non-resident stay:	You need a permit for a day trip. There is a lengthy process required for longer stays up to four days. If you want to become a monk, you will need to be Greek Orthodox and have permission.
Personal Tax:	0%.
Religion:	Greek Orthodox 100%.
Stability:	Ultra stable.

This is a bit different from all the tax havens we have covered so far. I added this, as some of you might wish to take up the monastic lifestyle. If you are Greek Orthodox and wish to dedicate your life totally to the monastic life of worship, then this may be for you. Mount Athos is perhaps the most beautiful place in Greece and levies no taxes whatsoever to its 1700 resident monks. A long application process is required, which if successful will allow you to live the rest of your days serving God and your fellow monks in Mount Athos. Women are forbidden by law.

The surrounding areas also enjoy some tax advantages, and visitors may visit the Mount after a lengthy formal admittance process.

Azores

http://www.drtacores.pt

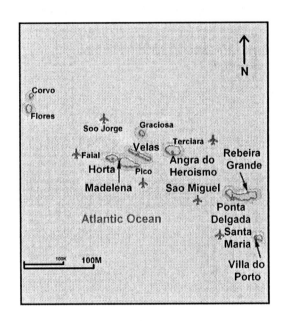

Associations:	Portugal.
Banking:	See section on Portugal.
Business:	See section on Portugal and *http://www.multi.pt/azores/business .html* for more details.
Climate:	Subtropical due to the Gulf stream. Very equable and slightly humid climate. The rainy season is from November to March.
Communications:	Good.
Currency:	Euro (EUR).
Entry and exit:	Six Airports.
GDP per capita:	$16,300.
Language:	Portugeuse.

Location: In the Atlantic Ocean, c.900 mi (1,448 km) west of mainland
                        Portugal.

Main industry: Sugar refining and liquor distilling.

National disasters: Volcanic activity and tsunamis.

Non-resident stay: See section on Portugal.

Religion: Roman Catholicism.

Stability: Very stable.

This winter tourist retreat is unspoilt and well connected to mainland Europe. It offers VAT advantages over Portugal.

Canary Islands

http://www.canary-islands.com

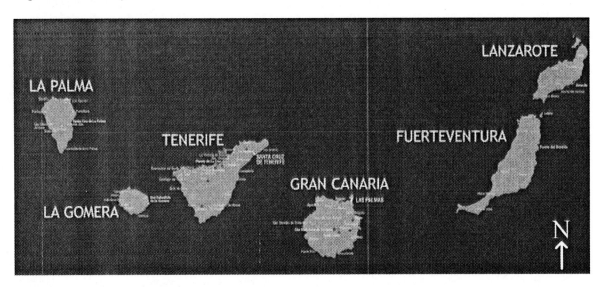

Associations:	Spain.
Climate:	The climate in the northern islands of the Canaries is subtropical; the south of the islands tends to be hotter and drier. Mainly moderate with the weather varying only by six degrees throughout the year.
Currency:	Euro (EUR).
Language:	Spanish.
Location:	Southwest of Spain and northwest of Africa, directly in front of the coast of Morocco.
Religion:	Catholic.
Tax:	See *http://www.cistia.es/ref/ref_ingles/titulo67_i.html* for further details.

This EU haven levies no VAT or duty on capital increases, and offers tax advantages for trading in Spain. It uses Spanish law and operates on a Spanish tax law framework with some special advantages. These irelands are popular for establishing a retirement or holiday home. In addition, many Brits and Mediterraneans choose it for this purpose.

Cyprus

http://www.cyprus.gov.cy

http://kypros.org/Government/

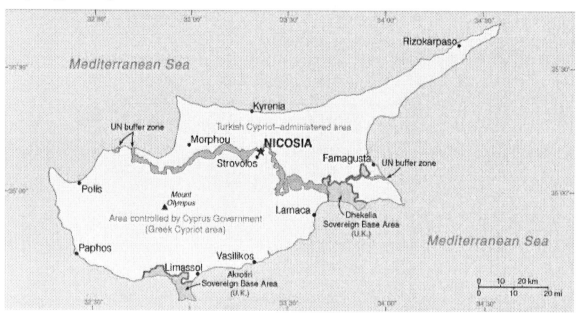

Associations:	Greece and Turkey.
Banking:	See *http://www.cyprus-net.com/browse/29/Banks* for more details.
Business:	There are eight main structures offered through the Cyprus offshore sector, which are:

Private companies limited by shares.
Public companies limited by shares.
Companies limited by guarantee.
Branches of overseas companies.
General partnerships.
Limited partnerships.
Sole proprietorships
Trusts.

	Local trusts. Offshore trusts. International trusts. Find out more about all these at *http://www.lowtax.Net/lowtax /html/jcycos.html*.
Climate:	Temperate: Mediterranean with hot, dry summers, and cool winters.
Communications:	Good.
Corporate Tax:	If you have an office or carry out business in Cyprus (whether your company is based in Cyprus or not), you will incur a 10% corporate tax, a 2% wave bill tax, and a military tax. For 2003 to 2004, an additional 5% tax was imposed on all profits exceeding CY£1,000,000. Permanently non-resident companies are exempt. To avoid the 10% withholding tax, make sure you have no business operation, royalty, or dividend income in Cyprus.
Currency:	Greek Cypriot area: Cypriot pound (CYP) Turkish Cypriot area: Turkish lira (TRL). See *www.xe.com*.
Entry and exit:	17 airports (13 paved, and 4 unpaved).
GDP per capita:	Greek Cypriot area: purchasing power parity - $16,000 (2003 est.); Turkish Cypriot area: purchasing power parity - $5,600 (2003 est.).
Language:	Greek, Turkish, and English.
Location:	Middle East, island in the Mediterranean Sea, south of Turkey.
Main industry:	Food, beverages, textiles, chemicals, metal products, tourism, and wood products.
National disasters:	Moderate earthquake activity and droughts.
Non-resident stay:	Do not stay over 183 days in a 12-month period. Residents are taxed on their world income.
Personal Tax:	Income, rental income derived from Cyprus, and pensions from employment in Cyprus. There is no withholding tax on dividend payments to non-residents. Estate duty is exempted on the following: Shares in a company owning a Cyprus ship. Shares in an offshore company. Bank deposits in Cyprus, whether onshore or offshore. In case of

death, the serving family will receive deductions on the first CY£150,000 of the value of a residence. The rest is charged as follows:

Estate value	Tax rate
Up to CY£20,000l	Nil
CY£20,001-25,000	20%
CY£25,001-35,000	25%
CY£35,001-55,000	30%
CY£55,001-80,000	35%
CY£80,001-105,000	40%
Over CY£105,000	45%

Every year you will also have to pay real estate tax on your property. This tax is levied as follows:

Property value	Tax Rate
Up to CY£100,000	Nil
CY£100,001-250,000	0.2%
CY£250,001-500,000	0.3%
Above £500,000	0.35%

The local authorities also charge property taxes from 0.1% to 0.5% annually.

If you transfer or sell your property, you will have to pay real estate transfer tax. These are calculated as follows:

Market Value	Tax Rate	Cumulative tax upper limit
Up to CY£10,000	5%	CY£500
CY£10,001-20,000	6%	CY£1,100
CY£20,001-35,000	6.5%	CY£2,075
CY£35,001-50,000	7%	CY£3,125
CY£50,001-75,000	7.5%	CY£5,000
Above CY£75,000	8%	

The gift transfer tax is levied on real estate and gifts you give to your family. These are very small however.

VAT. There are excise duties on alcohol, tobacco, motor vehicles, petrol, and soft drinks.

Religion: Greek Orthodox 78%, Muslim 18%, Maronite, Armenian Apostolic, and other 4%.

Stability: Point of concern - hostilities in 1974 divided the island into two de facto autonomous areas: a Greek Cypriot area controlled by the internationally recognized Cypriot government and a Turkish-Cypriot area, separated by a UN buffer zone. March 2003 reunification talks failed, but Turkish-Cypriots later opened their borders to temporary visits by Greek Cypriots. A UN-brokered peace plan attempts to break the stalemate over final status before the Greek Cypriot area enters the EU in May 2004.

Because of Turkey, there is a large Muslim community in Cyprus. Whilst Cyprus is a lovely place to visit, I am not sure about the long-term development in the Turkey and Greece division issue. Deciding to settle in a haven that may develop political or military problems in the future may not be wise. I advise you evaluate this for yourself before deciding. Aside from this issue, you also have the resident world tax problem. There are better options than this island for setting upon residency. You can visit and stay up to 183 days, but no more, if you want to avoid the taxes.

Portugal

http://www.portugal.gov.pt

Associations:	European Union.
Banking:	See *http://www.business.com/directory/financial_services/ban king/banking_institutions/commercial_banks/portugal/* for further information.

Business:	Portugal offers the following business benefits:

- Madeira free trade zone.
- Madeira holding companies.
- Special corporate income tax regimes.

Climate:	Maritime temperate; cool and rainy in north, warmer and drier in south.
Communications:	Very good.
Corporate Tax:	30% plus a 3% local rate.
Currency:	Euro (EUR).
Entry and exit:	66 airports (40 paved, and 26unpaved).
GDP per capita:	$18,000 (2003 est.).
Language:	Portuguese (official), and Mirandese (official - but locally used).
Location:	Southwestern Europe, bordering the North Atlantic Ocean, west of Spain.
Main industry:	Textiles and footwear, wood pulp, paper, cork, metalworking, oil refining, chemicals, fish canning, wine, and tourism.
National disasters:	The Azores are subject to severe earthquakes.
Non-resident stay:	Do not over stay 183 days.
Personal Tax:	Resident income tax

Income Bracket	Tax Rate
Up to €4,100	12%
€4,100 - €6,200	14%
€6,200 - €15,375	24%
€15,375 - €35,363	34%
€35,363 - €51,251	38%
Above €51,251	40%

Residents are also taxed on their worldwide income.
Annual municipal property tax for rural properties is 0.8%, and for urban properties, it is between 1.1% and 1.3%. Non-residents pay a flat rate of 25% with no deductions allowed for all rental or property incomes.
Capital gains tax
To defer 80% of the capital gains on property sales (property, shares etc), residents can reinvest the takings from the sale into

another Portuguese property. The deferral is to the next year, and inflation is taken into account on calculating capital gains.

In the sale of a primary home, only 50% can be deferred. Reinvesting the sale funds into the purchase of another primary residence within two years of the sale will exempt the funds from tax.

Inheritance and gift tax

	Up to €70K	From €70K to €275K	From €275K to €700K	From €700K to €1,375K	From €1,375K to €3,450K	From €3,450K to €6,850K	Over €6,850K
Minor children	-	4%	7%	10%	14%	18%	23%
Spouses and other descendants	-	6%	9%	12%	16%	20%	25%
Ascendants or between brothers and sisters	7%	10%	13%	16%	21%	26%	32%
3rd degree collaterals	13%	17%	21%	25%	31%	38%	45%
Any other persons	16%	20%	25%	30%	36%	43%	50%

Non-residents tax is 15% to 25% depending on the type of income.
There are withholding taxes on rental income.

Religion: Roman Catholic 94% and Protestant (1995).

Stability: Very stable - some Portuguese groups assert dormant claims to territories ceded to Spain around the town of Olivenza.

Christian community information:
http://www.catholic-hierarchy.org/country/pt.html

Jewish community information:
http://www.maven.co.il/synagogues/synagogues-search.asp?C=426

Hindu community information:
www.communidadehindu.org

Buddhist community information:
http://www.xs4all.nl/~verbooma/members/Uniao%20Budista%20Portuguesa.htm

Community Addresses
Hindu Community of Portugal, Rua da Madalena, 121, 1100-319 Lisbon, Ph : 21 88 75 434
Fax : 21 88 76 132, (*interbrinca@mail.telepac.pt*).

Ismaili Cultural Centre , Rua Abranches Ferrao, 1600-001, LISBON Ph : 21 722 9000/21
313 80 20 , Fax : 21 722 90 01.

Casa da Goa , Baluarte do Livramento, Calcada do Livramento, 17 , 1350-188,   LISBOA.
Ph : 21 39 30 078 Fax : 21 393 0167.

Porto Hindu Assocition, Av. Da Republica, 755-3 Sala 31,4430-201 Vila Nova de Gaia,
PortoPh : 22 375 8750 Mobile : 93 976 43 45 Fax : 22 375 8824.

Gurdwara Sikh Sangat Sahib Rua Padre Americo Monteiro Agular,   Vivenda da Luz, Serra
da Luz , 1675, Pontinha, Ph : 21 479 11 25 Mobile : 91 795 94 95.

Communidade Islamica de Lisboa, Mesquita Central de Lisboa, Avenida Jose Malhoa, 1070
238 Lisbon , Ph : 21 38 74 142/220   Fax: 21 38 72 230.

Portugal is not a low tax country, but by using the Madeira offshore structures, you will be
able to minimise your tax overhead. I advise you consider taking up residency elsewhere if
you are looking to shelter your world income. Seek professional tax and real estate advice if
you are considering buying in Portugal.

Spain

http://www.sispain.org

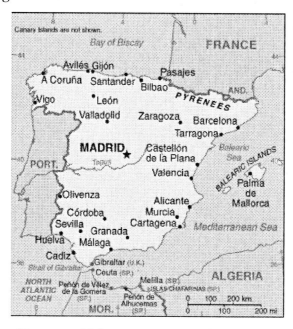

Associations:	European Union.
Banking:	See *http://209.15.138.224/inmonacional/banks.htm* for further details.
Business:	Spain offers the following structures and incentives to businesses: Co-ordination centres (Basque and Navarre). Spanish holding companies (ETVE). Venture capital funds. The Canary Islands Special Zone. See *www.lowtax.com/lowtax/html/offon/spain/spnhom .html* for a full explanation.
Climate:	Temperate; clear, hot summers in interior; more moderate and cloudy along coast; cloudy, cold winters in interior; partly cloudy, and cool along coast.
Communications:	Very good.

Corporate Tax:	30% for the first € 90,000 of taxable income, and 35% after that.
	If your company's taxable income is less than € 3 million, it qualifies for these tax incentives:
	If certain job creation requirements are met, you can apply accelerated depreciation to tangible fixed assets up to certain limits.

- New units whose values do not exceed €600 (up to an aggregate limit of € 12,000) will be allowed the application of accelerated depreciation without having recording for accounting purposes.
- Entitlement to increase by a coefficient of 1.5 the maximum depreciation rates permitted by the official depreciation tables. When your company reinvests proceeds from the sale of tangible fixed assets in the purchase of similar replacement assets, the special amortization coefficient multiplier is increased from 2.5 to 3.
- At the end of the tax period, 1% of the balance can be recorded as provisions for bad debts.

Internet, information technology, communications investments, and expenses receive a 10% tax credit.

- There is special treatment of multinational corporations headquartering in Spain.

Currency:	Euro (EUR). See *www.xe.com* for conversion rates.
Entry and exit:	156 airports (94 paved, and 62 unpaved).
GDP per capita:	$22,000 (2003 est.).
Language:	Castilian Spanish 74%, Catalan 17%, Galician 7%, and Basque 2%. Note: Castilian is the official language nationwide, the other languages are official regionally.
Location:	South-western Europe, bordering the Bay of Biscay, Mediterranean Sea, North Atlantic Ocean, and Pyrenees Mountains, southwest of France.
Main industry:	Textiles and apparel (including footwear), food and beverages, metals and metal manufactures, chemicals, shipbuilding, automobiles, machine tools, and tourism.
National disasters:	Periodic droughts.
Non-resident stay:	Do not over stay 183 days.

Personal Tax:	Non-residents pay wealth tax. For values up to $196,956.52 of assets, the wealth tax is 0.2%. Above this level, the rates of tax increase slowly. Income tax is calculated on 2% of property value and is 25% of this base. Capital gains tax is 35% for non-residents selling a Spanish property. The buyer will also have to deposit 5% of the cost of the house with the Spanish government.
Religion:	Roman Catholic 94%, and other 6%.
Stability:	Stable – Recent terrorist attacks by militant Basque activists. Since Gibraltar residents voted over-whelmingly by referendum in 2003 against a total shared sovereignty arrangement, talks between the UK and Spain over the fate of the 300-year old UK colony have stalled. Spain disapproves of UK plans to grant Gibraltar greater autonomy. Morocco protests Spain's control over the coastal enclaves of Ceuta, Melilla, and the islands of Penon de Velez de la Gomera, Penon de Alhucemas and Islas Chafarinas, and surrounding waters. Morocco serves as the primary launching area of illegal migration into Spain from North Africa. Morocco rejected Spain's unilateral designation of a median line from the Canary Islands in 2002 to set limits to undersea resource exploration and refugee interdiction, but agreed in 2003 to discuss a comprehensive maritime delimitation. Some Portuguese groups assert dormant claims to territories ceded to Spain around the town of Olivenza.

Jewish community information:
http://www.kosherdelight.com/SpainJewishHistory.htm

Buddhist community information:
http://www.dharmanet.org/Dir/World/ctr_es.html

Sikh community information:
http://www.geocities.com/gurdwaraworld/europe.html

Hindu community information:
http://siddhanta.shaivam.org/toi_spain.htm

Christian community information:
http://church-of-christ.org/churches/Spain/Spain.htm

Spain's high taxes should be avoided, unless using structures from the Canary Islands or if setting up an international headquarters. Spanish holding companies do not compete with Danish holding companies. The use of ZEC companies from the Canary Islands can drastically cut your Spanish taxes sometimes to less than a quarter.

Ceuta and Melilla

http://www.ciceuta.es/inicio.htm
http://www.camelilla.es

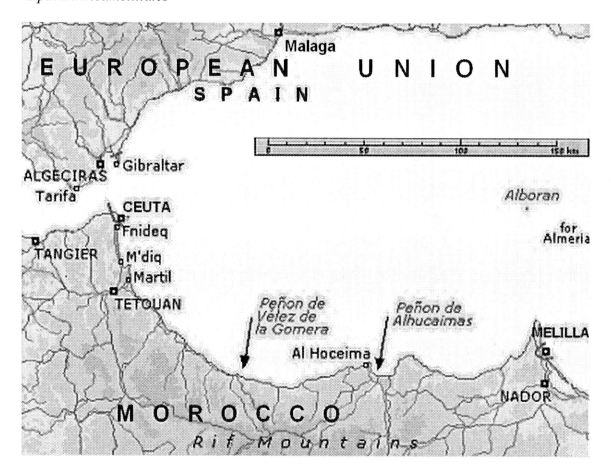

These two Spanish enclaves are little known offshore tax havens. Situated off the coast of Africa and easily accessible by ferry and plane, they offer half the tax of Spain. They also offer the possibility of being a resident without domiciliation. Tax is not levied against your world assets. They operate under the same tax laws as Spain, but charge approximately half the taxes with no VAT. They also operate duty free ports, making it ideal for mooring your Yacht.

Being a resident of these two towns automatically makes you a Spanish resident and thus, all the Spanish double taxation treaties will apply to you. Another benefit is to EU members who will automatically be able to gain residency there.

The culture is fairly mixed and you can find all religions living peacefully there. See *http://www.turiceuta.com/eng/infop/servr.htm* for more information. There are sizeable Indian owned shops and commercial traders. Many Moroccans pass through the towns daily to work or trade.

For tourist information, see *http://www.turiceuta.com/indexe.htm* and *http://www.i-melilla.com/*.

Gibraltar

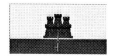

http://www.gibraltar.gov.gi

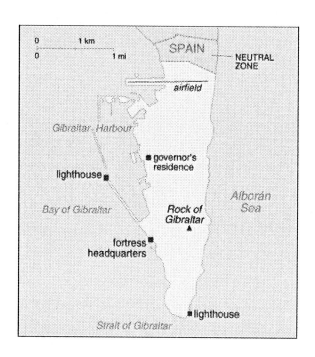

Associations:	United Kingdom.
Banking:	See *http://www.qualisteam.com/Offshore/Gibraltar* for more information.
Business:	If you own a Gibraltar licensed bank and/or branches of foreign banks, you are eligible to apply for a qualifying certificate entitling your bank to pay tax at a prescribed rate of between 0% and 35%. Usually the rate prescribed for banks is 5%, unless you do business with Gibraltar residents, then your profits are subject to taxation at the normal corporate rate of 35% in common with local trading companies.
Climate:	Mediterranean with mild winters and warm summers.
Communications:	Very good.

Corporate Tax:	The tax year runs from 1st July to the following 30th June. Do not run a local business, live there, or visit there. However, you can set up a trust, qualifying company, or exempt company there. These are the most tax efficient offshore solutions for businesses. You can also set up an offshore bank there and only pay 5% tax as long as you do not have any residents as clients of the bank.
Currency:	Gibraltar pound (GIP).
Entry and exit:	One Airport.
GDP per capita:	$17,500 (1997 est.).
Language:	English (used in schools and for official purposes), Spanish, Italian, and Portuguese.
Location:	South western Europe, bordering the Strait of Gibraltar, which links the Mediterranean Sea and the North Atlantic Ocean, on the southern coast of Spain.
Main industry:	Tourism, banking and finance, ship repairing, and tobacco.
National disasters:	None.
Non-resident stay:	Set foot or own property there.
Personal Tax:	0%, unless you gain a benefit in Gibraltar from external sources of income. A social insurance of £42.34, of which you pay £18.87, and your employer pays the rest. This affords 18 to 65 year olds disability, injury, childbirth, unemployment etc insurance. All income in Gibraltar is taxable from 17% to 45%. The following allowances apply: Personal allowance = £2,430 pa. Allowance for wife = £2,275 pa. First child only = £850 pa. One-parent family = £2,275 pa. 1st child study abroad = £955 pa. 2nd child study abroad = £795 pa. Disabled individual = £1,390 pa. Age allowance (single) = £570 pa. Age allowance (married) = £805 pa. Blind allowance = £500 pa. Home purchasers allowance = £14,000. Mortgage interest: 100% is allowed for Gibraltar property only. £10,000 is allowed as a one-off allowance on the first time purchase of a property in Gibraltar. Life insurance premiums are 100% allowed, as long as the premiums do not exceed 1/6th of the assessable income, or 7% of

the capital sum assured.

Non-residents can bypass all taxes by using a Gibraltar trust, exempt company, or qualifying company.

Religion: Roman Catholic 76.9%, Church of England 6.9%, Muslim 6.9%, Jewish 2.3%, and none or other 7% (1991).

Stability: Stable - since Gibraltar residents voted overwhelmingly by referendum in 2003 against a total shared sovereignty arrangement, talks between the UK and Spain over the fate of the 300-year-old UK colony have stalled. Spain disapproves of UK plans to grant Gibraltar greater autonomy.

Religious community information:
http://www.gibraltar.gov.gi/about_gib/Ecclesiastical/ ecclesiastical_index.htm

This is the first time I am going to advise not actually going to a country to save tax. Gibraltar residency laws state that if you set foot in Gibraltar or own property there, you are considered a resident. To avoid their 17% to 45% taxes, I advise you stay out and utilise their offshore structures (exempt and qualifying companies, or a trust).
See *http://www.lowtax.net/lowtax/html/gibraltar/jgilcos.html* for more details.

Greece

http://www.greece.gr

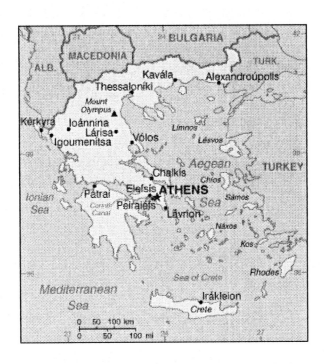

Associations:	European Union.
Banking:	See *http://www.worldwide-tax.com/greece/greinvestbank s.asp* for further details.
Business:	The Greek market encourages foreign investments. In all that concerns the grant of benefits, there is no difference between overseas investors and local investors. Nevertheless, there are restrictions for reasons of national security on the purchase of real estate in border areas and on certain islands in Greece. The types of business structures offered in Greece are:

- Foreign branches.
- Bank lending to mining, industrial, and shipping companies.

- Ships and ship management companies.
- Venture capital companies.
- Companies Investmenting in small islands.
- Mutual funds and portfolio investment companies.

For these companies there are Investment incentive allowances.

Climate:	Temperate; mild, wet winters; hot, dry summers.
Communications:	Very good.
Corporate Tax:	Taxation of employee An employer is obligated to deduct tax at source from an employee, and to make additional contributions to social security. Social security The employer's contribution is 28% of the salary. The employee's contribution is 15.9%. The contribution to social security for employees from before January 1, 1993 is to the limit of the salary as specified in law. A self-employed person makes payments to social security himself. The insurance covers pension, unemployment, and care insurance. Other deductions Tax must be deducted at source from the following payments, based on the following: Dividends - 0%. Interest - 35% (maximum). Royalties on patents -20%. Rent 25%.
Currency:	Euro (EUR).
Entry and exit:	79 airports (65 paved, and 14 unpaved).
GDP per capita:	$19,900 (2003 est.).
Language:	Greek 99% (official), English, and French.
Location:	Southern Europe, bordering the Aegean Sea, Ionian Sea, and the Mediterranean Sea, between Albania and Turkey.
Main industry:	Food and tobacco processing, textiles, chemicals, metal products, mining, tourism, and petroleum.
National disasters:	Severe earthquakes.
Non-resident stay:	Do not stay over 183 days.

Personal Tax:

Non-residents are taxed on their Greek incomes. Deposits made into Greek banks in foreign currencies are exempted from withholding tax. Capital gains for residents are treated as follows: Capital gains in Greece is added to regular income and is taxable at the same rate as regular income for both an individual and a company, other than in specific instances as defined in law.

A capital loss from the sale of an asset may in most cases be offset against regular taxable income.

A capital gain from the sale of real estate is exempt from capital gains tax.

A capital gain from the sale of shares traded on the Athens Stock Exchange is in most cases tax-exempt.

A capital gain from the sale of shares that are not traded on the Athens Stock Exchange is taxable at 20%.

Greece sourced income tax is as follows:

Tax %	The Tax Base (EUR)
5	1 - 8400
15	8401 - 13,400
30	13,401 - 23,400
40	23,401 and over

Religion:

Greek Orthodox 98%, Muslim 1.3%, and other 0.7%.

Stability:

Stable - Greece and Turkey have resumed discussions to resolve their complex maritime, air, territorial, and boundary disputes in the Aegean Sea. Greece shares the administration of Cyprus with Turkey, the issue of who owns Cyprus is still unresolved. There is a dispute with the former Yugoslav Republic of Macedonia over its name.

Religious community information:
http://www.britishembassy.gov.uk/servlet/Front?pagename=OpenMarket/Xcelerate/ShowPa ge&c=Page&cid=1042718516092

Greece will be hosting the 2004 Olympics, has strong business ties with Balkan states, and receives a large development grants from the EU (24 billion from 2000 to 2006). These are all good reasons to do business with Greece. If you are not planning to do business there then look elsewhere for your tax sheltered residency. You can stay for 183 days but no more, or you will be entitled to pay 5% to 40% in taxes on your world income.

Madeira

http://www.madeira-web.com

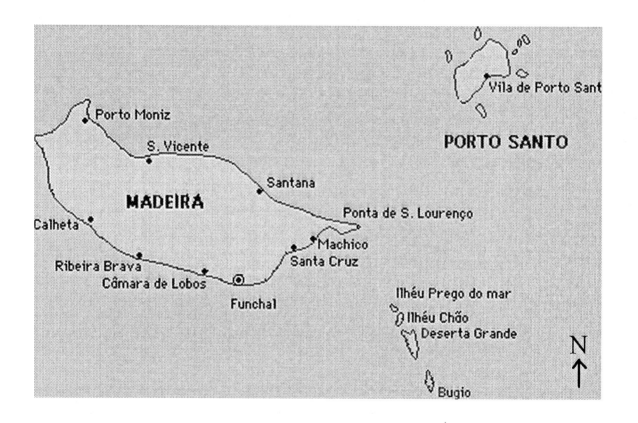

Climate:	Mild subtropical climate with warm summers, and extremely mild winters.
Currency:	Euro (EUR). See *www.xe.com*.
Personal Tax:	If you exceed 183 days stay or establish permanent residence there, you will pay tax on your world asset incomes. Taxable incomes: Employment income. Self-employment income. Commercial or industrial profits.

Agricultural income.
Income from capital.
Rental income.
Capital gains.
Pensions.
Other income.

If you are a non-resident, you will only pay taxes on your Portuguese-source income. The incomes covered are:
Scientific, artistic, or technical services performed in Portugal.
A commercial permanent establishment.
Investment income.
Pensions.
Income and capital gains from movable or immovable property.
Income tax and withholding taxes are levied and vary from 20% to 40%.
See *http://www.lowtax.net/lowtax/html/jmddctx.html*.

Corporate Tax:	Dividends from quoted companies are exempted from tax. Deductions are allowed on: 20% of representation expenses, employees' travel allowances, and passenger car expenses are disallowed. Interest on loans to finance production can usually be capitalised if they last for at least two years. Social costs up to 15% of an employee's salary are deductible (25%, if the employee has no right to social security). Losses can be carried forward for six years as long, as there is continuity of business activity. Group relief is available for 90% subsidiaries. Bad debt relief is given on a tapered scale; some types of debt are not considered bad. Depreciation is normally on a straight-line basis; there are limits on the depreciation of cars.
Language:	Portuguese and English.
Location:	850km (527 miles) southwest of Portugal.
Religion:	Catholic.
Stability:	Very stable - some Portuguese groups assert dormant claims to territories ceded to Spain around the town of Olivenza.
Communications:	Good.
GDP per capita:	US $5620.

Entry and exit:	One airport in Funchal.
Main industry:	Embroidery, agriculture, wine, wickerwork, sugar, honey, and rum.
National disasters:	Drought and tsunamis.
Banking:	See *http://www.bes.pt* and *http://www.banif.pt.*
Business:	Main offshore options are:

- Private limited liability companies.
- Stock corporations.
- Holding companies.
- Trusts.
- Shipping companies.

A company is considered resident if a rep or office operates for 120 days out of the year on Portuguese territory.

Non-resident stay:	183 days, or establish permanent residency there through property ownership.
Associations:	European Union and Portugal.

Religious community information:
http://www.a-zoftourism.com/Places+of+Worship-in-Madeira-id12903-p0.htm

For North West Africans and southern Europeans, this may be a location to spend six months of the year in without paying taxes on your offshore income. If you want to run a summer tourist or other seasonal business (120 days or less spent in Madeira), a local enterprise may also suit you. However, to avoid complications with the Portuguese government and your world income, do not over stay your tax free welcome. Look elsewhere.

Chapter 7

- *Africa*

Africa

For those seeking a tax haven within or close to Africa, you can choose from at least five. Northern Africans can also look at the Mediterranean havens, and North West Africans can look to Madeira.

Somalia

http://www.somalilandgov.com

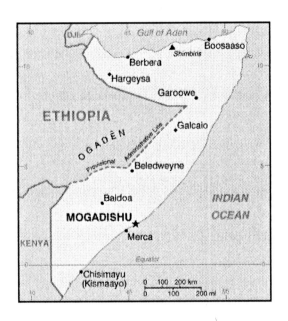

Associations:	United Nations.
Banking:	Open your own. (See *http://www.profile.co.za/fmd/data/m00938/m0093 8.asp* for the national reserve bank).
Business:	Incorporate a company there and get a tax holiday for the first three years. After the tax holiday period, you will only pay taxes on 50% of your profits. Setup offshore banks or re-domicile a bank there. There is an annual charge of 0.25% of the deposits held in the bank.

Climate:	Principally a desert; December to February - northeast monsoon, moderate temperatures in north and very hot in south; May to October - southwest monsoon, torrid in the north and hot in the south, irregular rainfall, hot and humid periods (tangambili) between monsoons.
Communications:	Poor in parts, but good in large population areas. Has internet, landline, and cellular.
Corporate Tax:	0%, apart from port taxes.
Currency:	Somali shilling (SOS). See *www.xe.com* for conversion.
Entry and exit:	60 airports (6 paved, and 54 unpaved).
GDP per capita:	$500 (2003 est.).
Language:	Somali (official), Arabic, Italian, and English.
Location:	Eastern Africa, bordering the Gulf of Aden and the Indian Ocean, east of Ethiopia.
Main industry:	A few light industries, including sugar refining, textiles, petroleum refining (mostly shut down), and wireless communication.
National disasters:	Recurring droughts; frequent dust storms over eastern plains in summer; floods during rainy season.
Non-resident stay:	You need a visa, visit at your own risk.
Personal Tax:	0%, however, taxes are collected by armed militia at illegal roadblocks.
Religion:	Sunni Muslim.
Stability:	Very unstable with numerous factions and clans maintaining independent militias, and the Somaliland and Puntland regional governments maintaining their own security and police forces. Somaliland secessionists provide port facilities to land-locked Ethiopia and establish commercial ties with regional states. Puntland secessionists clash with Somaliland secessionists to establish territorial limits and clan loyalties, each seeking support from neighbouring state.Ethiopia maintains only an administrative line with the Oromo region of southern Somalia, and maintains alliances with local Somali clans opposed to the unrecognized Transitional National Government in Mogadishu.

This tax haven is 100% off limits for residency, unless you are hunted everywhere else. The literacy levels of the residents are below 50% for men, and under 25% for women.

It is neither safe nor secure to obtain permanent residency there. The various clan leaders cannot agree on unifying their part of the country. Although currently rebuilding some form of stability, civil war could break out again in the near future. My advice here is if you want a cheap place to run a bank from, and your clients do not mind that the bank is licensed in Somalia, then register your bank there (some Muslim clients would be glad to invest in Somalia). However doing anything locally is high risk, and to be avoided.

Anjouan

http://www.anjouangov.com

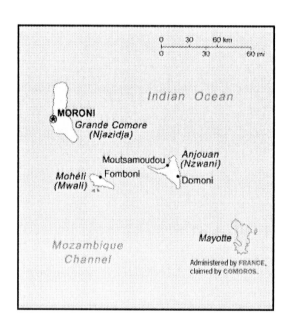

Associations:	Comoros, and French governments.
Banking:	A $17,000 fee and $10,000 reserve will get you a banking licence.
Business:	Airlines, airline companies ($20,000 for ready made),yachts, container ship registration, as well as betting and gaming ($20,000 per year charge) licences.
Climate:	From April to October, the season is fresh and dry; from November to March, the temperatures rise, and it can get very hot and humid with heavy rainfall.
Communications:	Microwave and high frequency radio. Has internet and landline phone services. Currently developing a GSM network.
Corporate Tax:	0%.
Currency:	Comoran franc (KMF). See *www.xe.com*.

Entry and exit:	Four airports in Comoros with one in Anjouan. Travel by boat to the main island, Moroni.
GDP per capita:	$700. One of the world's poorest countries and the average monthly wage is under €80 Euros.
Language:	Arabic (official), French (official), and Shikomoro (a blend of Swahili and Arabic).
Location:	Southern Africa, group of islands at the northern mouth of the Mozambique Channel, about two-thirds of the way between northern Madagascar and northern Mozambique.
Main industry:	Exporter of vanilla, ylang-ylang, orange flowers, perfume oil, cloves, and financial services.
National disasters:	Cyclones are possible during the rainy season (December to April). Le Kartala on Grand Comore is an active volcano.
Non-resident stay:	Visas are granted on entry.
Personal Tax:	0%.
Religion:	Sunni Muslim 98%, and Roman Catholic 2%.
Stability:	Comoros has endured 19 coups or attempted coups since 1975, and claims French-administered Mayotte.

This may not be a safe place to live long-term and the area has had many civil wars previously. Bottled water is advised, as tap water is unsafe. Precautions against malaria are advisable as mosquitoes are common.

Unless you invest in a company there, you cannot have a bank account. It is a good place to register aircraft, ships, and gambling companies. Registration can be carried out without local inspection. The relaxed ship and airline registration benefits makes Anjouan worth considering if you were looking to register a ship, aircraft, or airline.

Another point of interest about Anjouan is the mainly Sunni Muslim population. The custom of purdah is not upheld, and the majority of women tend to wear traditional colourful saris or chiromani. Alcohol is forbidden here and there are as many mosques as there are pubs in the UK. Literacy among women is fewer than 60% because of Sunni Moslem Shari a laws. Women are second-class citizens. This may be a dream tax haven for a Muslim. However, it may prove restrictive for non-Muslims.

Botswana

http://www.gov.bw

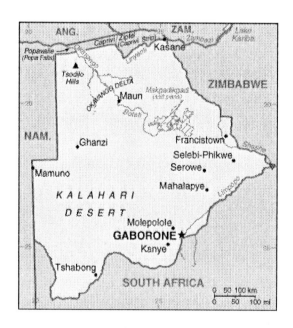

Associations:	British.
Banking:	See *http://www.financewise.com/public/edit/africa/links/af-bank.htm* for a list of African banks.
Business:	The types of structures available in Botswana are:

- Private or public limited liability companies.
- External companies (branch of foreign companies).
- Companies limited by guarantee.
- Partnerships.
- Common law trusts.
- Sole proprietorships.
- Societies, being associations of persons.
- Company setup fees are very low, and are normally less than BWP 10,000, although this depends on the type of

company and nominal capital registered in the company. (At time of writing in 2005, 10,000.00 BWP = 2,165.58 USD).

Climate:	Semiarid; warm winters and hot summers.
Communications:	Good.
Corporate Tax:	Companies whether resident or otherwise will be charged 12.5% for capital transfers. However, if you dispose of any business assets you will be taxed as follows: Taxable gains between P15,500 and 43,750: 5%. Taxable gains between P43,750 and 62,500: 10%. Taxable gains between P62,500 and 81,250: 15%. Taxable gains between P81,250 and 100,000: 20%. • Taxable gains over P100,000: 25%.
Currency:	Pula (BWP).
Entry and exit:	85 airports (10 paved, and 75 unpaved).
GDP per capita:	$8,800 (2003 est.).
Language:	English (official) and Setswana.
Location:	Southern Africa, north of South Africa.
Main industry:	Diamonds, copper, nickel, salt, soda ash, potash, livestock processing, and textiles.
National disasters:	Periodic droughts; seasonal August winds blow from the west, carrying sand and dust across the country, which can obscure visibility.
Non-resident stay:	Do not stay over 183 days or you will be taxed on Botswana sourced income.
Personal Tax:	Residents earning over BWP 25,000.00 are taxed as follows: • Taxable income between P25,000 and 43,750: 5%. • Taxable income between P43,750 and 62,500: 10%. • Taxable income between P62,500 and 81,250: 15%. • Taxable income between P81,250 and 100,000: 20%. • Taxable income over P100,000: 25%.

Non-resident individuals, trusts falling under section 14(2) of the Income Tax Act 1995, and the estates of deceased persons are taxed at the following rates:
- Taxable income between zero and P43,750: 5%.
- Taxable income between P43,750 and 62,500: 10%.

- Taxable income between P62,500 and 81,250: 15%.
- Taxable income between P81,250 and 100,000: 20%.
- Taxable income over P100,000: 25%.

If you sell or otherwise dispose of your home, you will not be required to pay any taxes on the proceeds.

The receiver of any gifts or inheritance except your spouse will pay a transfer tax. If you died, P100,000.00 will not be taxed. After this figure, the balance will be taxed as follows:
On the first P100,000: 2%.
On the next P200,000: 3%.
On the next P200,000: 4%.
- On the balance: 5%.

Religion:	Indigenous beliefs 85% and Christian 15%.
Stability:	Stable - established a commission with Namibia to resolve small residual disputes along the Caprivi Strip, including the Situngu marshlands along the Linyanti River. Downstream Botswana residents protest Namibia's planned construction of the Okavango hydroelectric dam at Popavalle (Popa Falls). Botswana, Namibia, Zambia, and the Zimbabwe boundary convergence is not clearly defined or delimited.

Muslim community information:
http://institutions.africadatabase.org/data/i157348 .html

Jewish community information:
Spiritual Leader to the Botswana Jewish community, Moshe Silberhaft, member of the African Jewish Congress and the SA Jewish Board of Deputies, PO Box 87557, Houghton 2041, South Africa.
Fax: +2711 6464940; Tel: +2711 4861434.
E-mail: *Msilber@global.co.za*.

Hindu community information:
http://www.geocities.com/Athens/2583 /toigaborone.htm

Sikh community information:
Go to *http://www.sikhnet.com/Sikhnet/directory.nsf/0/cad2bf6559a20a888725 66d3004bd0fc?OpenDocument* and ask the contact for the Sikh council of Botswana's contact details.

Buddhist community information:
http://www.buddhanet.net/africame/africadir.htm

Botswana is the perfect retreat for Africans looking for tax shelter to take up residence. As long as you do not work there and earn an income, you will avoid the majority of the residency taxes. With some planning and the use of an offshore trust, you can shelter your inheritance from taxes as well.

Liberia

http://www.executive-mansion.gov.lr/

http://www.micat.gov.lr/

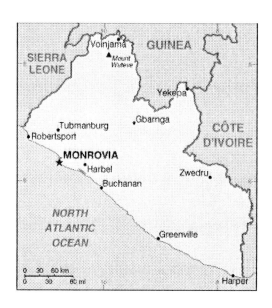

Associations:	United Nations.
Banking:	I advise you do not bank locally. Central Bank of Liberia PO Box 2048 Warren & Carey Streets Monrovia, Liberia 231-227 928 231-227 685 or 231-226 144 telex: 937-44 215.
Business:	Ship and corporation registration.
Climate:	Tropical; hot, humid; dry winters with hot days and cool to cold

nights; wet, cloudy summers with frequent heavy showers.

Communications:	Poor.
Corporate Tax:	0% for non-resident companies (offshore companies).
Currency:	Liberian dollar (LRD). See *www.xe.com* for current conversion rate.
Entry and exit:	53 airports (2 paved, and 51 unpaved).
GDP per capita:	$1,000 (2003 est.).
Language:	English 20% (official), and some 20 ethnic group languages, of which a few can be written and are used in correspondence.
Location:	Western Africa, bordering the North Atlantic Ocean, between Cote d'Ivoire and Sierra Leone.
Main industry:	Rubber processing, palm oil processing, timber, and diamonds.
National disasters:	Dust-laden harmattan winds blow from the Sahara (December to March).
Non-resident stay:	I would not advise becoming a resident here for security reasons. You will need a visa to visit.
Personal Tax:	0% for non-residents.
Religion:	Indigenous beliefs 40%, Christian 40%, and Muslim 20%.
Stability:	Unstable - domestic fighting among disparate rebel groups, warlords, and youth gangs in Guinea, Liberia, and Sierra Leone have created insurgencies, street violence, looting, arms trafficking, ethnic conflicts and refugees in border areas. The Cote d'Ivoire government accuses Liberia of supporting Ivorian rebels.

Liberia is perhaps the oldest tax haven. It has no infrastructure of local attorneys or accountants. It is simply in the business of registering corporations and ships. There are no other services offered and the tax haven clientele often never actually visit the islands. The registration of new companies is carried out by representative offices in New York, Zurich, Hong Kong, Tokyo, and Rotterdam. There are no taxes on offshore companies registered there. Liberia has been through many years of bloody civil wars and currently militia. Rebels still control some parts of this small country, therefore I would advise you not to settle there.

Sao Tome and Principe

http://www.sao-tome.com

http://www.saotome.st/

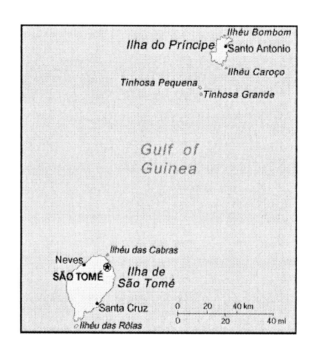

Associations:	United Nations.
Business:	There is a free trade zone on Principe, and currently there are many projects and import requirements due to preparation for the exploitation of the oil resources discovered. See *http://www.worldtravelguide.net/data/stp/stp490.asp* for more information. For further contact details, see *http://www. worldtravelguide.net/ data/stp/ stp000.asp.*
Climate:	Tropical; hot, humid, and one rainy season (October to May).
Communications:	Good.

Currency:	Dobra (STD). See *www.xe.com* for conversion rates.
Entry and exit:	2 paved airports.
GDP per capita:	$1,200 (2002 est.).
Language:	Portuguese (official).
Location:	Western Africa, islands in the Gulf of Guinea, straddling the Equator, west of Gabon.
Main industry:	Light construction, textiles, soap, beer, fish processing, and timber.
National disasters:	None.
Non-resident stay:	A visa is three months from the date of issue for single entry, and six months from date of issue for multiple-entry. Extensions are possible; apply at the Immigration Department in São Tomé.
Religion:	Christian 80% (Roman Catholic, Evangelical Protestant, and Seventh - day Adventist).
Stability:	Unstable - although independence was achieved in 1975, democratic reforms were not instituted until the late 1980s. Though the first free elections were held in 1991, the political environment has been one of continued instability with frequent changes in leadership, and coup attempts in 1995 and 2003.

Although recently plagued with civil war, this small African Island group offers economic growth and stability due to oil resources discovered off its coast. It is currently more stable than most African countries, and thus West Africans wanting to stay within West Africa but enjoy tax advantages and a more stable environment should consider São Tomé.

Republic of Cape Verde

http://www.capeverdeusembassy.org/

Associations:	Portugal.
Business:	See *http://www.tradepartners.gov.uk/cape_verde* for further details.
Climate:	Temperate; warm, dry summer; precipitation meagre and very erratic.
Communications:	Good.
Currency:	Cape Verdean escudo (CVE). See *www.xe.com* for current exchange rates.
Entry and exit:	7 airports (1 paved, and 6 unpaved).
GDP per capita:	Purchasing power parity - $1,400 (2002 est.).

Language: Portuguese, and Crioulo (a blend of Portuguese and West African words).

Location: Western Africa, group of islands in the North Atlantic Ocean, west of Senegal.

Main industry: Food and beverages, fish processing, shoes and garments, salt mining, and ship repair.

National disasters: Prolonged droughts; seasonal harmattan wind produces obscuring dust. Volcanically and seismically active.

Religion: Roman Catholic (infused with indigenous beliefs), and Protestant (mostly Church of the Nazarene).

Stability: Very stable

This African haven is highly stable and offers great incentives for business (especially exportation to EU countries), and many tax-exemptions for investors and resident businesses. If you want to do business in West Africa, consider Cape Verde. See *http://www.tradepartners.gov.uk/cape_verde /doingbusiness/* for more information.

Mayotte

http://ctt.mayotte.free.fr/

http://www.mayotte-island.com/

http://www.mayotte-tourisme.com/

http://www.rfo.fr/mayotte_ie17m.php

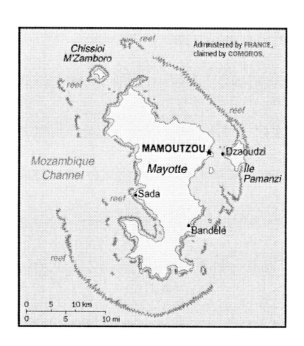

Associations:	France.
Banking:	Use foreign banks.
Business:	Heavily dependent on imports in machinery, chemicals, and food. See *http://www.rfo.fr/mayotte_ie17m.php* for more information.
Climate:	Tropical, marine, hot, and humid. Rainy season is during the

north eastern monsoon (November to May); dry season is cooler (May to November).

Communications:	Poor.
Corporate Tax:	This is 33.33% for businesses based in Mayotte. There is trading tax for all persons and companies pursuing a business. This is based on a fixed duty and the rentable value of the property used to carry out the taxable activity. The trading tax for importers is payable by importers of goods, and comprises a fixed duty and a variable tax. Deductions for capital investments for the start up or business expansions are allowed for some industries (hotel industry, tourism, and transport, and audiovisual and cinematographic production). This includes share ownership in, or investments to companies that carry out this work.
Currency:	Euro (EUR).
Entry and exit:	1 paved airport.
GDP per capita:	$2,600 (1998 est.).
Language:	Mahorian (a Swahili dialect), and French (official language) spoken by 35% of the population.
Location:	Southern Africa, island in the Mozambique Channel, about one-half of the way from northern Madagascar to northern Mozambique.
Main industry:	Newly created lobster and shrimp industry; and construction.
National disasters:	Cyclones during rainy season.
Non-resident stay:	EU and US passport holders need no visa, and length of stay is determined when you get there. You do have to bring sufficient funds to assist your case of length of stay, as well as always carry your return tickets with you whilst there.
Personal Tax:	0%, unless you earn an income in Mayotte.
Religion:	Muslim 97% and Christian (mostly Roman Catholic).
Stability:	Stable.

This remote territory is highly dependent on French assistance. Its main advantage is as a port of call for ships passing through the area. There are flights to and from Reunion Island, but due to Mayotte's location, a thriving tourist industry is proving difficult to establish. Mayotte is very close to the Comoros Islands and Anjouan, which offer many offshore tax structures. See the full listing of sections for Anjouan in *www.lowtax.net/lowtax/html /jajhom.html.*

Swaziland

http://www.swazi.com/government/

http://www.mintour.gov.sz/

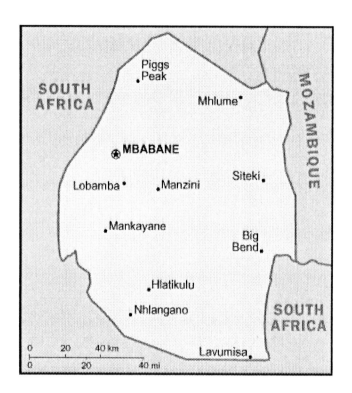

Associations:	South Africa.
Banking:	See *http://www.reserve-bank.com/szbank.htm* and *http://www.centralbank.org.sz* for details.
Business:	Partnerships. Foreign companies. Branches. Public. Private companies.

The Articles of Association of public companies include the following clauses:

A restriction of the right to transfer shares.
Membership is limited to a maximum of 50, excluding employees of the company.
Any offer for subscriptions of any shares or debentures to the public is not allowed.

Public companies are not subject to the above restrictions.

With a private company, the minimum number of shareholders is two, and directors one. However, in a public company, the requirement is a minimum of two directors and seven shareholders. So far, there is no legal requirement with regard to the nationality of the directors or shareholders. However, in some cases, exclusion of Swazi nationals may be considered as political.

In certain instances, it may be more beneficial to register a Swaziland company, for an enhanced image, easier access to credit facilities, and for obtaining government contracts.

Membership of a partnership is restricted to 20 persons, who can be either a natural or a juristic person, except for some recognised professionals such as lawyers and accountants.

Instead of operating through a subsidiary, a foreign company may operate through a branch in Swaziland, and as such, is classified as an external company. It is obligatory to register with the Registrar of Companies, and companies must in any event comply with the provisions of the Companies Act.

If you earned gratuities or leave pay in Swaziland whilst a temporary resident, you have to remit gratuities of up to 30% gross earned income, up to 30 days of leave pay, and up to a months pay in bonuses to your country of normal residence. The rest must remain in Swaziland.

Only agreements submitted to the Central Bank for approval may be used to make payments to non-residents in respect of royalties and fees from the use of patents, trademarks,

	copyrights, designs etc.
Climate:	Varies from tropical to near temperate.
Communications:	Good.
Corporate Tax:	Companies and branches pay 37.5% tax on Swaziland source profits. Foreign income is not taxed.

Three provisional tax payments are made in respect of each tax year. Any balance is payable on assessment after an annual tax return is lodged, whilst overpayments are refunded.

If your Swaziland based company receives dividends, the dividends are exempt from company tax, whilst dividends paid to non-residents whether company or individual, are subject to shareholders tax of 15% or 12.5% if paid to a company incorporated in Botswana, Lesotho, South Africa or Namibia.

A 10% non-residents' tax on interest is deductible from interest payable to non-residents, whether individuals or companies.

Tax losses may be carried forward indefinitely, provided there is continuous trade.

Companies in a group may not share tax losses with profitable companies.

Trading profits are taxable in Swaziland if the business is conducted in there.

Income for services is sourced in Swaziland if the services are rendered there.

There are certain deemed source rules.
No unilateral relief in cases of where double taxation is provided under Swazi tax law. The only possible relief for taxes paid abroad on income, also subject to Swazi tax, is under a double taxation agreement. As Swaziland only levies tax on Swaziland source income, the question of foreign tax relief does not usually arise.
Swaziland has concluded a number of double taxation agreements. The most significant are with South Africa and the United Kingdom, and concern dividends, interest, royalties, and fees.

Transfer duty is payable on land, buildings, and leases are by the purchaser at 2% on the first E40,000, 4% on the next E20,000, and 6% on amounts exceeding E60,000.

There is stamp duty on issue and transfer of shares at 1.5%.

Customs and Excise duties at varying rates are levied on a wide range of products manufactured in or imported into Swaziland. There are no taxes on wealth, estates, or gifts.

Currency:	Lilangeni (SZL). See *www.xe.com* for current conversion.
Entry and exit:	18 airports (1 paved, and 17 unpaved).
GDP per capita:	$4,900 (2003 est.).
Language:	English (official, government business conducted in English), and siSwati (official).
Location:	Southern Africa, between Mozambique and South Africa.
Main industry:	Mining (coal), wood pulp, sugar, soft drink concentrates, textile and apparel.
National disasters:	Drought.
Non-resident stay:	Entry is allowed for 60 days without a visa. A work permit is required to work in Swaziland. These are generally easily obtained if you offer specialised skills that will help in the development of Swaziland.
Personal Tax:	Income tax is levied only on Swaziland source incomes, as follows: E 0 to E 13,000 = 0% tiered until E 40,000 upwards = 30% Gratuities = 0% Gifts = 0% Dividend tax = 10% Sales tax = 12% or 20% is charged on certain transactions, importation of goods, sale of locally manufactured goods and services. Foreign income = 0% Husbands and wives are taxed individually. There are no income tax rebates. Tax year ends on the last day on June. See *http://www.globeafrica.com/Swazi/swazi2.htm* for further details.

Religion:	Zionist (a blend of Christianity and indigenous ancestral worship) 40%, Roman Catholic 20%, Muslim 10%, Anglican, Bahai, Methodist, Mormon, Jewish and other 30%.
Stability:	Very Stable

This country is one of the few countries in Africa that offer a genuine stable environment to relocate, as well as do business. If settling in the south of Africa is in your plans, then take a real serious look at Swaziland.

South Africa

http://www.gov.za/index.html

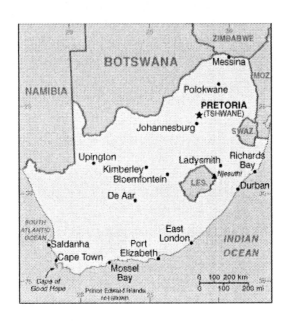

Associations:	United Kingdom.
Banking:	See *http://www.finforum.co.za/fininsts/bankdir.htm* for more details.
Business:	Incorporated partnerships, limited companies, trusts and exempt companies. International headquarters qualify for tax breaks. To see if your corporation qualifys, see *http://www.Sars .gov.za/it/brochures*.
Climate:	Mostly semiarid, subtropical along east coast, sunny days, and cool nights.
Communications:	Very good.
Corporate Tax:	The taxes levied on companies in South Africa are: • 30% for income tax.

- 35% if your company trades through a branch or an agency in South Africa.
- Partnerships in a joint partnership are taxed separately. Unincorporated partnerships are not a separate legal entity in South Africa. If you incorporate a joint partnership, it will be a legal entity, and thus pay tax in its own name.
- 40% for trusts.
- 12.5% for secondary tax on net dividends declared.
- You can deduct capital allowances. In South Africa there are various allowances granted by South African Revenue Service (SARS).
- 14% VAT unless exempt (see the note on VAT in the Personal tax section).
- Tax losses may be carried forward and set off against future trading profits.
- 12.5% is charged on dividends to discourage distribution of profits and encourage reinvestment. Gifts and other bonuses will be deemed dividends.
- All imports of goods and services are subject to VAT.
- There is special tax treatment for mining and insurance companies, and total exemption for suppliers of financial services, providers of road and rail transport for passengers, and suppliers of residential accommodation, etc.

The following are capital expenditures that businesses can claim back tax on:

- Three or five year write-off period on plant and machinery used in a manufacturing process.
- Three year write-off period in the ratio of 50:30:20 on farming equipment and machinery.
- 10% p.a. on pipelines used for transporting natural oil.
- 5% p.a. on electricity and telephone transmission lines.
- 5% p.a. on railway lines.
- 5% p.a. aircraft hangars, runways, aprons, and taxiways.
- 50%, R300m, 100% where the project is approved with preferred status, or R600m for additional

industrial investment allowance for qualifying strategic industrial projects. This deduction is in addition to any other deduction allowable.

- From 5% to 10% p.a. allowances for expenditure in connection with patents and similar rights.
- Various percentages on building allowances (buildings used in the process of manufacture, hotels, leasehold improvements, housing for employees, and residential building allowances under housing projects).

The following points are on taxation of public benefit organisations. If your organisation meets the following criteria, you will be exempt from tax. The types of activities that qualify are:

- Welfare and humanitarian.
- Healthcare.
- Land and housing.
- Education and development.
- Religion, belief, or philosophy.
- Cultural.
- Conservation, environment, and animal welfare.
- Research and consumer rights.
- Sport.
- Provision of funds, assets, or other resources.
- Other taxes include:
- Customs and excise duties.
- Donations tax.
- Estate duty.
- Transfer duty on real estate transactions not subject to VAT.
- Various stamp duties.
- Fuel levies.
- Motor vehicle licence fees.
- Municipal taxes on owners of real estate.

Capital allowances:

- Movable fixed assets that do not qualify for other capital allowances, and are used for the purposes of trade, can be claimed for depreciation through wear and tear. The asset is effectively written off over its anticipated useful lifespan.

- Buildings and other permanent structures do not qualify for wear and tear allowances (except for industrial and some other types of buildings for which there are special provisions).
- You can also claim capital allowances for expenditure on hotels, patents, trademarks, expertise, scientific research, mining capital expenditure, agricultural capital expenditure, aircraft, and ships.

Taxation Of Non-Residents
Dividends and branch profits:

- Companies and close corporations are exempt from withholding tax (not to be confused with secondary tax on companies) on dividends and distributed taxed profits.

Interest :

- Interest received by non-residents not ordinarily resident in South Africa, and by companies that are not managed, controlled, or trading in South Africa, is exempt from both normal and withholding tax.

Royalties:

- Unless reduced in terms of a Double Taxation Agreement (DTA), non-residents not trading in South Africa, but who receive royalties from South Africa, are taxed at an effective rate of 10.5%. The current withholding tax on royalties is set at a flat rate of 12% and the difference of 1.5% may only be refunded when the company is assessed for South African tax on this income.

Currency:	Rand (ZAR).
Entry and exit:	728 airports (145 paved, and 583 unpaved).
GDP per capita:	$10,700 (2003 est.).
Language:	11 official languages including Afrikaans, English, Ndebele, Pedi, Sotho, Swazi, Tsonga, Tswana, Venda, Xhosa, and Zulu.
Location:	Southern Africa, at the southern tip of the continent of Africa.
Main industry:	Mining (the world's largest producer of platinum, gold, chromium), automobile assembly, metalworking, machinery, textile, iron, and steel, chemicals, fertilizer, and foodstuffs.

National disasters:	Prolonged droughts.
Non-resident stay:	Do not exceed 91 days a year for any three years in a row, and do not spend over 549 days in any three years, as you will be subject to tax on your world income.
Personal Tax:	The taxes levied on individuals in South Africa are as follows:

- Resident tax is paid on a sliding scale. 40% is the current maximum and is payable if your income exceeds R270000 p.a.
- Residents and special trusts pay 25% Capital Gains Tax (CGT) on capital gains earned, whereas companies and trusts pay 50% CGT on capital gains earned.
- The resident annual allowance is R10000 on total capital gains earned in a year, and an additional R1m exclusion on the capital gain earned on your home. Companies and trusts have no exclusion. Residents are taxed on their worldwide assets.
- Non-residents only pay CGT on South African homes and assets of a permanent establishment in the Republic. As a non-resident, you pay no CGT on anything else.
- If your royalty income has any South African sources or rights, then you should pay 12% withholding tax.
- Resident employees are taxed at source monthly.
- There are two rates for VAT:
- Standard-rate (at 14%).
- Zero-rated (at 0%). These supplies include:
- Basic foodstuffs (e.g. brown bread, maize meal, rice, milk powders, and fruit & vegetables, etc.).
- The sale of petrol and diesel.
- Exports.
- Certain services rendered to non-residents.
- The sale of a going concern.

Etc.

Taxation of non-residents:
- As a non-resident, you are only taxed on your South African based income. The only exception is South African branches of foreign companies. These are taxed at 35%.
- Non-resident taxpayers are taxed at the same rates

applicable to residents, unless you have non-South African associated royalty income taxed at 0%.

- All dividends and interest you get from a South African source are exempt from income taxes, and no withholding tax is applied to dividends or interest.

Type	Rate for 2004/05
Individuals(non-mining)	18%-40% (Progressive System)
Companies (non-mining)	30%
South African Branches of Foreign Companies	35%
Secondary Tax on Companies (STC) on net dividends declared	12.5%
Trusts	40%
VAT	14%
Capital Gains Tax (CGT) inclusion rates (portion of capital gain included in taxable income)	Individuals = 25% Trust & Companies = 50%
Withholding Tax on Royalties Paid to Non-Residents	12%

Religion: Christian 68%, Muslim 2%, Hindu 1.5%, and indigenous beliefs and Animist 28.5%.

Stability: Stable but high crime in parts - managed dispute with Namibia over the location of the boundary in the Orange River.

Jewish community information:
http://www.jewishgen.org/safrica/synagogues/ #southafrica

Religious community information:
http://www-sul.stanford.edu/depts/ssrg/africa/ southafrica/rsareligion.html

There are many advantages in incorporating in South Africa as you have seen. Residency there however, is not advisable, as they levy taxes on your world assets. Double check the residency rules every year and keep a close eye on the DTA.

Chapter 8

- ***The Indian Ocean***

The Indian Ocean

Mauritius

http://ncb.intnet.mu/govt/house.htm

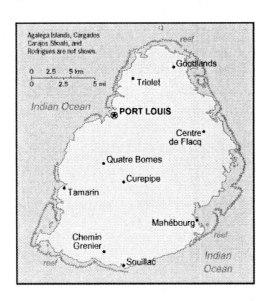

Associations:	United Kingdom.
Banking:	See *http://www.aaadir.com/countries.jsp?ID=237* for more details.
Business:	The offshore structures offered by Mauritius are:

Private companies limited by shares.
Companies limited by guarantees.
Public companies limited by shares.
Foreign companies.
GBC1 companies (offshore companies).
GBC2 (international companies).
Limited life companies.
General partnerships.
Limited partnerships.
Sole proprietorships.

	Trusts. For a full explanation of each of the above structures, see *http://www.lowtax.net/lowtax/html/jmucos.html*.
Climate:	Tropical, modified by southeast trade winds, warm. Dry winter (May to November); hot, wet, humid summer (November to May).
Communications:	Excellent.
Corporate Tax:	There are no withholding taxes per se in Mauritius, but the government achieves the same effect by charging residents income tax, and resident benefactors of foreign dividends, interests, and royalty payments. The latter is considered an agent, and thus the tax on such foreign payments is charged to the agent. This is a very complex matter, so you will need a local specialised legal adviser before proceeding. The following deductions are permitted along with the normal losses incidental to production of gross taxable income:

Capital and investment allowances based on actual cost at varying rates depending on the type of asset.
Interest costs.
Exchange losses from trading.
Reasonable directors' remuneration.
Bad and irrecoverable debts.
Approved pension contributions.
Royalties.
Past trading losses.
Rent premiums.
200% of overseas marketing costs for tourist or export businesses.
Local taxes.

The following are some particular types of deduction that are not permitted:
Depreciation.
Exchange losses on capital assets (added to cost base).
Debenture interest, when the debentures are issued in proportion to shareholdings (treated as distributions).
Excessive fees paid to directors or their families (treated as distributions).
Corporate income and capital gains (morcellement) taxes and land transfer tax.
Provisions.
Entertainment expenses.
Carried back losses.

Currency:	Mauritian rupee (MUR).
Entry and exit:	5 airports (2 paved, and 3 unpaved).
GDP per capita:	$11,400 (2003 est.).
Language:	English (official), Creole, French (official), Hindi, Urdu, Hakka, and Bhojpuri.
Location:	Southern Africa, island in the Indian Ocean, east of Madagascar.
Main industry:	Food processing (largely sugar milling), textiles, clothing, chemicals, metal products, transport equipment, non-electrical machinery and tourism.
National disasters:	Cyclones (November to April), and almost completely surrounded by reefs that may pose maritime hazards.
Non-resident stay:	Do not stay over 183 days or 270 days in three consecutive tax years. A tax year ends on 30th June.
Personal Tax:	Income tax is charged in Mauritius on:

Income from employment, including allowances, bonuses, commissions, and gratuities (in cash or in kind).
Pensions and annuities resulting from past employment, and compensation for loss of office.
Dividends.
Interest.
Rent.
Business income.

The following incomes are exempted from income tax:
Free travel between Mauritius and another country obtained under an employment contract is not taxed.
Members of the main professional bodies may deduct the costs of attending seminars, conferences, and training courses etc.
A proportion of retirement allowances is exempt.
Dividends received from incentive companies, from listed companies, or from companies which are full-rate (35%) taxpayers are exempt.
Many types of interest on governments borrowings and securities are exempt.
The first MR 1m received as a severance payment is exempt.
Personal and children's deductions.
Earned income relief (15%).
Retirement scheme premiums.
Loan interest.

A proportion of any investments made into incentive companies.

Employee pension contribution of 3% by the employee, and 6% by the employer, is required for each employee.

There is a registration duty (12% with 10% surcharge) and land transfer tax at 10% for transfers made within five years of the property's acquisition, and 5% after five years of the property's acquisition respectively.

Stamp duty is levied at 15MR per page of a property transaction including the mortgage.

Capital gains tax is levied on immovable property that is divided into at least five lots and sold. The rate varies from 20% to 30% depending on the purchase dates.

VAT is charged at 10% on most goods and services (exports and supplies to non-residents are exempted).

Religion:	Hindu 52%, Christian 28.3% (Roman Catholic 26%, Protestant 2.3%), Muslim 16.6%, and other 3.1%
Stability:	Very stable - Mauritius claims the Chagos archipelago (UK-administered British Indian Ocean Territory), and its former inhabitants, who reside chiefly in Mauritius, were granted UK citizenship and the right to repatriation in 2001. In addition, Mauritius claims French-administered Tromelin Island.

Muslim community information:
http://www.islamicfinder.org/cityPrayer.php? country=Mauritius

Hindu community information:
http://mandir.webmauritius.com/

Sikh community information:
http://www.sikhnet.com/Sikhnet/directory.nsf/0/6ea34f9b0950d0138725681a0014d3a6?OpenDocument

Christian community information:
http://pages.intnet.mu/sumau/

Seychelles

http://www.virtualseychelles.sc/

Associations:	Great Britain.
Banking:	See *http://www.cbs.sc/financial_institution_in_seychelles .htm* for more details.
Business:	The following are the types of structures offered in Seychelles: International business companies. Special licence companies. Limited partnerships. Protected cell companies. Trusts.
	For full explanation of each of the above structures, see *http://www .lowtax.net/lowtax/html/jsycos.html.*
Climate:	Tropical marine; humid. Cooler season during southeast monsoon (late May to September), warmer season during northwest monsoon (March to May).
Communications:	Good.

Corporate Tax: There is a business tax that is exempt from foreign incomes and any incomes that have been taxed with withholding or payments in which social security tax has been paid. Business tax is charged as follows:

Taxable Income, SCR		Tax on lower bands, SCR	Rate on Excess, %
Exceeding	Not Exceeding		
	24,000		0
24,000	48,000		25
48,000	96,000	6,000	30
96,000		20,400	40

NB: income with withholding tax below the 10% and 40% already applied is exempted from business tax. Withholding tax is levied on the following:
A final tax of 15% on dividends paid to non-residents.
A final tax of 10% on interest paid to non-residents other than financial institutions (for whom a nil rate applies).
A final tax of 40% on interest payments by a Seychelles financial institution at maturity of a bearer security issued by that institution.
15% on royalties paid to residents.
15% on royalties paid to non-residents on certain types of royalty. (Patent, copyrights, royalties, design and trademark are exempted).

Currency: Seychelles rupee (SCR).

Entry and exit: 15 airports (8 paved, and 7 unpaved).

GDP per capita: $7,800 (2002 est.).

Language: English (official), French (official), and Creole.

Location: Eastern Africa, group of islands in the Indian Ocean, northeast of Madagascar.

Main industry: Fishing, tourism, processing of coconuts and vanilla, coir (coconut fiber) rope, boat building, printing, furniture, and beverages.

National disasters: Lies outside the cyclone belt, so severe storms are rare; short droughts are possible.

Non-resident stay: Do not stay over 180 days in any 12 months.

Personal Tax: 0%, unless you work there, then you pay social security tax from your wages, as illustrated. The employee pays 5% whilst the employer pays according to the following scale:

Monthly remuneration, SR		Employer's Contribution, %
Exceeding	Not Exceeding	
	1,000	10
1,000	2,000	20
2,000	10,000	35
10,000		40

Religion: Roman Catholic 86.6%, Anglican 6.8%, other Christian 2.5%, and other 4.1%.

Stability: Very stable - together with Mauritius, Seychelles claims the Chagos archipelago (UK-administered British Indian Ocean Territory).

This is a fantastic haven residency at a very low price. It is less advanced than Mauritius, but then, Mauritius is less than 30 minutes from Seychelles and has a non-resident period of 183 days. So you could live on Seychelles, and spend your allocated 183 days in Mauritius as a non-resident.

Maldives

http://www.visitmaldives.com/intro.html

http://www.investmaldives.com/welcome.htm

http://www.presidencymaldives.gov.mv

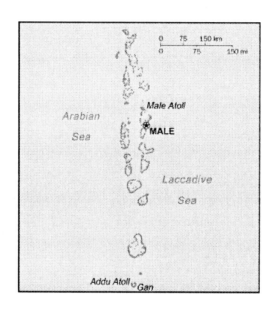

Associations:	None.
Banking:	See banking pages at *http://www.muslimtrade.net/tradeguideline /maldives* for further details.
Business:	See *http://www.investmaldives.com/incentives.htm* for full details.
Climate:	Tropical; hot, humid, dry. Northeast monsoon (November to March); southwest monsoon (June to August).
Communications:	Good.
Corporate Tax:	0% to non-residents. However, there are customs taxes that vary wildly depending on the imported items. See *http://www.Muslim trade.net/tradeguideline/maldives* for more details.

Currency:	Rufiyaa (MVR).
Entry and exit:	5 airports (2 paved, and 3 unpaved).
GDP per capita:	$3,900 (2002 est.).
Language:	Maldivian Dhivehi (dialect of Sinhala, script derived from Arabic), and English, spoken by most government officials.
Location:	Southern Asia, group of atolls in the Indian Ocean, south-southwest of India.
Main industry:	Fish processing, tourism, shipping, boat building, coconut processing, garments, woven mats, rope, handicrafts, and coral and sand mining.
National disasters:	The low level of the islands makes them very sensitive to sea level rise.
Non-resident stay:	You have to convert to Islam to be considered for citizenship.
Personal Tax:	0% to non-residents. However, there are customs taxes that vary wildly depending on the imported items. See *http://www.muslim trade.net/tradeguideline/maldives* for more details.
Religion:	Sunni Muslim.
Stability:	Very stable.

The Republic of Maldives is 100% Muslim and intolerant to any other faiths. People of other faiths may visit but cannot bring any articles representing deities. These will be confiscated at the airport. Non-Muslims cannot become citizens of the republic. These islands however, are extremely beautiful and very worth visiting. You may also wish to consider setting up a resort there, as the tax incentives are phenomenal. The republic is also classified by the OECD as a non tax haven. These advantages make commercial sense for setting up a tourist resort in this region.

Chapter 9

- ***The Middle East***

The Middle East

Moving further east, we will now consider tax havens ideally located for Middle Easterners to make use of.

Dubai

http://web-vgn.dubai-e.gov.ae:8083

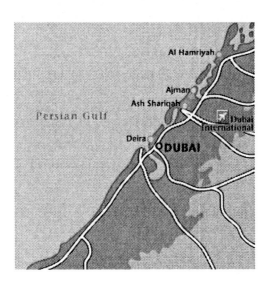

Associations:	United Arab Emirates.
Banking:	See *http://www.dwtc.com/directory/banks.htm* for further details.
Business:	The offshore structures offered are:

- General partnership companies (the chairman and a majority of directors must be UAE nationals).
- Partnership-en-commandites (the chairman and a majority of directors must be UAE nationals).
- Joint venture companies (local equity participation in the joint venture must be at least 51%).
- Public shareholding companies (the chairman and a majority of directors must be UAE nationals).

- Private shareholding companies (the chairman and a majority of directors must be UAE nationals).
- Limited liability companies (foreign equity in the company may not exceed 49%).
- Share partnership companies. (100% foreign owned, provided a local agent is appointed. Only UAE nationals or companies 100% owned by UAE nationals may be appointed as local agents).
- Partnerships (100% foreign owned, provided UAE nationals or 100% UAE owned companies are appointed as local agents).

Climate:	Sub-tropical arid climate, characterized by hot humid summers and mild temperate winters. From November until March, the weather is mild and pleasant with temperatures ranging from 14 degrees centigrade to 30 degrees centigrade. From May until September, temperatures can reach as high as 45 degrees centigrade with occasional severe humidity.
Communications:	Excellent.
Corporate Tax:	Oil companies pay up to 55% tax on UAE sourced taxable incomes, and the banks pay 20% on taxable income. You can store goods at the airport for up to six months free. Business properties pay 10% of their rental value annually.
Currency:	Emirati dirham (AED).
Entry and exit:	One airport.
GDP per capita:	$23,200 (2003 est.).
Language:	Arabic (official), Persian, English, Hindi, and Urdu.
Location:	Middle East, bordering the Gulf of Oman and the Persian Gulf, between Oman and Saudi Arabia.
Main industry:	Petroleum, fishing, petrochemicals, construction materials, some boat building, handicrafts, and pearling.
National disasters:	Frequent sand and dust storms.
Non-resident stay:	Owning a local property satisfies the residency requirements.
Personal Tax:	0%, except for import duties (up to 10%); 5% residential tax assessed on rental value; 5% tax on hotel services and entertainment; 100% tax on cigarettes; and 10% on luxury goods.

Religion: Muslim 96% (Shi'a 16%), Christian, Hindu, and other 4%.

Stability: Very stable.

Hindu community information:
http://siddhanta.shaivam.org/toi_dubai.htm

Sikh community information:
http://allaboutsikhs.com/gurudwaras/gurud_110.htm

Muslim community information:
http://www.islamicfinder.org/getitWorld.php?id= 34681&lang=

Christian community information:
http://www.arabicbible.com/directories/churches /dubai.htm

Seychelles offers the simplest residency requirement we have seen so far. The acquisition or rental of a home in the Seychelles satisfies residency application requirements.

There are three laws in Dubai, UAE law, Dubai law, and Shari a law. When considering buying freehold, be aware that Dubai law has defined that foreigners can buy freehold, but UAE law has not. If UAE law nullifies Dubai law, your freehold will not be worth the paper it is written on.

Dubai is a beautiful modern place to live and although a Muslim state, it is very cosmopolitan and liberal compared to some other Muslim countries. Its airport accommodates 170 airlines flying all over the world. There is nowhere you cannot leave Dubai to get to.

The single drawback with Dubai is the heat, as the hotter months there almost unbearable. February until May are the best months for many reasons including the weather. Everywhere you go, there will be air conditioning systems on, from the hotels, to the shops, and the cabs. You will not be too uncomfortable in the evening and night, as the temperature falls to a pleasant range.

If you are considering running a business from there, make sure you understand their laws correctly, and the compulsory 51% ownership of your enterprise by a local Dubai business, investor, or the government. There is a huge expatriate community there, and a thriving tourist industry.

Lebanon

http://www.presidency.gov.lb/

http://www.tourisminlebanon.com/

Associations:	Syria and Arab League.
Banking:	See *http://www.abl.org.lb/ABL/index.html* for further details.
Business:	A tax haven for offshore companies. See section above on Corporate Tax.
Climate:	Mediterranean; mild to cool wet winters; hot, dry summers; Lebanon mountains experience heavy winter snows.
Communications:	Good.
Corporate Tax:	Offshore companies receive special tax treatment, but are prohibited from manufacturing, banking, insurance, holding, industrial, or any commercial activity within Lebanese territory. There is a $600 flat rate charge on offshore companies. Offshore companies are subject to the 6% capital gains tax.

Currency:	Lebanese pound (LBP). See *www.xe.com* for current conversion rates.
Entry and exit:	8 airports (5 paved, and 3 unpaved).
GDP per capita:	$4,800 (2003 est.).
Language:	Arabic (official), French, English, and Armenian.
Location:	Middle East, bordering the Mediterranean Sea, between Israel and Syria.
Main industry:	Banking, food processing, jewellery, cement, textiles, mineral and chemical products, wood and furniture products, oil refining, and metal fabricating.
National disasters:	Dust storms and sandstorms.
Non-resident stay:	Consult your local consulate. See *http://dir.yahoo.com/Regional/Countries/Lebanon/Governme nt/Embassies_and_Consulates* for more information.
Personal Tax:	Residents pay income tax; this is tiered from 3% to 10% with many exemptions. See *http://www.dm.net.lb/tmalouli/practice/tax.htm* for more details. There is capital gains at 6%, dividends at 5%, profits made by foreign companies at 10%, and stamp duty at 0.3% on various documents.
Religion:	Muslim 70% (including Shi'a, Sunni, Druze, Isma'ilite, Alawite or Nusayri), Christian 30% (including Orthodox Christian, Catholic, Protestant), and Jewish negligible.
Stability:	Stable - Syrian troops have been in central and eastern Lebanon since October 1976. The Lebanese government claims the Shab'a Farms area of Israeli-occupied Golan Heights.

Lebanon is a great place for offshore companies, as long as you do not manufacture or provide financial services through your offshore company. See the Corporate Tax section above. Lebanon operates a military draft system that may be restrictive to your purpose of going offshore; because of this, I would not advice seeking citizenship there.
See *http://www.lebanonembassyus.org/consular_affairs/military.html* for more details.

Qatar

http://www.mofa.gov.qa/

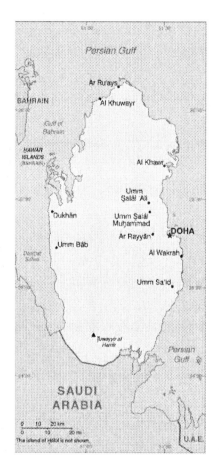

Associations:	September 1971, independence was gained from the United Kingdom.
Banking:	See *http://www.hejleh.com/countries/qatar.html#2* for a list.
Business:	The business sectors that offer the best prospects in Qatar are as follows: Beverages and Tobacco. Chemicals and related products.

Food and live animals.
Animal and vegetable oils; fat and waxes.
Inedible crude materials, except fuel.
Machinery and transport equipment.
Mineral fuels, lubricants, and related materials.
Manufactured goods classified chiefly by materials.
Miscellaneous manufactured goods.
See *http://www.hejleh.com/countries/qatar.html#2* for further details.

Climate:	Arid; mild, pleasant winters; very hot, humid summers.
Communications:	Excellent.
Corporate Tax:	0% to non-resident corporations. All Qatar source corporate incomes are liable to income tax as follows:

Amount of Income	Tax Rate
Less than QR 100,000	Exempt
QR 100,001 to QR 500,000	10%
QR 500,001 to QR 1,000,000	15%
QR 1,000,001 to QR 1,500,000	20%
QR 1,500,001 to QR 2,500,000	25%
QR 2,500,001 to QR 5,000,000	30%
QR 5,000,001 and above	35%

Taxable income is determined after allowable deductions are made for interest payments, rentals, salaries and bonuses, taxes and fees (other than income tax), depreciation, losses from the sale of assets, and humanitarian or scientific donations. See *http://incometaxindia.gov.in/double%20taxa tion%20agreement/qatar.asp* and *www.infoprod.co.il/country/ qatar2e.htm* for more details.

Currency:	Qatari rial (QAR). See *www.xe.com* for current exchange rates.
Entry and exit:	2 paved airports.
GDP per capita:	$17.54 billion (2003 est.).
Language:	Arabic (official), and English is commonly used as a second language.
Location:	Middle East, peninsula bordering the Persian Gulf and Saudi Arabia.

Main industry:	Crude oil production and refining, fertilizers, petrochemicals, steel-reinforcing bars, and cement.
National disasters:	Haze, dust storms, and sandstorms are common.
Non-resident stay:	See *http://www.qatarembassy.net/visa.asp*. Requires you have a work permit and sponsorship. Exit may be blocked if you have not completed your contract (this is rare). You can gain extended stays as long as your stay is in the interest of the Qatari government. Check with your embassy about obtaining permanent resident stay. If you are a US citizen and want to seek employment in Qatar, see *http://www.qatar.tamu.edu/orientation/* for useful advice.
Personal Tax:	0% for all non-residents. Residents pay income tax on Qatar based incomes. See the income tax chart in the Corporate Tax section. Salaries, wages, personal bank interest, and other forms of personal income are not subject to tax.
Religion:	Muslim 95%.
Stability:	Stable – Qatari military is comprised of Pakistani and Yemeni soldiers and high-ranking officers. Some of this group and others are opposed to Qatar helping the US during the Iraq war. A coup was thwarted in October 2002, which may reoccur if the Qatari government continues to assist the US in Middle Eastern campaigns. See *www.freerepublic.com/focus /news/775276/posts* for further information.

Especially popular with Pakistani, Yemeni, Arabs, and Indians, Qatar is a good choice for Muslims everywhere wanting a low tax, stable, and wealthy Muslim state to reside. You can avoid income tax as long as your income source is not in Qatar.

Bahrain

http://www.bahrain.gov.bh

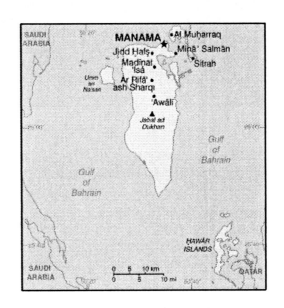

Associations:	Golf Corporation Council (GCC).
Banking:	See *http://www.newarabia.net/banking.htm* for more details.
Business:	See *http://www.newarabia.net/business_in_bahrain.htm* or *http://www.tradearabia.com/* for further information.
Climate:	Arid; mild, pleasant winters; very hot, humid summers.
Communications:	Excellent.
Currency:	Bahraini Dinar (BD) constituted of 1000 fils. Fixed against the US dollar at 1US$ = BD0.3768.
Entry and exit:	4 airports (3 paved, and 1 unpaved).
GDP per capita:	$17,100 (2003 est.).
Language:	Arabic is the official language, although English is widely used

	for business purposes, and is usually understood.
Location:	Middle East, archipelago in the Persian Gulf, east of Saudi Arabia.
Main industry:	Petroleum processing and refining, aluminium smelting, offshore banking, ship repairing, and tourism.
National disasters:	Periodic droughts and dust storms.
Non-resident stay:	A visa is required by all except nationals of GCC states. 72 hours or seven-day visas are available at the airport immigration desk and King Fahd Causeway. Visas are available at all Bahrain Embassies and Consulates. Extensions are available from the Department of Immigration, Manama.
Religion:	Shi'a Muslim 70% anf Sunni Muslim 30%.
Stability:	Stable.

Bahrain offers many tax advantages to do business in the Middle East. It has established itself as an international banking centre (see *http://www.bma.gov.bh/*), and there are many tax breaks for non-residents seeking to do business there. If you are a Muslim, Bahrain offers some of the best Islamic banking products offered in the world, ranging from traditional Islamic structures such as Murabaha, Ijara, Mudaraba, Musharaka, Al Salam and Istisna'a; restricted and unrestricted investment accounts; syndications; and other structures used in conventional finance, which have been accordingly modified to comply with Shari a principles.

Chapter 10

- ***Asia And The Orient***

Asia And The Orient

Moving further east, we will now consider tax havens ideally located for Asians and Orientals to make use of.

Hong Kong

http://www.info.gov.hk

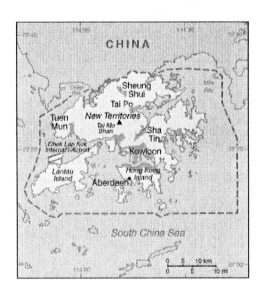

Associations:	China.
Banking:	See *www.hkab.org.hk/asp/public/memberBank.asp? Submit=Search&key=All&lan=en* for a full list.
Business:	The following are available in Hong Kong: Banking and financial services. The securities market. Venture capital sector. Investment fund management. Financial holding and investment activities. Headquarters companies. Booking centre companies. Professional services. Insurance.

	Ship management and maritime operations.
Climate:	Tropical monsoon; cool and humid in winter; hot and rainy from spring through summer, warm and sunny in fall.
Communications:	Excellent.
Corporate Tax:	16% on income with similar duties and deductions as above. For a full list, see *http://www.lowtax.net/lowtax/html/ hongkong /jhkdctx.html.*
Currency:	Hong Kong dollar (HKD).
Entry and exit:	4 paved airports.
GDP per capita:	$28,700 (2003 est.).
Language:	Cantonese and English, both are official.
Location:	Eastern Asia, bordering the South China Sea and China.
Main industry:	Textiles, clothing, tourism, banking, shipping, electronics, plastics, toys, watches, and clocks.
National disasters:	Occasional typhoons.
Non-resident stay:	There is a Capital Investment Entrant Scheme for wealthy applicants. To qualify for admission under this scheme, the entrant must pass the below criteria: Be aged 18 or above when applying for entry under the scheme. Have net assets of not less than HK$6.5 million, to which he/she is absolutely beneficially entitled throughout the two years preceding his/her application. Have invested within six months before submission of his/her application to the Immigration Department; or will invest within six months after the granting of approval in principle by the Immigration Department not less than HK$6.5 million in permissible investment asset classes (except Certificates of Deposit which must be invested within the latter period). Have no adverse record both in Hong Kong and his/her country/region of residence. Be able to demonstrate that he/she is capable of supporting and accommodating himself and his dependants, if any, on his/her own, without relying on any return on the permissible investment assets, employment, or public assistance in Hong Kong. All others not eligible for the above may apply for entry, a visa, and work permit.

Personal Tax:

Salary tax is levied on Hong Kong based salaries, bonuses, commissions, and payments by the employer into a pension fund for the employee, and gratuities at 16% or according to this schedule:

Income	Tax rate
Nil to HK$35000	2%
HK$35000 to HK$70000	7% (8% from 2004)
HK$70000 to HK$105000	12% (14% from 2004)
HK$105000 upwards	17% (20% from 2004)

If you are an employee who worked less than 60 days in Hong Kong, your salary is exempted. Moreover, even if you work over 60 days, only your salary earned in Hong Kong is taxed according to the proportion of time spent in Hong Kong. Employees working in Hong Kong companies operating outside Hong Kong pay no tax on their salary.

Housing provided by an employer is taxed at 10% of the employees' wages.

Capital gains on share options are taxable.

Employee child payments are taxable.

Any payment by an employer that can be cashed in is taxed.

Charitable contributions representing up to 10% of an individual's income, are allowed, as long as the following apply:
If you care for a parent or grandparent at home, you will be allowed US$7,700 per annum.
You get up to US$12,800 per annum for home loan interest deductions.
A pension allowance of up to US$1,550 per annum is allowed on the condition that the money is being invested in a recognised pension fund.
Depreciation of plant and machinery essential to the production of income is allowed subject to salaries tax.
US$13,850 is the single person's allowance.
US$27,700 is the married person's allowance.
US$3,850 is the first and second child allowances, and US$1,925 is the allowance on other children thereafter.
US$3,850 per person is allowed for dependent family members,

(note this is only on your immediate family and not your relations).

US$7,700 is the dependent disabled person's allowance.

US$3,850 is the education allowance for any courses that assist in your employment.

Estate duty is levied on Hong Kong based property. This is according to progressive rates up to 15% (from US$962,000 to US$1,350,000). There is an 8% per annum penalty for delayed payment, plus an annual doubling of the estate duties owed on every year you are late.

Exemptions apply to the below:

To gifts of up to US$26,000 within three years of your death, all gifts to your spouse within three years of your death, or gifts that are part of your normal expenditures made within three years of your death.

To your marriage home. However, this is exempt if you leave the home to your spouse.

To proceeds from life insurance policies under US$962,000.

To all assets outside Hong Kong.

To all assets you give to charity within a year of your death.

To any property passed on where you were a trustee (formed over three years from your death).

To pension, annuity, lump sum gratuity, or other similar benefits passing on your death from an occupational retirement scheme under the terms of that scheme.

Gift Tax:

0% for property worth less than US$128,000.

Progressive rates of stamp duty with a maximum up to 2.75% on property over US$513,000.

0.1% stamp duty is payable on shares or marketable securities, unless the transfer is a voluntary disposition inter vivo.

The following are all exempt from stamp duty:

Transactions on loan capital.

Bills of exchange.

Promissory notes.

Certificates of deposit.

Exchange fund debt instruments.

Hong Kong multilateral agency debt instruments.

Debentures transactions.

Loan stocks.
Fund bonds.
Non-Hong Kong currency denominated notes (as long as they are redeemable in that currency).
Public trusts and charitable bodies' donations of stock.

Property tax:
16% of rental income (non-resident owners pay the same as resident owners).
Deductions (rates paid, any bad debts, and repairs and outgoings allowance) up to 20% of rental income.
You are advised to keep records up to seven years.
Use a Hong Kong company to purchase property, as you will be able to allow for depreciation, financing costs, and interest costs.

Social taxes:
This is a private arrangement unless you earn over HK$4000 monthly, then you have to contribute a minimum of 5% of your salary, up to maximum of HK$20,000 per month.
Payments to pension schemes are tax deductible up to 15% of your salary.

Religion: Eclectic mixture of local religions 90%, and Christian 10%.

Stability: Stable.

List of communities and associations:
http://newton.uor.edu/Departments&Programs /AsianStudiesDept/hk-commun.html

Muslim organisation information:
http://www.islam.org.hk/eng/E-association.asp

Jewish community information:
http://www.jcc.org.hk/
Hindu community information:
http://www.hinduismtoday.com/archives/1989/10 /1989-10-03.shtml

Sikh community information:
http://www.geocites.com/gurdwaraworld/gurd8.html

Christian community information:
http://www.freeway.org.hk/hkci/

Buddhist community information:

http://www.manjushri.com/TEMPLES/Asia /HongKong.html

For those living in the east and pacific region, Hong Kong is a godsend of a tax haven. You can live there for literally no tax, as long as your income is not from there. It is a cosmopolitan business centre with connection to the rest of the world. Now under the protection of China, it has never been better.

Singapore

http://www.gov.sg

Associations:	Malaysia and United Kingdom.
Banking:	See *www.abs.org.sg/members_brieflist.htm* for further details.
Business:	Singaporean holding companies:

Withholding taxes on incoming dividends.
Corporate income tax on dividend income received.
Capital gains tax on the sale of shares.
Withholding taxes on outgoing dividends.

Fiscal incentives (service & manufacturing industries):
Pioneer status.
Development & expansion scheme.
Expansion incentives.
Export incentives.
Investment allowance incentives.
Overseas enterprises incentives.
R & D double deduction.

Fiscal incentives (financial services industry):
Fund management.
Bond market.

Foreign securities companies.
Credit rating agencies.
Research & development (financial products research).
Approved trustee & custodian companies.
Offshore insurance business.

Fiscal incentives (special economic sectors):
International trading companies.
Approved oil traders.
International aircraft leasing companies.
Interest repayments.
International shipping operations.
International consultancy service companies.
Plant & machinery service companies.

Fiscal incentives (all economic sectors):
Operational headquarter companies.
Approved royalties' incentives.
Accelerated depreciation allowances.
Interest repayments to non-residents.

For a fuller explanation of all these business advantages, see *http://www.lowtax.net/lowtax/html/offon/singapore/sinhom.html*

Climate:	Tropical; hot, humid, rainy; two distinct monsoon seasons - North eastern monsoon from December to March, and South western monsoon from June to September; inter-monsoon - frequent afternoon and early evening thunderstorms.
Communications:	Excellent.
Corporate Tax:	The corporation tax is charged at 22% (20% from 2005), on all income derived from sources in Singapore, together with income from sources outside Singapore if received in Singapore. The goods & services tax (3%) is their equivalent of VAT, and exporting companies are exempted.
Currency:	Singapore dollar (SGD). See *www.xe.com* for current conversion rates.
Entry and exit:	9 paved airports.
GDP per capita:	$23,700 (2003 est.).
Language:	Chinese (official), Malay (official and national), Tamil (official), and English (official).
Location:	South-eastern Asia, islands between Malaysia and Indonesia.
Main industry:	Electronics, chemicals, financial services, oil drilling equipment, petroleum refining, rubber processing and rubber products, processed food and beverages, ship repair, offshore platform construction, life sciences, and entrepot trade.

National disasters:	None.
Non-resident stay:	Do not over stay over 183 days, or you will be entitled to pay taxes on all Singapore based incomes.

Exceptions are for those on short-term employment under 60 days, and those whose home countries have tax treaties with Singapore entitling them to tax-exemptions. Singapore currently has tax treaties with 36 countries.

Personal Tax:	Capital gains tax is rare and only levied in certain circumstances.

Gift taxes do not exist in Singapore.

Estate duty is 5% for estates up to US $5.7m, and 10% above that level.

Personal income tax ranges from 2% on the first S$7,500 of chargeable income up to 26% for an income of S$400,000.

Singapore-sourced investment income derived by individuals from financial instruments is tax-exempt from 2005.

Social contribution is as below:

Employee	16% (may be raised to 20% in coming years).
Employer	20%.

For non-resident individuals, withholding taxes are levied on Singapore-source income at varying rates; foreign-source income is untaxed whether remitted or not.

Religion:	Buddhist (Chinese), Muslim (Malays), Christian, Hindu, Sikh, Taoist, and Confucians.
Stability:	Very stable - disputes with Malaysia over deliveries of fresh water to Singapore. Singapore's land reclamation works, bridge construction, maritime boundaries, and Pedra Branca Island/Pulau Batu Putih persists. Parties have agreed to the International Court of Justice (ICJ)'s arbitration on island disputes within three years.

Muslim organisation information:
http://www.littleindia.com.sg/religion/religion_index.htm
Jewish community information:

www.maven.co.il/synagogues/synagogues-search.asp?C=431 and *www.bh.org.il/Communi ties/Archive/Singapore.asp*

Hindu community information:
http://www.mandirnet.org/singapore_list.html

Sikh community information:
http://www.singaporesikhs.com/

Christian community information:
http://www.geocities.com/PicketFence/4745 /index2.html

Buddhist community information:
http://www.buddhist.org.sg/

Singapore offers a very high quality of life, security, and a cosmopolitan business environment with considerably low taxes for residents. There are many business incentives offered by the government to attract corporations to invest into Singapore. In addition, the government's current decision to stop taxing foreign-based incomes has now made this tax haven worthwhile looking at.

Malaysia

http://www.gov.my

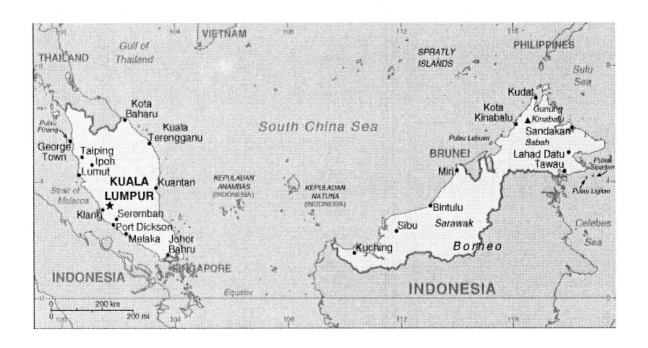

Associations:	Great Britain.
Banking:	See *http://www.ibbm.org.my/links/* for full details.
Business:	The following are some of the business incentives offered by Malaysia:

Investment tax allowances
Manufacturing companies.
High technology companies.
SMEs.
Tourist development.
R & D.

Income tax incentives

Pioneer status.
Double deduction tax allowances.
Operational headquarters offices.
Malaysian shipping companies.

The Malaysian Satay Holding Company
This is a holding company structure involving the ownership of a foreign subsidiary by a resident Malaysian company, which in turn is wholly owned by an offshore Labuan parent corporation. The benefits are:
Withholding taxes on incoming remittances.
Corporate income tax on dividend income received (special economic sectors).
Fiscal incentives (all economic sectors).

Climate:	Tropical; annual southwest (April to October), and northeast (October to February) monsoons.
Communications:	Very good.
Corporate Tax:	All companies are assessable on income accrued in or derived from Malaysia. Income from outside Malaysia remitted by a resident company is free from tax, except for banking, insurance, sea, and air transport companies. Malaysia resident companies are those with control and management of their affairs in Malaysia. The location of board meetings determines the location of a company's control and management. A tax rate of 28% is applicable to both resident and non-resident companies. In the case of a company carrying on petroleum production, the applicable tax rate is 38%.
Currency:	Ringgit (MYR). See *www.xe.com* for current conver-sion rates.
Entry and exit:	117 airports (37 paved, and 80 unpaved).
GDP per capita:	$9,000 (2003 est.).
Language:	Bahasa Melayu (official), English, Chinese dialects (Cantonese, Mandarin, Hokkien, Hakka, Hainan, and Foochow), Tamil, Telugu, Malayalam, Panjabi, and Thai. Note - in addition to these above, in East Malaysia several indigenous languages are spoken; the largest are Iban and Kadazan.

Location:	Southeastern Asia, peninsula bordering Thailand and the northern one-third of the island of Borneo, bordering Indonesia, Brunei, and the South China Sea, south of Vietnam.
Main industry:	Peninsular Malaysia - rubber and oil palm processing and manufacturing, light manufacturing industry, electronics, tin mining and smelting, logging and processing timber, Sabah - logging, petroleum production, Sarawak - agriculture processing, petroleum production, refining, and logging.
National disasters:	Flooding, landslides, and forest fires.
Non-resident stay:	Do not over stay 182 days.

Personal Tax: Residents are taxed on their world incomes remitted to Malaysia or based there.

Resident individual

Income	Tax rate
Under RM 2,500	0%
Above RM 2,500	Graduated from 2% to 30%

Personal relief

The chargeable income of an individual resident is arrived at by deducting from his total income the following personal reliefs:

- RM 5,000 for you (a further relief of RM 5,000 if you are a disabled person).
- RM 3,000 for your wife (a further relief of RM 2,500 if the wife is a disabled person).
- RM 5,000 (maximum) for medical expenses of parents.
- RM 5,000 (maximum) for medical expenses for serious illnesses for the individual, his wife, or child.
- RM 5,000 for the purchase of basic support equipment for the individual, his wife, child, or parent, who is disabled.
- RM 5,000 (maximum) for contributions to the Employees Provident Fund (EPF) and insurance, or takaful[5] premiums for life policies are allowed.
- The maximum relief for unmarried children (regardless of age) receiving full-time education in universities and institutions of higher education in Malaysia is four times the normal relief.
- Incapacitated children (RM 5,000 per child).
- A further RM 2,000 tax relief is given for insurance or takaful premiums with respect to medical and educational purposes.

---

[5] Al-Takaful (social guarantee) refers to the act of a group of people reciprocally guaranteeing one another by providing mutual financial assistance, should anyone amongst them be inflicted with a pre-defined mishap. Participants shall contribute an agreed sum regularly into a Tabarru' (donation) fund. The Takaful operator (insurance company) agrees to manage the Tabarru' fund based on a set of guidelines and on the Al-Mudharabah (profit sharing) concept. Participants are the sahibul-mal (capital providers), while the Takaful operator is the Mudharib (entrepreneur).

- RM 3,000 for wife relief if your wife opts for joint assessment. A married woman whose income is separately assessed generally has her overall tax liability reduced, although this may not always be the case. The separate assessment covers all her income sources.

Sales tax
This is an ad valorem[6] stage tax imposed at the import and manufacturing levels.

Manufacturers are required to be licensed under the Sales Tax Act 1972.
Manufacturers whose annual sales turnovers do not exceed RM100, 000 are exempted from licensing.
These companies are taxed based on their inputs.
However, to alleviate the burden of small manufacturers from sales tax upfront on their inputs, these companies can opt to be licensed under the Sales Tax Act 1972 in order to purchase tax free inputs.
With this option, manufacturers will only have to pay sales tax on their finished products.

The general rate for sales tax is 10%.
0% for raw materials for use in the manufacture of taxable goods.
0% for primary commodities, basic foodstuffs, basic building materials, certain agricultural implements and heavy machinery for use in the construction industry.
0% for certain tourist and sports goods, books, newspapers and reading materials.
0% for inputs for selected non-taxable products.
5% for certain non-essential foodstuffs and building materials
15% for cigarettes and liquor.

Tax rebate
Tax liability of a resident individual is reduced by rebates that are granted as follows:
- For an individual with income not exceeding RM 10,000, a rebate of RM 110 is given. A further

---

[6] Ad valorem is a tax, based on the assessed value of real estate or personal property. In other words, ad valorem taxes can be property tax or even duty on imported items. Property ad valorem taxes are the major source of revenues for state and municipal governments.

rebate of RM 60 is given for his wife. A wife who is assessed separately will be entitled to a rebate of RM 110 if her chargeable income does not exceed RM 10,000.

- The equivalent of the amount paid in respect of any zakat, fitrah, or other Islamic religious dues, which are obligatory.
- A sum of RM 400 for the purchase of a computer by an individual or his wife.
- The amount of fee paid to the government for the issue of an employment pass, visit passes, or work permit.

Non-resident individual

Generally, as a non-resident individual, you are liable to tax at the rate of 30%, and you are not entitled to any personal relief. However, for the following types of income, non-residents are subject to a withholding tax, which is a final tax:

Special income of classes	10%
Technical advice, assistance, or services	10%
Installation services on the supply of plant, machinery, etc.	10%
Personal services associated with the use of intangible property	10%
Services of a public entertainer	15%
Interest rate	15%
Contract payments to nonresident contractors	20%
Other income	30%

Employees staying less than 60 days will not be taxed on any incomes. However, the income of a non-resident individual who performs independent services such as consultancy services, is not exempted from tax. See the following link for more detail:

http://www.asiatradehub.com/malaysia/tax1.asp-top# top.

Real property gains tax

There are generally no capital gains taxes in Malaysia. Real property gains tax is charged on gains arising from the selling of real property situated in Malaysia; or on interest; options; or other rights in, or over such land; as well as the selling of shares in real property companies. The rates of tax are as follows:

Disposal before the 6th year	
Disposal within 2 years	30%
Disposal in the 3rd year	20%
Disposal in the 4th year	15%
Disposal in the 5th year	5%

Disposal in the 6th year and thereafter	
Company	5%
Individual	Nil

Residents selling property after five years of ownership are exempt from real property tax, and are entitled to RM 5,000 or 10% (whichever is greater) exemption on the gains.

Residents also enjoy a one-time tax-exemption on the gains arising from the disposal of one private residence.

Non-residents
A 30% tax rate is chargeable to non-residents selling property within five years ownership, and disposal after the fifth year is taxed at 5%.

Service Tax
Tax is imposed on companies with an annual turnover ranging from RM 150,000 to RM 500,000 and covers spending on:
Food.
Drinks and tobacco.
Provision for premises for meetings.
Conventions, cultural shows, and fashion shows.
Health services.
Legal.
Engineering.
Surveyor.
Architectural.
Accounting.
Advertising.
Insurance companies.
Motor vehicles service and repair centres.
Telecommunication services.
Security and guard services.
Recreational clubs.

Estate agents.
Parking space services.
Courier service firms.
Dentist.
Veterinary doctors.
Provision of accommodation and food by private hospitals.
Credit cards companies.
Hotels having more than 25 rooms.
Restaurants within or outside hotels.
Car rental agencies.
Employment having an annual sales turnover of RM150,000.
Project management coordinating services having an annual sales turnover of RM300,000 and above.

Religion: Muslim, Buddhist, Daoist, Hindu, Christian, and Sikh. Note - in addition, Shamanism is practiced in East Malaysia.

Stability: Stable - involved in complex dispute with China, Philippines, Taiwan, Vietnam, and possibly Brunei over the Spratly Islands. The 2002 Declaration on the Conduct of Parties in the South China Sea has eased tensions, but falls short of a legally binding code of conduct desired by several of the disputants. There are disputes with Malaysia over deliveries of fresh water to Singapore. Singapore's land reclamation works, bridge construction, maritime boundaries, and Pedra Branca Island/Pulau Batu Putih persists. Parties have agreed to the International Court of Justice (ICJ)'s arbitration on island disputes within three years. ICJ awarded Ligitan and Sipadan islands off the coast of Sabah, also claimed by Indonesia and Philippines, to Malaysia. A 1-kilometer segment at the mouth of the Golok River remains in dispute with Thailand. Philippines retains a now dormant claim to Malaysia's Sabah State in northern Borneo based on the Sultanate of Sulu's granting the Philippines Government power of attorney to pursue the Sultanate's sovereignty claim. In 2003, Brunei and Malaysia ceased gas and oil exploration in their offshore and deepwater seabeds until negotiations progress to an agreement over allocation of disputed areas. Malaysia's land boundary with Brunei around Limbang is in dispute.

Religiuos communities:
www.mycen.com.my/search/religion.html and *www.mycen.com.My/search/association.html.*

By combining Labuan offshore structures with Malaysian operations, you can achieve a sizeable tax advantage. Malaysian taxes are lower than in most European countries, and there are many business incentives. As a place to live however, I would advise you look to Laboun, which I will cover next.

Labuan

http://www.lofsa.gov.my

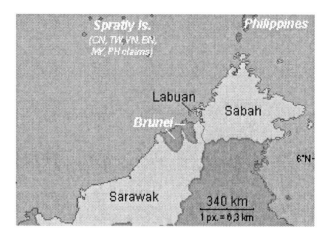

Climate:	Tropical balmy climate with two annual monsoon seasons - the South West monsoon from April to June, and the North East monsoon from September to December.
Currency:	Malaysia Ringgit (RM). See *www.xe.com* for current conversion rates.
Personal Tax:	The following incomes are exempt from taxes:

- Offshore dividends.
- Offshore trust distributions received by the beneficiaries.
- Royalties received by a non-resident.
- Offshore company interest (check conditions).
- Income from an offshore company for providing services.
- 65% of offshore entities income (the management companies and offshore service providers incomes are tax-exempt).
- Up to 50% of the income received for a period of five years by renting qualifying assets to an offshore company. (Great for property developers).
- 50% of public sector residents, offshore company housing, and regional allowances.
- Domestic company receipts from an offshore

company of second tier dividends declared out of dividends received.

- Beneficiary offshore trust distributions.
- Offshore company royalty payments to non-residents.
- Offshore company interest payments to non-residents.
- Offshore company interest payments to residents (as long as they are not in banking, finance companies, or insurance businesses in Malaysia).
- Non-resident payment to an offshore company for technical or management fees.
- 50% of employment income from a Labuan employed non-Malaysian citizen util 2004.

Travel cost within Malaysia
Leave passage up to three a year, or a single leave passage costs up to RM 3,000 outside of Malaysia.

Income tax

Income	Rate
Up to RM 2,500	0%
Up to RM 5,000	1%
Up to RM 20,000	3%
Up to RM 35,000	7%
Up to RM 50,000	13%
Up to RM 70,000	19%
Up to RM 100,000	24%
Up to RM 250,000	27%
Over RM 250,000	28%

Deductions for residents

- Interest on borrowings used to finance the purchase of income-producing property or investments.
- Donations of cash to the government, a local authority, or an institution or organization approved by the tax authorities.
- A rebate of RM 400 is allowed to individuals once every five years for the purchase of a personal computer, which may not be used for business purposes.
- Foreign employees may claim a rebate for amounts spent to obtain employment passes, visit passes, and work permits.
- Personal allowances include RM 8,000 for yourself,

and RM 3,000 for your spouse.
- Medical expenses for parents to RM 5,000.
- Expenses for disabled family members.
- Life insurance premiums/provident fund contributions to RM 5,000.
- Medical expenses for yourself, wife, or child with serious disease to RM 5,000.
- Medical and educational insurance premiums to RM 2,000.

Withholding tax for non-resident local source income
- Use of movable property (i.e. rental income) - 10%.
- Technical advice, assistance, or services - 10%.
- Installation services for the supply of plant, machinery, and similar assets - 10%.
- Personal services associated with the use of intangible property - 10%.
- Royalties for the use or conveyance of intangible property - 10%.
- Services of a public entertainer - 15%.
- Interest - 15%.
- Contract payments to non-resident contractors - 20%.
- Other income - 30%.

Short-term visitors are exempt from income tax as long as they do not work more than 60 days a calendar year.

If you are earning income in Malaysia, and you are from a country which has tax treaties with Malaysia, that income will be exempt from income tax as long as it is not paid by a resident (company or individual).

Social security tax

Expatriates earning over RM 2,500 per month	0%
Employee	11%
Employer	12%

NB. Expatriates choosing to pay Employees Provident Fund (EPF) will receive tax relief. You may withdraw your contributions tax free if you are leaving Malaysia permanently.

Corporate Tax: All companies are assessable on income accrued in or derived from Malaysia.
Income from outside Malaysia remitted by a resident company is

free from tax, except for banking, insurance, sea, and air transport companies.

Malaysia resident companies are those with control and management of their affairs in Malaysia.

The location of board meetings determines the location of a companies control and management.

A tax rate of 28% is applicable to both resident and non-resident companies. In the case of a company carrying on petroleum production, the applicable tax rate is 38%.

There is a 5% to 15% sales tax on goods imported for local consumption, and on locally manufactured goods.

There is a 5% service tax on restaurants, and hotels etc.

Rates of income tax
Income tax is imposed at the rate of 28% on chargeable income for resident companies.

A non-resident company pays 28% on chargeable income from Malaysian sources other than:

Source	Tax Rate
Branch remittance tax	0%
Interest	15%
Royalties	10%
Technical fees	10%
Payments for use of movable property	10%
Payments to non-resident contractors	20%

Bank interest paid to non-residents without a place of business in Malaysia is exempt from tax.

Development tax (the government plans to abolish this tax in stages)
There is 4% charge on net income from Malaysia registered or based royalties, businesses, or property rental.

Real property gains tax
There are generally no capital gains taxes in Malaysia. Real property gains tax is charged on gains arising from the selling of real property situated in Malaysia; or on interest; options; or other rights in, or over such land; as well as the selling of shares in real property companies. The rates of tax are as follows:

Disposal before the 6th year	
Disposal within 2 years	30%
Disposal in the 3rd year	20%
Disposal in the 4th year	15%
Disposal in the 5th year	5%

Disposal in the 6th year and thereafter	
Company	5%
Individual	Nil

Residents selling property after five years of ownership are exempt from real property tax, and are entitled to RM 5,000 or 10% (whichever is greater) exemption on the gains.

Residents also enjoy a one-time tax-exemption on the gains arising from the disposal of one private residence.

Language:	Bahasa Melayu is the national language. However, English, Chinese, and Tamil are widely spoken.
Location:	Labuan comprises of one main island, and six smaller islets, covering an area of 95 sq. km. It is located off the coast of Borneo at Latitude 5 N and Longitude 115 E.
Religion:	Islam is the official religion of Malaysia. Freedom of worship is guaranteed. Places of worship for Muslims, Hindus, Christians, and Buddhists are available.
Stability:	Very stable.
Communications:	Very good.
GDP per capita:	$941 (2000 est.).
Entry and exit:	One Airport.
Main industry:	See table below:

Sector	GDP (%)
Mining (Gas/Petroleum)	41.3%
Manufacturing	15.2%
Contractors/Retail/Hotel/Restaurant	11.2%
Finance/Insurance/Real Estate/Services	9.2%
Transportation/Store/Communication Services	8.3%
Community/Personal Services	6.7%
Construction	6%
Agriculture	1.7%

National disasters:	Flooding and landslides.
Banking:	See *www.privatebanking.info/user/category.jsp?Location_id=73*

	39&category_id=1&category_page_id=0&published=1 for more details.
Business:	The following structures are available in Labaun:
	Private companies limited by shares.
	Companies limited by guarantee.
	Public companies limited by shares.
	Foreign companies.
	Branches of foreign companies.
	Offshore Companies
	Offshore limited partnerships.
	Trusts
	See *http://www.lowtax.com/lowtax/html/jlbcos.html* for in-depth detail.
Non-resident stay:	Do not over stay 182 days in any three years, or if you are planning on regular stays, do not over stay 90 days in any three or four-year period.
Associations:	Malaysia.

Religious communities:
www.mycen.com.my/search/religion.html and *www.mycen.com.my/search/associa tion.html*.

Buddhist community information:
The Labuan Buddhist Association
    462-B, Jalan Tenaga, W.P.Labuan.
    P.O.Box : 80154,
    87011 W.P.Labuan
    Tel: 087-417699,
    Fax: 087-416128

Brunei Derussalam

http://www.brunei.gov.bn/index.htm

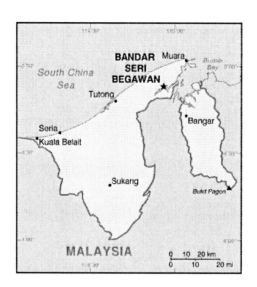

Associations:	Britain.
Banking:	Use *http://www.ibb.com.bn/*, and the following banks. Baiduri Bank. Berhad Development Bank of Brune. Berhad. Hong Kong Bank. Overseas Union Bank (OUB). Sime Bank Berhad. Citibank. Islamic Bank of Brunei Berhad (IBB)Berhad. Standard Chartered Bank.
Business:	See *http://www.offshore-fox.com/offshore-corporations/offshore_corporations_0414.html*, *http://www.bedb.com.bn/invguide.asp*, http://www.brunet.bn/org/bsmehp/business/taxes/smetaxa.htm and http://www.vyapaarasia.com/brunei/ for details.

Communications:	Excellent.
Currency:	Bruneian dollar (BND). See *www.xe.com* for current conversion rates.
Entry and exit:	2 airports (1 paved, and 1 unpaved).
GDP per capita:	$18,600 (2002 est.).
Language:	Malay (official), English, and Chinese.
Location:	Southeastern Asia, bordering the South China Sea and Malaysia.
Main industry:	Petroleum, petroleum refining, liquefied natural gas, and construction.
National disasters:	Typhoons, earthquakes, and severe flooding are rare.
Non-resident stay:	See *http://www.immigration.gov.bn/travel.htm* for more information.
Religion:	Muslim (official) 67%, Buddhist 13%, Christian 10%, and indigenous beliefs and other 10%.
Stability:	Very stable - in 2003 Brunei and Malaysia ceased gas and oil exploration in their offshore and deepwater seabeds until negotiations progress to an agreement over allocation of disputed areas. Malaysia's land boundary with Brunei around Limbang is in dispute. Brunei established an exclusive economic fishing zone encompassing Louisa Reef in southern Spratly Islands in 1984 but makes no public territorial claim to the offshore reefs. The 2002 Declaration on the Conduct of Parties in the South China Sea has eased tensions in the Spratly Islands but falls short of a legally binding code of conduct desired by several of the disputants.

Brunei offers some of the best medical care and education systems in the world. The economic climate is very buoyant, offers many operational, and tax benefits to the investor. This is a great location for Chinese or other Asian citizens seeking a better place to do business and live. For businesses seeking to protect assets, Brunei offers the Dedicated Cell Companies (DCC), also known as a Protected cell Company. This structure can be used to segregate your assets into subsidiaries so that creditors or lawsuits will only affect the associated subsidiary, and not the whole mother company.

Christmas Island

http://www.nic.cx

http://www.christmas.net.au/

http://www.tourism.org.cx/

http://www.dotrs.gov.au/terr/xmas/index.htm

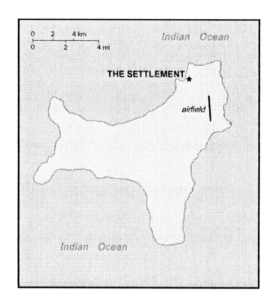

Associations:	Australia.
Climate:	Tropical with a wet and dry season; heat and humidity moderated by trade winds; wet season December to April.
Communications:	Good.
Currency:	Australian dollar (AUD).
Entry and exit:	One paved airport (*http://www.christmas.net.au/flights.html*).
GDP per capita:	Low.

Language:	English (official), Chinese, and Malay.
Location:	South-eastern Asia, island in the Indian Ocean, south of Indonesia.
Main industry:	Tourism, phosphate extraction (near depletion), and satellite launch facility.
National disasters:	The narrow fringing reef surrounding the island can be a maritime hazard.
Non-resident stay:	Same as Australia.
Religion:	Buddhist 36%, Muslim 25%, Christian 18%, and other 21% (1997).
Stability:	Very stable.

This island is popular with Malay, Chinese, and Australians. It has a Malay Muslim community, Chinese community, and Australian European community, with no conflicts. It operates under Australian law, and citizenship of the island automatically makes you an Australian citizen. I would not advise becoming a citizen of Christmas Island as you would automatically become an Australian citizen (see section on Australia). Income tax is as in Australia, for Christmas Island residents; but goods and services tax is exempt on the island. Trading with mainland Australia however, will bring you back into the Australian goods and services tax.

Aomen Tebie Xingzhengqu (Macau Special Administrative Region)

http://www.macau.gov.mo/

http://www.macau.gov.mo/index_en.html

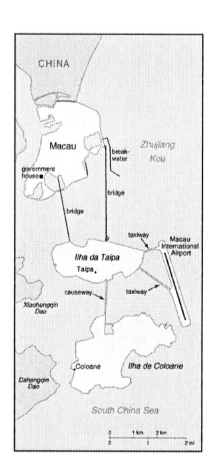

Associations:	China.
Banking:	See *www.financewise.com/public/edit/asia/macau/macau-links .htm* for further details.
Business:	See *http://www.macau.gov.mo/index_en.html* for further details.

Climate:	Subtropical; marine with cool winters, warm summers.
Communication:	Excellent.
Currency:	Pataca (MOP). See *www.xe.com* for current conversion rates.
Entry and exit:	1 paved airport.
GDP per capita:	$19,400 (2003 est.).
Language:	Portuguese, and Chinese (Cantonese).
Location:	Eastern Asia, bordering the South China Sea and China.
Main industry:	Tourism, gambling, clothing, textiles, electronics, footwear, and toys.
National disasters:	Typhoons.
Non-resident stay:	You have to be a Chinese citizen.
Religion:	Buddhist 50%, Roman Catholic 15%, and none and other 35% (1997).
Stability:	Ultra stable.

This is an ideal haven for Chinese citizens or Hong Kong businesses facing the new higher corporate taxes introduced in Hong Kong. As long as you do not sell your service or product to Macau residents or trade in the Macau market, you can apply for a Macau Offshore Company (MOC). If granted, you will be able to trade virtually tax free through it. Consult a specialist in Macau for further details. Also, see the following link for further details: *http://beijing.lehmanlaw.com/Macau/reading.htm*.

Chapter 11

- *Australasia*

Australasia

Australia

http://www.gov.au/

Associations:	Great Britain.
Banking:	See *http://www.quazell.com/bank/both_aus.htm* for further details.
Business:	Not very good. Avoid doing business here if tax relief is what you seek.
Climate:	Generally arid to semiarid; temperate in south and east, and tropical in north.
Communications:	Excellent.
Corporate Tax:	Do not incorporate a company in Australia, base your company's central management there, or carry out business and have

	Australians with voting rights in your company.
Currency:	Australian dollar (AUD).
Entry and exit:	147 airports.
GDP per capita:	$28,900 (2003 est.).
Language:	English, and native languages.
Location:	Oceania, continent between the Indian Ocean and the South Pacific Ocean.
Main industry:	Mining, industrial and transportation equipment, food processing, chemicals, and steel.
National disasters:	Cyclones along the coast, severe droughts, and forest fires.
Non-resident stay:	183 days or two years, if you can prove that your abode is abroad. To save complexity, do not stay longer than 183 days, and do not buy shares or any assets in Australia apart from your main residence. Do not do business in Australia.
Personal Tax:	Only on income sourced in Australia. Do not over stay 183 days. It is very difficult to unshackle yourself from the Inland Revenue once you are deemed an Australian resident.
Religion:	Anglican 26.1%, Roman Catholic 26%, other Christian 24.3%, non-Christian 11%, and other 12.6%.
Stability:	Very stable – the 1999 maritime delimitation established partial maritime boundaries with East Timor over part of the Timor Gap. However, temporary resource sharing agreements over an un-reconciled area, grants Australia 90% share of exploited gas reserves and hampers creation of a southern maritime boundary with Indonesia (consult Ashmore and Cartier Islands disputes). Australia asserts a territorial claim to Antarctica and to its continental shelf.

Because of its first world status and pleasant climate, Australia is a great place to stay. However, do not carry out business there, source any incomes from there, or exceed 183 days stay per annum there. Their government tax machinery is well oiled, so maintain privacy concerning your offshore financial and business activities at all times.

Cocos (Keeling) Islands

http://www.cocos-tourism.cc/

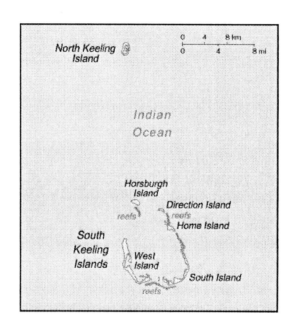

Associations:	Australia.
Business:	See *www.dotrs.gov.au/regional/northern_forum/formal_response/ cocos_islands* for government incentives and business opportunities.
Climate:	Tropical with high humidity, moderated by the southeast trade winds for about nine months of the year.
Communications:	Good.
Currency:	Australian dollar (AUD).
Entry and exit:	One airport.
GDP per capita:	Low.

Language: Malay (Cocos dialect), and English.

Location: South-eastern Asia, group of islands in the Indian Ocean, southwest of Indonesia, about halfway from Australia to Sri Lanka.

Main industry: Copra products and tourism.

National disasters: Cyclone season is October to April.

Non-resident stay: Same as Australia.

Religion: Sunni Muslim 80%, other 20% (2002 est.).

Stability: Very stable.

This idyllic island paradise is little known and understood by the majority of the world. With almost an all-Muslim population, Muslims seeking a slower paced life and better quality of life will feel right at home here. The population numbers are fewer than 700 people, and are very close knit; although, very welcoming to outsiders, especially other Muslims.

There is no goods and services tax on Cocos Island, and the Australian government offers further tax concessions for the region.

See *http://www.dotars.gov.au/terr/cocos/index.htm* for further details.

Chapter 12

- *Oceania*

Oceania

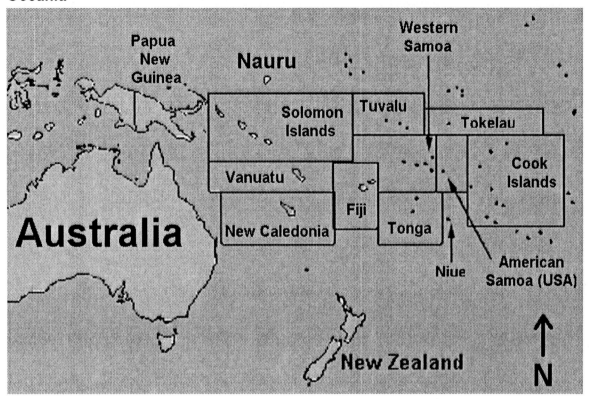

Figure 5-3: Map of Oceania

For citizens of the South Pacific Ocean, New Zealand, and Hawaii, the closest offshore tax havens are the Cook Islands and Vanuatu. Hawaiians can tap into the havens for U.S. and Canadian citizens, whilst New Zealanders can tap into havens for Australians. See Appendix 9 for a map of this area.

Cook Islands

http://www.ck/govt.htm

http://www.cook-islands.gov.ck

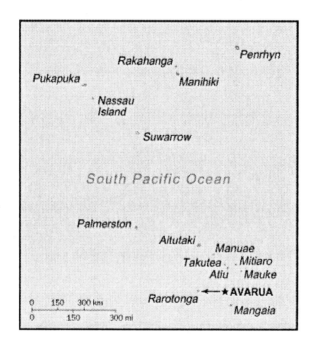

Associations:	New Zealand.
Banking:	Interest on non-resident deposits is free of withholding taxes.
Business:	A domestic company pays 20% on worldwide profits, with a non-domestic company only paying 20% on locally derived profits. There is a 15% withholding tax on all gains paid to your business by domestic businesses, and 5% to you as a resident. Domestic business bonus issues to shareholders are charged 20% tax.
Climate:	Tropical: moderated by trade winds.
Communications:	Very good, with cellular, landline, and internet.
Corporate Tax:	Only 12.5% VAT if you do not work there or engage in imports.

Income level	Tax rate
NZ$6,000	0%
NZ$6,000 to NZ$10,000	20%
NZ$10,000 to NZ$30,000	25%
Over NZ$30,000	30%

There is stamp duty on some official transactions, and commodities attract import duties.

Currency: New Zealand dollar (NZD). See *www.xe.com*.

Entry and exit: 9 airports (1 paved, and 8 unpaved).

GDP per capita: $5,000 (2001 est.).

Language: English (official) and Maori.

Location: Oceania, group of islands in the South Pacific Ocean, about one-half of the way from Hawaii to New Zealand.

Main industry: Fruit processing, tourism, fishing, clothing, and handicrafts.

National disasters: Typhoons (November to March).

Non-resident stay: Non-residents cannot buy freehold land, lease for over 60 years, and must seek permission before leasing land for more than five years. Non-residents need a job and working permit if they intend to work there. Non-residents may seek longer than the 31-day tourist visa term by applying for a work permit. If granted, you will have 12 months at a time. This stay is granted only to non-residents who bring a skill that is not available locally, or a lot of financial investment.

Personal Tax: 0% if not employed there.

Religion: Christian (the majority of population are members of the Cook Islands Christian Church). See *http://www.ck/religion.htm*.

Stability: Extremely stable.

This tax haven has an agenda of its own. The Cook Islands wants to improve its economic standing through foreign investments. At the same time, it does not want to loose land to any foreigner, thus you cannot acquire land there freehold. In addition, they want everyone coming in to have a job there, unless you are bringing funds to start a business that will benefit them. This rather selfish and frankly admirable attitude leaves this far-flung location unspoilt and a great holiday location.

Vanuatu

http://www.vanuatugovernment.gov.vu

Associations:	United Kingdom and France.
Banking:	There are over 100 offshore banks registered in Vanuatu. See *http://www.rbv.gov.vu/VanuatuBanks.htm* for a list.
Business:	Their import taxes vary widely according to the type of goods. Export tax is 5%. A business license tax is between VT 20,000 and VT 100,000, with a further turnover-tax as high as 4% for domestic businesses. Most offshore businesses are exempt. Bank registration and IBC as well as trusts are popular in Vanuatu.
Climate:	Tropical; moderated by southeast trade winds from May to October; moderate rainfall from November to April; may be affected by cyclones from December to April.

Communications: Very good, with cellular, landline, and internet.

Corporate Tax: 0%. Employees and employers contribute 3% of each salary to an approved superannuation scheme, usually the Vanuatu National Provident Fund.

Currency: Vatu (VUV) pegged against a dollar currency basket to 140VUV=$1. See *www.xe.com.*

Entry and exit: 30 airports (3 paved, and 27 unpaved).

GDP per capita: $2,900 (2002 est.).

Language: Three official languages: English, French, Pidgin (known as Bislama or Bichelama), plus more than 100 local languages.

Location: Oceania, group of islands in the South Pacific Ocean, about three-quarters of the way from Hawaii to Australia.

Main industry: Food and fish freezing, wood processing, and meat canning.

National disasters: Tropical cyclones or typhoons (January to April), volcanism causes minor earthquakes, and tsunamis.

Non-resident stay: You can go for a retirement permit that requires you have an income of US$2140 per month or more. Otherwise, the tariff for long-term stay in Vanuatu is as follows:

Investment (Vatu)	US$	Resident permit
15 Million	107,150	3 Years
25 Million	173,600	5 Years
50 Million	347,200	10 Years
100 Million	694,400	15 Years

Personal Tax: 0%.

Religion: Presbyterian 36.7%, Anglican 15%, Roman Catholic 15%, indigenous beliefs 7.6%, Seventh-Day Adventist 6.2%, Church of Christ 3.8%, and other 15.7% (including Jon Frum Cargo cult).

Stability: Extremely stable - Matthew and Hunter Islands east of New Caledonia are claimed by Vanuatu and France.

Muslim community information:
http://www.islamicfinder.org/getitWorld.php ?id=38233&lang=

Vanuatu is a beautiful but remote location suitable only those who want to really get away, or who live in the South Pacific Ocean. It is simple and fair to get residence there, and there are no taxes as long as you do not conduct business locally. The domestic taxes are nonexistent except for some import and business licence fees, so even if you do decide to do business there, you will be paying minimal amounts. For Australians, Fijians, Japanese Hawaiian, New Zealanders, and other South Pacific and Oceania residents, this may be your ideal tax haven.

See *http://www.lowtax.net/lowtax/html/jvahom.html* for further information.

Fiji

http://www.fiji.gov.fj

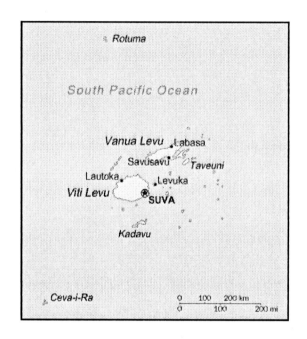

Associations:	Ex-English colony (independence gained in 1970).
Business:	See *http://www.mrd.gov.fj/gfiji/legislation/taxation.html* for notes on Fijian tax law.
Climate:	Tropical marine, only slight seasonal temperature variation.
Communications:	Very good.
Currency:	Fijian dollar (FJD). See *www.xe.com* for current conversion rates.
Entry and exit:	28 airports (3 paved, and 25 unpaved).
GDP per capita:	$5,800 (2003 est.).
Language:	English (official), Fijian, and Hindustani.
Location:	Oceania, island group in the South Pacific Ocean, about two-thirds of the way from Hawaii to New Zealand.
Main industry:	Tourism, sugar, clothing, copra, gold, silver, lumber, and small cottage industries.
National disasters:	Cyclonic storms can occur from November to January.
Non-resident stay:	Non-Fijian born residents can never own land. You can however, lease land and property.
Religion:	Christian 52% (Methodist 37%, Roman Catholic 9%), Hindu 38%,

Muslim 8%, and other 2%.

Stability: Stable - free and peaceful elections in 1999 resulted in a government led by an Indo-Fijian, but a coup in May 2000 ushered in a prolonged period of political turmoil.

Although a visual paradise, Fiji is not free from taxes. It levies income tax at 35% for resident companies, 45% for non-resident companies, as well as a 10% VAT and other taxes. See *http://www.mrd.gov.fj/gfiji/legislation/taxation.html* for more information. Having said all that, its taxes are still lower than Australia and most of the developed countries of the world.

Niue

http://www.gov.nu/
http://www.niueisland.com/

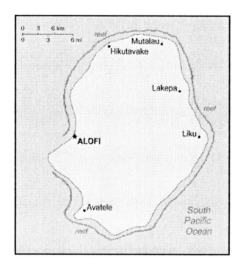

Associations:	New Zealand.
Banking:	None – look to New Zealand.
Business:	See *http://www.pitic.org.nz/countriesniue.htm* for further details. This country has a subsidised budget that is always in deficit. The population has all but migrated to New Zealand, and there is a gross shortage of raw materials.
Climate:	Tropical, modified by southeast trade winds.
Communications:	Very poor.
Currency:	New Zealand dollar (NZD).
Entry and exit:	1 paved airport.
GDP per capita:	$3,600 (2000 est.).
Language:	Niuean, a Polynesian language closely related to Tongan and Samoan; and English.
Location:	Oceania, island in the South Pacific Ocean, east of Tonga.
Main industry:	Tourism, handicrafts, and food processing.
National disasters:	Typhoons. On 7 January 2004, Cyclone Heta (registered at Force 5, the strongest a cyclone can reach) struck the island nation, devastating the country's infrastructure. Many of the

	island's residents have chosen to immigrate to New Zealand.
Non-resident stay:	A visa is required for stays over three months. US, New Zealand, Australia, and EU, as well as some other first world countries, may not require a visa to stay for less than three months.
Religion:	Ekalesia Niue (Niuean Church - a Protestant church closely related to the London Missionary Society) 75%, Latter-Day Saints 10%, and other 15% (mostly Roman Catholic, Jehovah's Witnesses, and Seventh-Day Adventist).
Stability:	Stable but their economy is erratic.

The offshore advantages of Niue were all removed when the government shut the offshore businesses down due to pressures from OECD, and the discovery operation of fraudsters and money launderers utilising the structures. The cyclone's destruction of many properties on the island has caused economic stress, as well as the financial minister's dismissal due to fraudulent activities. All together, this island will have to wait a long time to become a place worth considering as a potential tax haven home.

Tonga

http://www.pmo.gov.to/
www.tongaholiday.com

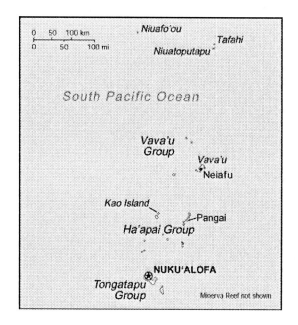

Associations:	None.
Banking:	For further information, see *http://www.reservebank.to/com_ banks.htm.*
Business:	Contact: Director of Trade, Investment & Promotion
	Ministry of Labour, Commerce & Industries
	PO Box 110
	Nuku'alofa
	Kingdom of Tonga
	Tel: (676) 25 483
	Fax: (676) 25 410
	Website: *www.mlci.gov.to.*
Climate:	Tropical, modified by trade winds, warm season (December to May), and cool season (May to December).
Communications:	Poor.
Corporate Tax:	The company tax rates in Tonga are as follows:

Resident company:

Tax Rate	Income
15%	for the first US$72,290
30%	over US$72,290

Non-Resident company:

Tax Rate	Income
37.5%	for the first US$36,145
42.5%	over US$36,145

Sales tax, customs duty, and port and services taxes, are levied on most imported goods and commodities sold in Tonga.

The are no taxes falling into the below categories:

- Provisional tax
- Payroll tax
- Local government tax
- Capital gains tax
- Export tax
- Probate tax
- Death duties
- Repatriation of funds (including dividends, profits, capital gains, salaries, interest on capital and loan repayment) is permitted.

See *www.adb.org/Documents/Books/Business_Reference_Guides/ big/ton.pdf* for details.

Currency:	Pa'anga (TOP).
Entry and exit:	6 airports (1 paved, and 5 unpaved).
GDP per capita:	$2,200 (2001 est.).
Language:	Tongan and English.
Location:	Oceania, archipelago in the South Pacific Ocean, about two-thirds of the way from Hawaii to New Zealand.
Main industry:	Tourism and fishing.
National disasters:	Cyclones (October to April); earthquakes and volcanic activity on Fonuafo'ou.
Non-resident stay:	For the visa period applied for, you need proof of financial ability to support yourself. One-month application is free of charge as long as you hold a passport and return ticket.
Personal Tax:	Income tax:

Tax rate	Income
10%	Over US$1,807

Religion:	Christian (Free Wesleyan Church claims over 30,000 adherents).
Stability:	Stable.

This low tax rate paradise could be used to eliminate business taxes. The government offers long-term tax-exemptions to foreign businesses that will develop the islands. Tonga is a great place to invest, and its people are great to live with.

Tuvalu

http://www.tuvaluislands.com/
http://www.tcsp.com/destinations/tuvalu/index.shtml

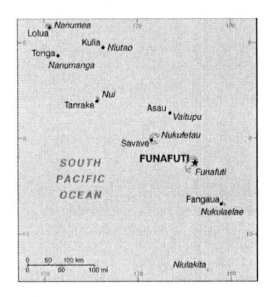

Associations:	None.
Banking:	Use foreign banks.
Business:	Contact:
	Tuvalu Trade & Investment Agency
	Ministry of Finance, Economic Planning & Industry
	Private Bag
	Vaiaku,
	Funafuti
	Tuvalu
	Tel: (688) 20 183 / 20 190
	Fax: (688) 20 191
	Email: *tbc@tuvalu.tv*
	http://www.tcsp.com/spto/export/sites/SPTO/investment/tuvalu.shtml
Climate:	Tropical; moderated by easterly trade winds (March to November); westerly gales and heavy rain (November to March).
Communications:	Poor.
Corporate Tax:	Exemptions for industrial and business building materials, plant,

	and machinery. 40% tax on non-resident company income, and 30% on resident companies.
Currency:	Australian dollar (AUD). Note - there is also a Tuvaluan dollar.
Entry and exit:	1 unpaved airport.
GDP per capita:	$1,100 (2000 est.).
Language:	Tuvaluan, English, Samoan, and Kiribati (on the island of Nui).
Location:	Oceania, island group consisting of nine coral atolls in the South Pacific Ocean, about one-half of the way from Hawaii to Australi.a
Main industry:	Fishing, tourism, and copra.
National disasters:	Severe tropical storms are usually rare, but in 1997, there were three cyclones. The low level of the islands makes them very sensitive to changes in sea level.
Non-resident stay:	No visa is required, but a visitor's permit is issued, allowing you a one-month stay, providing you have sufficient funds, proof of accommodation, and an onward ticket.
Personal Tax:	No tax on the first 2,220, but 30% after. A variety of sales taxes is levied on goods and services.
Religion:	Church of Tuvalu (Congregationalist) 97%, Seventh - day Adventist 1.4%, Baha'i 1%, and other 0.6%.
Stability:	Ultra Stable.

These underdeveloped islands are more unspoilt than some other South Pacific islands. Businesses that bring development and jobs to the islands can obtain exemptions from many of the taxes of the islands. Tuvalu is ideal for those seeking a less developed location to settle. The islands are low-lying, and thus vulnerable to sea level changes, so be sure to have a sea-going vessel nearby during cyclones and increment weather, just in case.

New Caledonia

http://www.newcaledoniatourism-south.com

http://www.gouv.nc/

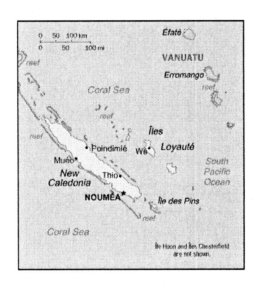

Associations:	France.
Banking:	Use Australian or French banks.
Business:	See *www.tcsp.com/spto/export/sites/SPTO/investment/ new_ caledonia.shtml* for further details.
Climate:	Tropical; modified by southeast trade winds; hot and humid.
Communications:	Good.
Corporate Tax:	0% for non-resident companies, and 30% corporation tax (35% for mining companies).
Currency:	Comptoirs Francais du Pacifique franc (XPF). Note – they may adopt the Euro in 2003.
Entry and exit:	25 airports (11 paved, and 14 unpaved).

GDP per capita: $15,000 (2002 est.).

Language: French (official), and 33 Melanesian-Polynesian dialects.

Location: Oceania, islands in the South Pacific Ocean, east of Australia.

Main industry: Nickel mining and smelting.

National disasters: Cyclones, most frequent from November to March.

Non-resident stay: Three months, with no possibility of an extension.

Personal Tax: Resident income tax:

Personal Tax Rates (Brackets)	Income
No tax	<8,900
rate of 5%	8,900-11,570
rate of 6%	
rate of 8%	
rate of 10%	11,570-14,240
rate of 12%	
rate of 15%	14,240-19,580
rate of 20%	19,580-24,920
rate of 30%	24,920-40,050
rate of 40%	>40,050

Residents are taxed on their world income. There are taxes on property and other income sources. 0% for non residents.

Religion: Roman Catholic 60%, Protestant 30%, and other 10%.

Stability: Very Stable.

These idyllic islands are not tax free and you risk your world income if you seek to settle there. Look to Vanuatu, or some of the other tax free islands already mentioned instead. New Caledonia is a great playground, and vacationing there is definitely recommended.

French Polynesia

http://www.polynesianislands.com/fp
http://www.tahiti-tourisme.com/
http://www.presidence.pf/

Associations:	France.
Business:	See *http://www.tahiti-invest.com*, *http://www.tahiti-export.pf/*, and *http://www.pitic.org.nz/countriesfrench polynesia.htm* for details.
Climate:	Tropical, but moderate.
Communications:	Very good.
Corporate Tax:	0% income tax. However, VAT is levied up to 10%.
Currency:	Comptoirs Francais du Pacifique franc (XPF). See *www.xe.com* for current conversion rates.
Entry and exit:	49 airports (37 paved, and 12 unpaved).
GDP per capita:	$17,500 (2001 est.).
Language:	French (official) and Tahitian (official).
Location:	Oceania, archipelago in the South Pacific Ocean, about one-half of the way from South America to Australia.
Main industry:	Tourism, pearls, agricultural processing, handicrafts, and phosphates.
National disasters:	Occasional cyclonic storms in January.
Non-resident stay:	You can stay for three months without special permission. To stay

	for over three months, you need to apply for long-term stay. See *http://www.france. diplomatie.fr/venir/visas/index.html* for further details.
Personal Tax:	0% income tax. However, VAT is levied up to 10%.
Religion:	Protestant 54%, Roman Catholic 30%, other 10%, and no religion 6%.
Stability:	Very Stable.

In French Polynesia, there are no income taxes. They do charge a VAT (TVA in French) for services and goods. These can be as much as 10%. France tested nuclear bombs on Maruroa Island up until 1995. These included high altitude tests, as well as underground tests. This has somewhat affected locals in the region to varying degrees, and some radioactivity is still leaking out of Maruroa and the neighbouring areas. I advise you stay clear of Maruroa, and also from 300 miles radius of Marutoa if possible.

Samoa

http://www.interwebinc.com/samoa/

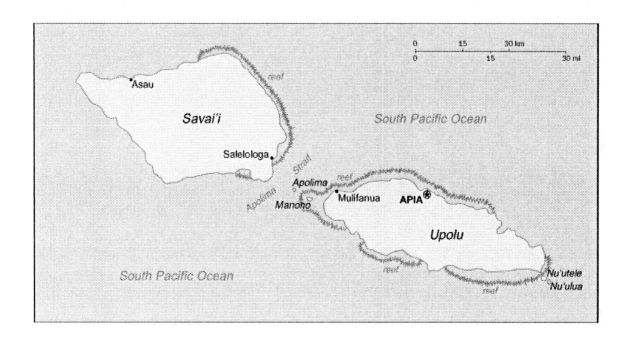

Associations:	New Zealand.
Banking:	See *http://www.cbs.gov.ws*, *http://www.privatebanking.info/user/ category.jsp?location_id=331&category_id=1&category_page_i d=0&published=1* and *http://www. sterlingbank.ws/* for details.
Business:	See *http://www.tradeinvestsamoa.ws* for further details. Samoa offers tax-exempt offshore company structures. In addition, see *http://www.taxhavenco.com/osm/taxhavens/WesternSamoa.html* and *www.milonline. com /mil-wsamoa1.html* for details.
Climate:	Tropical: rainy season (November to April), dry season (May to October).
Communications:	Good.
Corporate Tax:	You can use one of their offshore business company structures to

gain exemption from Samoan taxes. A 39% tax is levied for resident companies, and 48% for non-resident companies. There are investment incentives for industrial investments. (See *http://www.interwebinc. com/samoanew/invest/ invest14.html* for further details).

Currency:	Tala (SAT).
Entry and exit:	4 airports (3 paved, and 1 unpaved).
GDP per capita:	$3,000 (2004 est.).
Language:	Samoan (Polynesian) and English.
Location:	Oceania, group of islands in the South Pacific Ocean, about one-half of the way from Hawaii to New Zealand.
Main industry:	Food processing, building materials, and auto parts.
National disasters:	Occasional typhoons and active volcanism.
Non-resident stay:	Do not stay over 30 days. You may apply for permanent resident status if you have stayed five uninterrupted years in Samoa. A $500 cost is associated, and you may be required to invest into a Samoan property. Residents of Samoa are taxed on their worldwide income.
Personal Tax:	This is on a sliding scale of 10% to 45% for residents. Non-residents however, do not pay any taxes unless carrying out business activities or drawing an income in Samoa. Samoa does not tax capital gains, and dividend income of residents is taxed at a top rate of 10%. See *http://www.interwebinc.com/samoanew/invest/invest12.html* for details
Religion:	Christian 99.7%. (About one-half of population is associated with the London Missionary Society, which includes Congregational, Roman Catholic, Methodist, Latter-Day Saints, and Seventh-Day Adventist).
Stability:	Very stable.

Samoa is a high tax country for residents and any locally operating businesses. However, non-resident individuals can enjoy a better tax position as long as they do not draw a Samoa based income or become a resident. There are stamp duties and other duties levied on imports, as well as dividend and income taxes on your world income. If you are looking to avoid the payment of high taxes, then avoid residing in Samoa. If you are looking for a private offshore company in a country with no double taxation treaties, then look closer at Samoa.

Nauru

http://www.spc.int/

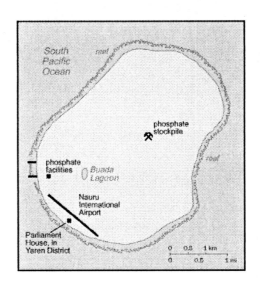

Associations:	Australia, New Zealand, United Kingdom, and United Nations.
Banking:	Nauru has more registered offshore banks than citizens have. See *www.taxhavenco.com/osm/BankCharter.html* for further details.
Business:	Offshore banking and companies.
Climate:	Tropical with a monsoonal pattern; rainy season (November to February).
Communications:	Good.
Corporate Tax:	0%.
Currency:	Australian dollar (AUD).
Entry and exit:	1 paved airport.
GDP per capita:	$5,000 (2001 est.).

Language:	Nauruan (official, a distinct Pacific Island language), and English is widely understood, spoken, and used for most government and commercial purposes.
Location:	Oceania, island in the South Pacific Ocean, south of the Marshall Islands.
Main industry:	Phosphate mining, offshore banking, and coconut products.
National disasters:	Periodic droughts.
Non-resident stay:	Not advisable due to pollution from intensive phosphate mining.
Personal Tax:	0%.
Religion:	Christian (two-thirds Protestant, one-third Roman Catholic).
Stability:	Ultra Stable.

This island used to be an unspoilt paradise; today it faces economical and environmental challenges. Its phosphate mining dependent economy is collapsing due to depleted resources. It is now dependent on foreign aid. Nauru has developed an offshore banking centre and offers banking licences for a relatively low cost. Other offshore structures are also available here.

See *http://www.offshore-manual.com/taxhavens/Nauru.html* for further details.

Tokelau Islands (Atafu, Nukunonu and Fakaofo Islands)

http://www.tokelau.org.nz/

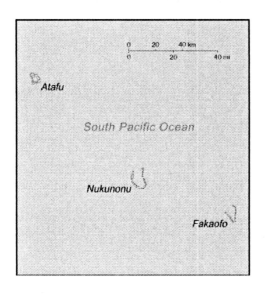

Associations:	New Zealand.
Banking:	None.
Business:	None.
Climate:	Tropical; moderated by trade winds (April to November).
Communications:	Poor.
Currency:	New Zealand dollar (NZD).
Entry and exit:	No airports, only accessible via ship.
GDP per capita:	$1,000 (1993 est.).
Language:	Tokelauan (a Polynesian language), and English.
Location:	Oceania, group of three atolls in the South Pacific Ocean, about one-half of the way from Hawaii to New Zealand.
Main industry:	Small-scale enterprises for copra production, woodworking, plaited craft goods, stamps, coins, and fishing.
National disasters:	Lies in the Pacific typhoon belt.
Non-resident stay:	See *http://www.traveldocs.com/tk/* for further details.
Religion:	Roman Catholic 28%, Congregational Christian Church 70%, and other 2%.
	Note: on Atafu, 100% are Congregational Christian Church of Samoa; on Nukunonu, 100% are Roman Catholic; and on Fakaofo, both denominations exist, with the Congregational Christian

Church predominant.

Stability: Ultra stable.

This untouched island group has no tourism, capital city, banks, harbour, or airport. It is a beautiful paradise with few modern amenities, but suffers from rising sea levels. Its highest point is five meters above sea level. This is an interesting place to visit but very inconvenient for anything else, including visiting.

Territory of American Samoa

http://www.asg-gov.net/

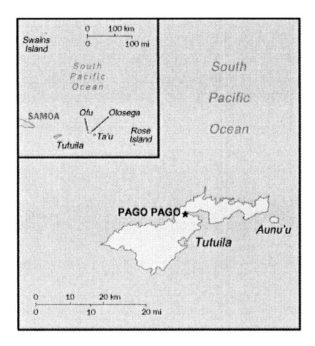

Associations:	USA
Banking:	See *www.anz.com.au/AmericanSamoa/default.asp* for further details.
Business:	Office of the Governor
	Executive Office Building
	Third Floor, Utulei
	Pago Pago
	American Samoa
	96799
	administrator@asg-gov.net
Climate:	Tropical marine moderated by southeast trade winds; annual rainfall averages about 3m, rainy season from November to April, dry season from May to October; little seasonal temperature variation.
Communications:	Good.
Currency:	US dollar (USD).

Entry and exit:	3 airports (2 paved, and 1 unpaved).
GDP per capita:	$8,000 (2000 est.).
Language:	Samoan (closely related to Hawaiian and other Polynesian languages), and English. Note: most people are bilingual.
Location:	Oceania, group of islands in the South Pacific Ocean, about half way between Hawaii and New Zealand.
Main industry:	Tuna canneries (largely supplied by foreign fishing vessels), and handicrafts.
National disasters:	Typhoons are common from December to March.
Non-resident stay:	*See http://www.amsamoa.com/indexdoc.html* for further details.
Religion:	Christian Congregationalist 50%, Roman Catholic 20%, Protestant and other 30%.
Stability:	Ultra stable.

Solomon Islands

http://www.commerce.gov.sb/

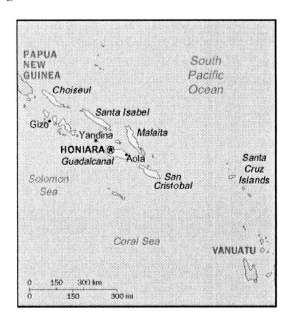

Associations:	Australia and Britain.
Banking:	See *http://www.nbsi.com.sb/* for further details.
Business:	See *www.solomon.emb.gov.au/invest_index.html* for details.
Climate:	Tropical monsoon; few extremes of temperature and weather.
Communications:	Very good.
Currency:	Solomon Islands dollar (SBD). See *www.xe.com* for current value.
Entry and exit:	33 airports (2 paved, and 31 unpaved).
GDP per capita:	$1,700 (2001 est.).
Language:	Melanesian Pidgin in much of the country is lingua franca, and English is official, but spoken by only 1%-2% of the population. Note: 120 indigenous languages.
Location:	Oceania, group of islands in the South Pacific Ocean, east of Papua New Guinea.
Main industry:	Fish (tuna), mining, and timber.
National disasters:	Typhoons, but rarely destructive; geologically active region with frequent earth tremors; volcanic activity.

Non-resident stay:	Contact Information: Department of Commerce, Employment and Trade, P O Box G26, Honiara, Solomon Islands, South Pacific Telephone: +677 22808 / 25095 Fax: +677 22808 General enquiries: *commerce@commerce.gov.sb* Webmistress: *moira@commerce.gov.sb* Government Information Service: Office of the Prime Minister tel: +677 21300 fax 20401.
Religion:	Anglican 45%, Roman Catholic 18%, United (Methodist and Presbyterian) 12%, Baptist 9%, Seventh-Day Adventist 7%, other Protestant 5%, and indigenous beliefs 4%.
Stability:	Very Stable - Australian defence personnel are dispatched at the invitation of the Solomon Islands' government to restore law and order on the islands, and reinforce regional security.

Norfolk Island

http://www.norfolkisland.com.au

http://www.norfolk.gov.nf/

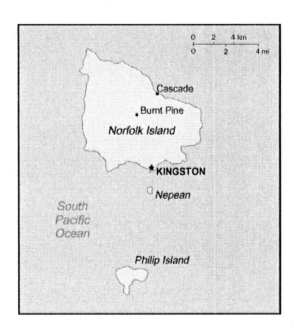

Associations:	Australia.
Banking:	See *http://www.norfolk.gov.nf/Norfolk%20Banks.htm* for further details.
Business:	Tourist related businesses.
Climate:	Subtropical; mild, little seasonal temperature variation.
Communications:	Poor.
Corporate Tax:	0% for non-residents.
Currency:	Australian dollar (AUD).
Entry and exit:	One paved airport.

GDP per capita:	Low.
Language:	English (official), and Norfolk (a mixture of 18th century English and ancient Tahitian).
Location:	Oceania, island in the South Pacific Ocean, east of Australia.
Main industry:	Tourism.
National disasters:	Typhoons (especially May to July).
Non-resident stay:	30 days, with the option of an extension to 120 days.
Personal Tax:	0% for non-residents. There is a $25 departure tax.
Religion:	Anglican 37.4%, Uniting Church in Australia 14.5%, Roman Catholic 11.5%, Seventh-Day Adventist 3.1%, none 12.2%, unknown 17.4%, and other 3.9% (1996).
Stability:	Very Stable.

This beautiful island with its easygoing cheerful locals is a great place for settling and doing business. It has a small resident population (less than 3,000). If you are seeking a quiet location near Australia and the south pacific region, you may wish to look at the Norfolk Islands.

Wallis and Futuna Islands

http://www.wallis-islands.com/index.gb.htm

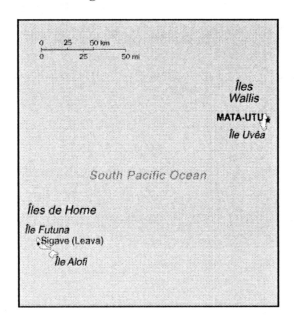

Associations:	France.
Climate:	Tropical; hot, rainy season (November to April); cool, dry season (May to October); rains 2,500-3,000 mm per year (80% humidity); average temperature 26.6 degrees C.
Communications:	Good.
Currency:	Comptoirs Francais du Pacifique franc (XPF).
Entry and exit:	2 airports (1 paved, and 1 unpaved).
GDP per capita:	$3,700 (2001 est.).
Language:	French, and Wallisian (indigenous Polynesian language).
Location:	Oceania, islands in the South Pacific Ocean, about two-thirds of the way from Hawaii to New Zealand.
Main industry:	Copra, handicrafts, fishing, and lumber.
National disasters:	None.
Non-resident stay:	See *http://www.diplomatie.gouv.fr/venir/visas/documents/vdtc_001.html* for further details.
Religion:	Roman Catholic 99%, and other 1%.
Stability:	Stable.

These islands are plagued with high unemployment (over 90%), and a France subsidised economy. This may be a good place to visit, but not to live or do business in. Look at other Polynesian islands in this section for alternatives.

Marshall Islands

http://www.rmiembassyus.org/geninfo.html

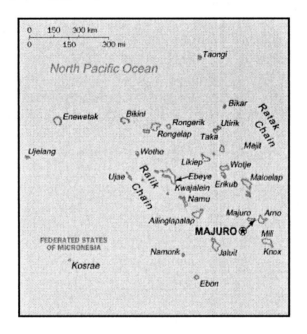

Associations:	USA.
Banking:	Offshore banks and insurance companies are not permitted in the Marshall Islands.

Bank Name: Standard Hellier (Marshall Islands) Inc.
URL: *http://www.standardhellierbank.com/*
Email: *shbank@caribsurf.com*
Street: Ajeltake Islands, P.O.Box 1405
City: Majuro
Zip: MH 96960
State: Majuro
Country: Marshall Islands
Phone: 1 473 444 0657
Fax: 1 473 444 0657
Telex: 3460 SHB GA
Bank Type: Development finance institution
Comments: Investment company full owned by Standard Hellier Bank, Koror, Palau Islands.

Business:	Ship and corporation registration. See *http://www.register-iri.com* and *http://www.bbp-net.com/cat/114* for further details.
Climate:	Tropical; hot and humid; wet season from May to November; islands border typhoon belt.
Communications:	Very good.
Corporate Tax:	0% for offshore businesses.
Currency:	US dollar (USD).
Entry and exit:	15 airports (4 paved, and 11 unpaved).
GDP per capita:	$1,600 (2001 est.).
Language:	English (widely spoken as a second language, both English and Marshallese are official languages), two major Marshallese dialects from the Malayo-Polynesian family, and Japanese.
Location:	Oceania, group of atolls and reefs in the North Pacific Ocean, about one-half of the way from Hawaii to Australia.
Main industry:	Copra, fish, tourism, craft items from shell, wood, and pearls.
National disasters:	Infrequent typhoons.
Non-resident stay:	You will require a visa unless you are from Australia, New Zealand, or other neighbouring islands. If staying over 30-days, you may be required to take an AIDS test. You can extend a 30-day stay to 90 days.
Personal Tax:	0% for non-residents.
Religion:	Christian (mostly Protestant).
Stability:	Very stable - claims US territory of Wake Island.

The Marshall Islands is an incorporation haven. It has no infrastructure of local attorneys or accountants, it is simply in the business of registering corporations and ships. There are no other services offered, and the tax haven clientele often never actually visit the Islands. The registration of new companies is carried out by representative offices in New York, Zurich, Hong Kong, Tokyo, Rotterdam and Piraeus. There are no taxes on offshore companies registered there. There are two archipelagic island chains of 30 atolls and 1,152 islands. Bikini and Enewetak are former US nuclear test sites. Kwajalein is used as a US missile test range. I advise you stay away from these three Islands.

Federal states of Micronesia

http://www.fsmgov.org

Associations:	United Nations and United States.
Banking:	See *http://www.reserve-bank.com/fmbank.htm* for further details.
Business:	See *http://www.fsmgov.org/nfc/* for further details.
Climate:	Tropical; heavy year-round rainfall, especially in the eastern islands; located on the southern edge of the typhoon belt, with some occasionally severe damage.
Communications:	Poor.
Currency:	US dollar (USD).
Entry and exit:	6 paved airports.
GDP per capita:	$2,000 (2002 est.).
Language:	English (official and common language), Trukese, Pohnpeian, Yapese, Kosrean, Ulithian, Woleaian, Nukuoro, and Kapingamarangi.
Location:	Oceania, island group in the North Pacific Ocean, about three-quarters of the way from Hawaii to Indonesia.
Main industry:	Tourism, construction, fish processing, specialized aquaculture, craft items from shell, wood, and pearls.
National disasters:	Typhoons (June to December).
Non-resident stay:	See *http://www.fsmgov.org/status.html* for further details.

Religion:	Roman Catholic 50%, and Protestant 47%.
Stability:	Very Stable.

Chuuk State

Governor: Hon. Ansito Walter
Lt. Governor: Hon. Manuel Sound
Weno, Chuuk FM 96942
Phone: (691) 330-2234
Fax: (691) 330-2233
http://www.visit-fsm.org/chuuk/

Kosrae (Kusaie) State

Governor: Hon. Rensley Sigrah
Lt. Governor: Hon. Gerson Jackson
P.O. Box 187,
Tofol, Kosrae FM 96944
Phone: (691) 370-3002/3303
Fax: (691) 370-3162
http://www.visit-fsm.org/kosrae/

Ponape (Pohnpei) State

Governor: Hon. Johnny David
Lt. Governor: Hon. Jack Yakana
Kolonia, Pohnpei FM 96941
Phone: (691) 320-2235
Fax: (691) 320-2505
http://www.visit-fsm.org/pohnpei/

Yap State

Governor: Hon. Vincent A. Figir
Lt. Governor: Hon. Andrew Yatilman
Box 39, Colonia, Yap FM 96943
Phone: (691) 350-2108/2109
Fax: (691) 350-4113
http://www.visit-fsm.org/yap/

The main, and I believe, best offshore tax havens have been presented here. There are more tax havens that I did not cover. For stability, economic, or other reasons, I have omitted them from this list. For a full list of tax havens, please see Appendix 2.

Chapter 13

- ***The PT Way: How To Become Invisible To Big Brother***

The PT Way: How To Become Invisible To Big Brother

Today more than ever, the word freedom has lost its meaning to many. Whilst countless hundreds of millions believe they are free, the truth is far from this. If you live in a high tax, high government involvement country, and your freedom is limited to the small portion granted by the regime. You are free to come and go as long as you follow the below:

- Do not break any of the countless laws (no matter how unfair they may be).
- Pay your taxes.
- Are not sued (whether guilty or innocent).
- Do not publicly take a stand against the government.
- Do not privately take a stand against the government.
- Do not support the ruling regime's enemies.
- Make too much money.

As you can see, all your current freedoms lie within the control of your government, police, courts, employer, and in many cases, your spouse, or those closest to you[7]. The PT lifestyle is the reclaiming of this control from your current hidden masters. To do this, you need to do the following:

1. Make your money in a different jurisdiction than the one you will live, or holiday in.
2. Hold at least one citizenship in a country that is not concerened about their non-residents' activities elsewhere.
3. Gain legal residence in a safe and secure tax haven.
4. Keep your assets and financial investments in a safe and private tax haven, separate to the location of all the points thus mentioned.
5. Spend your time in a location separate to those previously mentioned.

An example of this would be if you kept your money in Liechtenstein or Andorra through a Trust; you were domiciled in Campione; you carried out business in Dubai, Hong Kong, or Labuan; and you were a citizen of the UK or Ireland as well as any of the following countries in the Americas:

- Brazil
- Mexico
- Costa Rica
- Honduras
- Panama
- Guatemala

---

[7] Lawsuits and divorce proceedings are often the reason many choose the privacy and protection offered by the PT way.

- Argentina
- Uruguay
- Chile
- Venezuela
- Dominican Republic

In addition to the above countires, you could also be a citizen of any other country that allowed non-resident domiciliation. In this way, you would be a resident, but not living there long enough to attract taxes.

American citizens (the US taxes worldwide income) have a couple of choices:

- Give up your American citizenship and take up a UK or Irish citizenship.
- Consult professional tax and offshore consultants who can help you arrange your affairs through companies and trusts to minimise US taxes. See Appendix 1 for a list of tax consultants.

Be aware of the jurisdiction that you are in whilst on holiday. For instance, if you are a resident of Ceuta or Melilla (both operate on Spanish law and come under Spanish jurisdiction), and you spend time on holiday in any Spanish territory (Canary Islands, Ceuta and Melilla), the time spent there will count towards your allowed non-resident consideration for Spain (183 days per year etc). Therefore, make sure you do not exceed this allocation.

It is important to understand how precariously balanced your personal freedom is, and even more important, to protect against the possibilities of being wiped out financially or worse. To educate yourself further on these topics, obtain Dr WG Hill's books *PT* (ISBN: 0906619580 – Scope International Limited) and *PT 2 – The Practice* (ISBN: 0906619246 – Scope International Limited). Australians may want to read *The Invisible World* by Lance Spicer (ISBN: 0646310518 – Trident Consulting & Publishing).

Summary

Listed in this book are over 105 tax havens. Distributed all over the world, these tax havens offer security, privacy, and the opportunity to live your life the way you really would like it, without excessive government interferance and high taxes. If you are thinking of escaping the pressures, stresses, lack of personal freedoms and high taxes, look no further than this book to set you on the path to finding your ideal tax haven.

All the major tax havens are included as well as the not so obvious and the well kept secrets of the wealthy. From Navada to Sao Tome and Principe to Chuuk, you will find all the information you will need to narrow down your choice of havens. Religious information, climatic conditions, tax considerations, best types of international businesses to conduct as well as many more statistics and personal comments are offered on all the havens.

So whether you are considering being a PT or you just want to move somewhere safer, quiter, more beautiful with better weather, this book is your best choice for seeing all your choices in one convenient source.

I wish you happiness and prosperity in your future and hope we shall meet one dayon the beaches of an idealic offshore tax haven.

Appendices

Appendix 1

Offshore Tax Consultants

United Kingdom
Tax Consultants Guide
Info Guide Publications Ltd.
Mayfair House
14-18 Heddon Street
Mayfair
London
W1B 4DA
Phone: 0871 5045532
Email: *info@taxconsultantsguide.com*

Clark & Co
12 North Hill
Colchester
Essex
CO1 1AS
Tel: 01206 577422
Fax: 01206 562816
Email: *partners@clarke-colchester.co.uk*

Citycas Ltd
Valiant House
4-10 Heneage Lane
London
EC3A 5DQ
Tel: 0207 626 7171
Fax: 0207 626 7272
Email: *info@citycas.com*

MD Consulting Limited
St Mary's Court
The Broadway
Amersham
Buckinghamshire
HP7 0UT
01494 772765

TaxationWeb Ltd.
6 Coleby Avenue

Peel Hall
Manchester
M22 5HH
United Kingdom
Mark McLaughlin
Email: *martino@taxationweb.co.uk*

The Wells Partnership
The Old Rectory, Church Street
Weybridge
Surrey
KT13 8DE
England
Tel: 01932 704 700
Fax: 01932 855 049

Berg Kaprow Lewis
35 Ballards Lane,
London
Greater London
N3 1XW
England
Tel: 020 8922 9222
Fax: 020 8922 9223

Greenwood Barton
National Westminster Bank Chambers,
Heckmondwike
West Yorkshire
WF16 0HU
England

Bartlett Kershaw Trott
4 Pullman Court, Great Western Road
Gloucester
Gloucestershire
GL1 3ND
England
Tel: 01452 527000
Fax: 01452 304585

Harris Lipman
2 Mountview Court, 310 Friern Barnet Lane
Whetstone

London
N20 0YZ
England
Tel: 020 8446 9000
Fax: 020 8446 9537

Maskell, Moss & Co. Limited
24 Cathedral Road,
Cardiff
South Glamorgan
CF11 9LJ
Wales
Tel: 029 2025 6330
Fax: 029 2025 6331

The Institute Of Chartered Accountants in Ireland
CA House, 87/89 Pembroke Road
Dublin
Ir 4
Ireland
Tel: +353 1 637 7200
Fax: + 353 1 6680842

Conway, Conway & Co.
12 Basin Street,
Nass
Co. Kildare
KD
Ireland

Isle of Man
Isle of Man - Head Office
OCRA (Isle of Man) Limited
Grosvenor Court
Tower Street
Ramsey, Isle of Man IM8 1JA
British Isles
Tel: +44 (1624) 811000
Fax: +44 (1624) 811001
Email: *stevenson@ocra.com*
Contacts: David Stevenson, Colin Forster, Brian Monk

Italy
Faulkner International Ltd Italy, Rome

Via Carlo Passaglia No 11
Rome
Italy
Senior Financial Consultant email: *johnmpye@faulkner-international.com*

Faulkner International Ltd Italy Turin
Piemont
Turin
Italy
Financial Consultant email: *david.silk@faulkner-international.com*

Mary Jane Bridges
Tel: 06474-7069
Address: Via Urbana 116, 00184 Rome

Donald J. Carroll
Tel: 06570-281 Fax: 06570-282733
Address: Largo Angelo Fochetti 28, 00154 Rome
Email: *donald.carroll@studiopirola.com*

Cynthia J. Ehrlich
Tel: 06336-0340
Address: Via Cassia 595/F, 00189 Rome
Email: *USTAXhelp@yahoo.com*

Timothy Ellis
Tel: 06614-3216
Address: Via Paolo V 11- Int. 7, 00167 Rome

Vincent P. Gambino
Tel: 063751-1192 Fax: 063741-1420
Address: Via Asiago 1, 00195 Rome.
Email: *VPGambino@tiscalinet.it.*

Sally M. Silvers
Tel: 06853-57172
Address: Via Basento 37, 00198 Rome
Email: *sally.silvers@flashnet.it*

France
Faulkner International Ltd France, Paris
Faulkner Conseil SARL
116, Avenue du General Leclerc
75014 Paris

France
Email: *info@faulkner-international.com*

Faulkner International Ltd France, Valbone
Faulkner Conseil SARL
6, Rue Soutrane, 1er Etage
06560 Valbonne.
France
Regional Director email: *terry.hurley@faulkner-international.com*
Financial Consultants email: *maddie.goodden@faulkner-international.com, info@faulkner-international.com*

Czech Republic
Faulkner International Ltd Czech Republic
p. a. On-Target
Perlova 1 110 00 Prague 1
Czech Republic
Financial Consultant email: *david.newton@faulkner-international.com*

Germany
Faulkner International Ltd Germany
Kurfuerstendamm 21
Berlin, 10719
Germany
Financial Consultant email: *info@faulkner-international.com*

Tax Consultants Guide
Info Guide Publications
Lindenstrasse 2
Gelnhausen
Frankfurt
Germany
63571
Phone: +49 6051 618140
Email: info@taxconsultantsguide.com

Norway
Faulkner International Ltd Norway
Proffice, Lokkeveien 10,
4008 Stavanger,
Norway
Email: *ian.neil@faulkner-international.com, steve.calloway@faulkner-international.com*

Brazil

Faulkner International Ltd Brazil
Traversa do Ouvidor 50 (sobreloja)
Centro 20040 - 040 Rio de Janeiro
Brazil
Regional Director email: *tim.richards@faulkner-international.com*
Website: *http://www.faulkner-international.com*

Faulkner International Ltd Brazil
Rua Haddock Lobo 846
Conjuntura 1105
Edifficio Netware
Cerqueira César
01414-000 São Paulo
Brazil
Regional Director email: *robin.sanders@faulkner-international.com*
Consultant email: *info@faulkner-international.com*

Netherlands
Faulkner International Ltd Netherlands, Eindhoven
Faulkner Nederland BV
Fellenoord 130, 5611ZB
Eindhoven
Netherlands
Email: *info@faulkner-international.com*

Faulkner International Ltd Netherlands, Hoofddorp
Faulkner Nederland BV
De Horsten, Planetenweg 15A
2132HN Hoofddorp
Netherlands
Financial Consultant email: *clive.anderton@faulkner-international.com*

Vietnam
Faulkner International Ltd Vietnam
Ho Chi Minh
Vietnam
Financial Consultant email: *keith.bridger@faulkner-international.com*

Bahrain
Faulkner International Ltd Kingdom of Bahrain
Manama
Kingdom of Bahrain.
Regional Director email: *chris.watts@faulkner-international.com*

Latvia
Faulkner International Ltd Latvia
Latvia
Email: *info@faulkner-international.com*

Russia
Faulkner International Ltd Moscow
Moscow
Email: *info@faulkner-international.com*

Dubai
Faulkner International Ltd Dubai
Apt 307, Obedulla Tower
PO Box 52465
Bur Dubai
Dubai
United Arab Emirates.
Regional Director email: *eric.boardman@faulkner-international.com*

Thailand
Faulkner International Ltd Thailand
Bamboo Court Apartment 5
59 - 38 Sukhumvit Soi 26
Klongtoey
Bangkok 10110
Thailand
Regional Director email: *john.macgill@faulkner-international.com*

China
Faulkner International Ltd China, Shenzhen
1 Gong Ye 1st Road,
Shekou Industrial Zone,
518069 Shenzhen
The Peoples Republic of China
Email: *info@faulkner-international.com*

Faulkner International Ltd China, Shanghai
14C No:1051, Xin Zha Road
Jlng An District,
Shanghai 200041
The Peoples Republic of China
Regional Director email: *brian.mcandrew@faulkner-international.com*

OCRA (Hong Kong) Limited
3908 Two Exchange Square
8 Connaught Place
Central
Hong Kong
Tel: +852 2522 0172
Fax: +852 2522 4720
Email: hongkong@ocra.com.hk
Bart Dekker
Iris Lee

Korea
Faulkner International Ltd Korea
Seoul
Korea
Email: *info@faulkner-international.com*

Japan
Faulkner International Ltd Japan
9F Motoakasaka Building
1-7-10 Motoakasaka
Minato-Ku
Tokyo, 107-0051
Japan
Financial Consultants email: *asher.lepcha@faulkner-international.com*

Switzerland
Faulkner International Ltd Switzerland, Geneva
MPM Geneva (European International Office)
Avenue Louis-Casai 18
1211 Geneva 28
Switzerland
Email: *info@faulkner-international.com*

Faulkner International Ltd Switzerland, Basle
Basle
Switzerland

Email: *info@faulkner-international.com*

Spain
Faulkner International Ltd Spain
World Trade Center
Edificio Sur - 2ª Planta
Muelle de Barcelona
Barcelona, 08039
Spain
Regional Director email: *paul.evans@faulkner-international.com*
Training Manager email: *steve.carter@faulkner-international.com*

Australia
Ten-Forty Tax Preparation
P.O. Box 988
Bondi Junction, NSW 1355
Richard Grilliot
Email: *tenforty@bigpond.net.au*
Tel: 9362-0368
Fax: 9362-1102

Expatriate Tax Associates
1 Grove Street
Birchgrove, NSW 2041
Email: *evanhill@extax.com.au*
www.extax.com.au
Tel: 9555-5663
Fax 9810-0557

Ernst & Young
321 Kent Street
Sydney, NSW 2000
GPO Box 2646
Sydney, NSW 2001
G.S. Choong or Ron Crowe
Tel: 9248-5555
Fax: 9248-5314

Taylor Woodings Corporate Services
Level 26 Royal Exchange Building, 56 Pitt Street
Sydney
New South Wales, Australia
1225
International

Tel: (02) 8247 8000
Fax: (02) 8247 8099

Pricewaterhouse Coopers
201 Kent Street
Sydney, NSW 2000
GPO Box 4177
Sydney, NSW 2001
Jim Tait: 8266-2952
Helen Cudlipp: 8266-2995
Carol Separovich: 8266-5769
Rohan Geddes: 8266-7261
Fax: 8266-8910

Walter Jacenko
P.O. Box 247
Eastwood, NSW 2122
Tel: 9874-4558
Fax: 9874-6440

U.S. Tax Management P/L
1907/1 Sergeants Lane
St. Leonards NSW 2065
Al Simpson Email: *alsimpson@bigpond.com*
Tel: 9906-2633
Fax: 9906-2644

KPMG
KPMG Centre
45 Clarence St.
Sydney, NSW 2000
GPO Box H67 Australia Square
Sydney, NSW 2000
Rodney Moore
Tel: 9335-8202
Fax: 9299-7077

Darrel Causbrook
Causbrook & Associates
Suite 1204, Level 12
66 King Street
Sydney NSW 2000
Email: *darrel.causbrook@causbrooks.com.au*
Tel: 9299-1850

Fax: 9299-1860

Richard A. Bobb
155 Castlereagh St.
7th Floor
Sydney, NSW 2000
Richard Bobb or Kathryn Chow
Tel: 9261-2422
Fax: 9264-8701

Deloitte Ross Tohmatsu
225 George Street
Sydney, NSW 2000
C. J. Getz
Tel: 9322-7680
Fax: 9322-7025

Harry V. Turner & Co.
Suite 25
105 Longueville Rd.
Lane Cove, NSW 2066
P.O. Box 673
Lane Cove, NSW 1595
Harry Turner
Tel: 9427-0599 or 9427-0818
Fax: 9427-5976

Teresa D. West
C/- Cropper Parkhill
Solicitors
Level 20, 1 Castlereagh Street
Sydney NSW 2000
(P.O. Box 71 Burwood, NSW 2134)
Mobile: 0418-681-284
Tel: 9232-5000

Duthie Samurai & Co Pty Ltd
Charles A. Duthie
P.O. Box 97
Lane Cove, NSW 2066
Tel: 9418-6942
Fax: 9418-6855
Website: *www.dsco.info*

John L. Campbell
c/o - Zein El Hassan
Corrs Chambers Westgarth
Governor Philip Tower
Sydney NSW 2000
John L. Campbell
Tel: 9210-6500
Fax: 9210-6611
(for estate and gift taxes only)

Australian Capital Territory
Duesburys Chartered Accountants
7th Floor St. George Bank Building
60 Marcus Clarke Street
Canberra, ACT 2601
GPO Box 500
Canberra, ACT 2601
Tel: 02-6279-5400
Fax: 02-6279-5444
Michelle Horner - US Tax Specialist

Hallett and Company
Level 8 AMP Tower
1 Hobart Place
Canberra City, ACT 2602
Tel: 02-6257-5712
Fax: 02-6257-5958
Peter Radford - US Tax Specialist

Queensland KPMG
345 Queen St., Level 30
Brisbane, Qld 4000
GPO Box 223
Brisbane, Qld 4001
Bill Armagnacq
Tel: 07-3233-3111
Fax: 07-3220-0074

Perth
The Tax Lady
5 Malcolm Court
Noranda, WA 6062
Tel: 08-9375-5946
Email: *marv@starwon.com.au*

United States
US National Tax Associations
U.S. Accounting Associations
http://www.taxsites.com/associations2.html#accounting-us

American Bar Association - Section of Taxation
http://www.abanet.org/tax/home.html

American College of Trust and Estate Counsel - *http://www.actec.org/*

American Institute of Certified Public Accountants - *http://www.aicpa.org/*

American Payroll Association - *http://www.americanpayroll.org/*

American Property Tax Counsel - *http://www.aptcnet.com/*

American Society of IRS Problem Solvers
http://www.irsproblemsolvers.com/

American Taxation Association - *http://www.atasection.org/*

Appraisers Association of America - *http://www.appraisersassoc.org/*

Association for Computers and Taxation - *http://taxact.org/*

Center for State and Local Taxation
http://www.iga.ucdavis.edu/csltax.html

Council on State Taxation - *http://www.statetax.org/*

Federation of Tax Administrators - *http://www.taxadmin.org/*

Institute for Professionals in Taxation - *http://www.ipt.org/*

Multistate Tax Commission - *http://www.mtc.gov/*

National Association of Computerized Tax Processors - *http://www.nactp.org/*

National Association of Enrolled Agents - *http://www.naea.org/*

National Association of State Auditors, Comptrollers and Treasurers - *http://www.nasact.org/*

National Association of State Budget Officers - *http://www.nasbo.org/*

National Association of Tax Consultants - *http://www.natctax.org/*

National Association of Tax Professionals - *http://www.natptax.com/*

National Council of Property Taxation - *http://www.ncpt.net/*

National Society of Tax Professionals - *http://www.nstp.org/*

National Tax Association - *http://ntanet.org/*

National Taxpayers Conference - *http://www.statetaxes.net/*

Tax Executives Institute - *http://www.tei.org/*

US State Tax Associations
Alabama Society of EAs
Roland Fricke, EA
P.O. Box 242
Arab, AL 35016
Phone: 256-586-4111
Fax: 256-586-4138
Email: *buddy@bara.net*
Website: *www.alsea.org*

Alaska Society of EAs
H. Joi Soucy, EA
P.O. Box 2163
Kodiak, AK 99615
Phone: 907-486-6225
Fax: 907-486-4129
Email: *msbear@worldnet.att.net*

Arizona Society of EAs
Larry Martin, EA
7360 E. 22nd Street, #109
Tucson, AZ 85710
Phone: 520-722-8363
Fax: 520-722-8398
Email: *martinea@juno.com*
Website: *www.aztaxpros.org*

Arkansas Society of EAs
Sherry Main, EA

15493 Riches Rd.
Fayetteville, AR 72704
Phone:479-521-0310
Fax:479-521-2269
Email: *slmain@nwark.com*
Website: *www.arksea.org*

California Society of EAs
Richard J. Quarterman, EA
13204 Myford Road Ste 835
Tustin, CA 92782-9118
Phone: 949-261-2111
Fax: 949-261-7070
Email: *r.quarterman@att.net*
Website: *www.csea.org*

Colorado Society of EAs
Victoria Bell, EA
6535 S. Dayton Street
Englewood, CO 80111
Phone: 303-708-8077
Fax: 303-708-8079
Email: *bellsultax@aol.com*
Website: *www.taxpro.org*

CSEA Executive Office:
Catherine Apker, CAE
Executive Vice President
3200 Ramos Circle
Sacramento, CA 95827
Phone: 916-366-6646
Fax: 916-366-6674
Email: *evp@csea.org*

Connecticut Society of EAs
Caroline Frano, EA
1111 E. Putnam Ave.
Riverside, CT 06878
Phone: 203-637-3887
Fax: 203-637-7965
Email: *caroline.frano@snet.net*

Florida Society of EAs
Lynn Schmidt, EA

1495 Sixth Street, SE
Winter Haven, FL 33880
Phone: 863-295-9895
Fax: 863-298-8299
Email: *lynn@lyncotax.com*
Website: *www.fseaonline.org*

FSEA Executive Office: Jean Gates, EA
P.O. Box 3895
Clearwater, FL 33767
Phone: 727-442-2806
Fax: 727-442-2724
Email: *taxtiger@gte.net*

Georgia Society of EAs
Audrey L. Griffin, EA
Griffin Tax Service
100-C N. Houston Lake Blvd
Centerville, GA 31028-1713
Phone: 478-953-5016
Fax: 478-953-6092
Email: *griftax@grifsolu.com*
Website: *www.4gaea.org*

Hawaii Society of EAs
David Ramirez, EA
P.O. Box 61397
Honolulu, HI 96839-1397
Phone: 808-589-2322
Fax: 808-589-2422
Email: *irstaxrelief@msn.com*

Illinois Society of EAs
Karen Miller, EA
496 W. Boughton Road
Bolingbrook, IL 60440
Phone: 630-759-5070
Fax: 630-759-9101
Email: *eataxes@aol.com*

Illinois Society of EAs
Executive Director: Jacqueline Meyer, EA
1415 Matanuska Trail
McHenry, IL 60050

Phone: 815-385-6889
Fax: 815-363-1623
Email: *Meyer_JD@msn.com*

Indiana Society of EAs
Helen (Casey) Juza, EA
202 E. Main Street
Danville, IN 46122
Phone: 317-745-6051
Fax: 317-745-1735
Email: *execserv@aol.com*
Website: *www.indianaenrolledagents.com*

Iowa Society of EAs
David J. Adkins, EA
4415 Stone Ave.
Sioux City, IA 51106
Phone: 712-276-9240
Email: *Jeff@adkinstax.com*

Kentucky Society of EAs
John C. Frazier, EA
8333 Alexandria Pike
Suite 204
Alexandria, KY 41101
Phone: 859-694-3000
Fax: 859-448-2762
Email: *jctaxpro@aol.com*

Louisiana Society of EAs
Dexter Duhon, EA
114 S. State Street
Abbeville, LA 70510
Phone: 318-893-2702
Fax: 318-893-2780
Email: *djd@msis.net*

Maryland/DC Society of EAs
Robert Jacobs, EA
550M Ritchie Hwy., #145
Serverna Park, MD 21146
Phone: 410-544-4680
Fax: 410-544-1324
Email: *ataxguru@prodigy.net*

Massachusetts Society of EAs
Leon M. Rudman, EA
39 Powell Street
Stoughton, MA 02072
Phone: 781-344-9031
Fax: 781-344-9031
Email: *rudman@comcast.net*
Website: *www.maseaonline.org*

Michigan Society of EAs
Robert Hemenway, EA
602 West Main St.
Owosso, MI 48867
Phone: 989-723-5977
Fax: 989-725-8372
Email: *hbsowosso@michonline.net*

MiSEA Administrative Office:
1071 E. Nine Mile Rd.
Hazel Park, MI 48030
Phone: 248-547-99EA
Fax: 248-547-9934

Minnesota Society of EAs
Dorothy Anderson, EA
P.O. Box 748
Crosslake, MN 56442
Phone: 218-692-2650
Fax: 218-692-3364
Email: *aceinc@crosslake.net*
Website: *www.mnsea.org*

Mississippi Society of EAs
Bertha Page, EA
615 West Canal Street
Picayune, MS 39466-3916
Phone: 601-798-3116
Fax: 601-798-5650
Email: *pagetax@datasync.com*

Missouri Society of EAs
James Bales, EA
1800 Liberty Park Blvd., #6

Sedalia, MO 65301
Phone: 660-827-3212
Email: *taxpro@iland.net*
Website: *www.naea.org/mosea/*

Nevada Society of EAs
Cherene D. Cooper, EA
2585 S. Jones Blvd. Ste. 2D
Las Vegas, NV 89146-5604
Phone: 702-646-4646
Fax: 702-364-4697
Email: *cherene.cooper@gte.net*

New Mexico Society of EAs
Linda Ruckel, EA
3900 Paseo del Sol
Santa Fe, NM 87507
Phone: 505-988-9572
Fax: 505-988-9572
Email: *advancetax1@cs.com*

New Jersey Society of EAs
Martin Stein, EA
11 New York Blvd.
Edison, NJ 08820
Phone: 732-548-8023
Fax: 732-548-8023
Toll Free Referral Line: 866-652-6232
Email: *martystax@aol.com*
Website: *www.njsea.org*

New York State Society of EAs
Sandra Martin, EA
15 Reitz Pkwy
Pittsford, NY 14534
Phone: 585-381-8585
Fax: 585-442-8252
Email: *pats1040@aol.com*
Website: *www.nyssea.org*

North Carolina Society of EAs
Louis Arthur, EA
7610 Falls of The Neuse Road
Suite 100

Raleigh, NC 27615
Phone:919-844-6488
Fax: 919-844-6460
Email: *larthur@nbt-cpa.com*
Website: *www.nc-sea.org*

Northern New England
Society of EAs
David Landers, EA
P.O. Box 331
Rye, NH 03870
Phone: 603-964-7177
Fax: 603-964-9030
Email: *taxmayvin@aol.com*

Ohio State Society of EAs
Nancy Remus, EA
2901 Wexford Blvd.
Stow, OH 44224
Phone: 216-673-0463
Email: *nremus@aol.com*
Website: *www.ossea.org*

Oregon Society of EAs
Peter Mar, EA
P.O. Box 23402
Eugene, OR 97402
Phone: 541-607-9200
Fax: 541-607-1770
Email: *peter@helpmytaxes.com*

Oklahoma Society of EAs
Leslie Armstrong, EA
2000 S. Douglas Blvd.
Midwest City, OK 73130
Phone: 405-741-0832
Fax: 405-737-7600
Email: *leslie@armstrongtax.com*

Pennsylvania Society of EAs
George Meyers, EA
677 West DeKalb Pike
King of Prussia, PA 19406
Phone: 610-337-2220

Fax: 610-265-7801
Email: *gjmea@aol.com*

Rhode Island Society of EAs
D.J. Hadden, EA
27 Whipple Avenue
Westerly, RI 02891
Phone: 401-596-6179
Fax: 401-596-6179

South Carolina Society of EAs
Lawrence G. Picard Sr., EA
400 Stratford Drive
Summerville, SC 29485-8642
Phone: 843-871-1065
Fax: 843-871-1332
Email: *larrypicard@knology.net*

Tennessee Society of EAs
Caryle M. Breeden, EA
7345 Middlebrook Pike
Knoxville, TN 37909
Phone: 865-693-4274
Fax: 865-531-1846
Email: *tnigot2go@aol.com*

Utah Society of EAs
Dave Sheldon, EA
9449 Union Square, #200
Sandy, UT 84070
Phone: 801-571-2870
Fax: 801-571-2891
Email: *daveshel@concentric.net*
Website: *www.utsea.org*

Texas Society of EAs
Louis Powell, EA
408 W. College St.
Carthage, TX 75633
Phone: 903-693-7491
Fax: 903-693-7492
Email: *louispowel@aol.com*
Website: *www.txsea.org*

Virginia Society of EAs
J. Michael Boyle, EA
P.O. Box 7246
Richmond, VA 23221
Phone: 804-565-8055
Fax: 804-565-8055
Email: *j4m9b9@aol.com*
Website: *www.vaeas.org*

VASEA Executive Director: John M. (Mike) Hall
13208 Sherri Drive
Chester, VA 23831-4540
Phone: 804-748-4733
Fax: 804-748-2318
Email: *va.sea@verizon.net*

Washington State Society of EAs
Linda Shipway, EA
16605 152nd Place NE
Woodinville, WA 98072
Phone: 425-483-2956
Email: *linda.shipway2@verizon.net*
Website: *www.taxea.org*

WSSEA Administrative Office: Mariaane Kreycik, EA
222 E. Fourth Ave. Suite A
Ellensburg, WA 98926
Phone: 509-925-6931
Fax: 509-962-5807
Email: *taxpro@ellensburg.com*

Wisconsin Society of EAs
Diane M. Lotto, EA
200 South Washignton St.
Green Bay, WI 54301
Phone: 920-432-6466
Fax: 920-432-5751
Email: *dlotto@tds.net*

WiSEA Executive Office:
Donald Wollersheim, EA, Exec. Dir.
115 East Waldo Blvd.
Manitowoc, WI
Phone: 920-684-6940

Fax: 920-684-8208
Email: *donw@lsol.net*

International Tax Associations
International Accounting Associations
http://www.taxsites.com/associations2.html#international

Ad Concordiam - *http://www.adconcordiam.net/*

Canadian Payroll Association - *http://www.payroll.ca/*

Canadian Property Tax Association - *http://www.cpta.org/*

Canadian Tax Foundation - *http://www.ctf.ca/*

Canadian Taxpayers Federation - *http://www.taxpayer.com/*

Chartered Institute of Taxation - *U.K. - http://www.tax.org.uk/*

Council for International Tax Education - *http://www.fdta-cite.org/*

European-American Tax Institute - *http://www.eati.co.uk/*

European Association of Tax Law Professors - *http://www.eatlp.org/*

FSC/DISC Tax Association - *http://www.fdta-cite.org/*

Institute for Fiscal Studies - *U.K. - http://www1.ifs.org.uk/*

Institute of Taxation in Ireland - *http://www.taxireland.ie/*

Inter-American Center of Tax Administrations - *http://www.ciat.org/*

International Association of Assessing Officers - *http://www.iaao.org/*

International Fiscal Association - *http://www.ifa.nl/*

U.S. Branch - http://www.ifausa.org/

International Tax Planning Association - *http://www.itpa.org/*

North American Society of Tax Advisors - *http://www.taxadvisors.com/*

Swedish Taxpayers Association - *http://www.skattebetalarna.se/*

Taxation Institute of Australia - *http://www.taxinstitute.com.au/*

Taxpayers Association of Europe - *http://www.taxpayers-europe.org/*

Taxpayers Australia - *http://www.taxpayers.com.au/*

Appendix 2

Offshore Countries With Little Or No Taxes

Andorra

Anguilla

Antigua and Barbuda

Aruba

Bahamas

Bahrain

Barbados

Belize

Bermuda

British Virgin Islands

Canary Islands

Cayman Islands

Cook Islands

Costa Rica

Cyprus

Dominica

Dominican Republic

Gibraltar

Grenada

Guernsey

Channel Islands Guernsey / Sark / Alderney

Isle of Man

Jersey

Liberia

Liechtenstein

Maldives

Malta

Marshall Islands

Mauritius

Monaco

Montserrat

Nauru

Netherland Antilles
The Dutch Antilles

Niue

Panama

Samoa
Or Western Samoa.

San Marino

Seychelles
The Republic of Seychelles

St Lucia

St Kitts and Nevis
Or The Principality of St. Christopher and Nevis

St Vincent and the Grenadines
Or The Republic of St. Vincent

Switzerland

Tonga

Turks and Caicos

US Virgin Islands

Vanuatu

Appendix 3

States And Their Religions

Catholic Nations
Nations which recognise *Catholicism* as the official religion:
Argentina
Bolivia
Costa Rica
El Salvador
Holy See
Paraguay

Protestant Nations
Nations which recognise a form of *Protestant Christianity* as their official religion:
Vanuatu
Samoa
United Kingdom

Islamic Nations
Nations which recognise *Islam* as their official religion:
Afghanistan
Algeria
Bangladesh
Comoros
Libya
Mauritania
Morocco
Iran
Iraq
Jordan
Malaysia
Maldives
Oman
Pakistan
Saudi Arabia
Tunisia

Buddhist Nations
Nations which recognise *Buddhism* as their official religion:
Bhutan
Burma
Thailand

Hindu Nations
Nations which recognise *Hinduism* as their official religion:
Nepal

Appendix 4

Bahamian Banks

Atlantic Bank of Commerce Limited
http://www.firstatlanticcommerce.com/
P.O. Box N8865
Nassau, N.P., The Bahamas
Tel: 242-326-0740
Fax: 242-325-1272
Deputy General Manager: Mrs. Hilda Knowles

BankAmerica Trust and Banking Corporation
http://www.bankofamerica.com/
BankAmerica House
East Bay Street, P.O. Box n-9100
Nassau, Bahamas,
Tel: 8009 393 7411
Fax: 809 393 3030
Telex: 20 159

Bankers Trust Company
Claughton House
P.O.Box N-3234
Nassau, Bahamas
Tel: 809 325 4107
Fax: 20262

Bank of Bahamas Limited
http://centralbankbahamas.com/
50 Shirley Street, P.O. Box N-7118
Nassau, Bahamas
Tel: 809 326 2560
Fax: 809 325 2762
Telex: 20141 BBL

Bank of Boston Trust Company Limited
Charlotte House
P.O. Box N-3930
Nassau, Bahamas
Tel: 809 322 8531
Telex: 20189 BOSTRUST

Bank of Nova Scotia
http://www.scotiabank.com/cda/content/0,,CID50_LIDen,00.html
Box N-7545 Bay Street
Nassau, Bahamas
Tel: 809 322 4631
Fax: 809 328 8473
Email: 19163288473@faxsav.com

Bahamas Offshore Accounts
http://bahamas-offshoreaccounts.com/

Barclays Bank in the Bahamas
http://www.bahamas.barclays.co.uk/off-bahamas.html
Full range of banking services.

Chemical Bank & Trust Limited
http://www.chemicalbankmi.com/
P.O. Box N-4723
Nassau, N.P., The Bahamas
Tel: 242-322-1003
Fax: 242-326-7339
Senior Trust Officer: Mr. Michael Ranson

CIBC Trust Company
http://www.cibc-global.com/jur_bah_frm.html

Cititrust Bahamas
http://www.citibank.com/
Thompson Boulevard P.O. Box-1576
Nassau, Bahamas
Tel: 809 322 4240
Fax: 809 325 6147
Telex: 20420

Coutts & Company Limited
http://www.coutts.com/contact/bahamas.asp
P.O. Box N7788
Nassau, N.P., The Bahamas
Tel: 242-326-0404
Fax: 242-326-6709
Manager: Mr. James D. Graham

Darier Hentsch Private Bank & Trust Limited
http://www.darierhentsch.com/darier/nassau.htm
P.O. Box N4938
Nassau, N.P., The Bahamas
Tel: 242-322-2721
Fax: 242-326-6983
Vice President: Mrs. Anna Colebrooke

Demachy Worms & Co. International
P.O. Box N3918
Nassau, N.P., The Bahamas
Tel: 242-326-0282
Fax: 242-326-5213
Financial Controller: Mr. Ronald W. Springle

Eastland American Bank Limited
P.O. Box N4920
Nassau, N.P., The Bahamas
Tel: 242-325-9170
Fax: 242-325-1002
Manager: Mr. Tyrone Fowler

Euro-Dutch Trust Co. Limited
P.O. Box N9205
Nassau, N.P., The Bahamas
Tel: 242-325-1033
Fax: 242-323-7918
Managing Director: Mr. Anthony L.M. Inder Rieden

Fidinam Trust Corporation Limited
P.O. Box N9932
Nassau, N.P., The Bahamas
Tel: 242-326-5084
Fax: 242-328-0541
Resident Manager: Mr. Cedric B. Moss

Guta Bank & Trust Limited
http://www.interknowledge.com/bahamas/investment/guta-bank/index.html

Laurentian Bank & Trust Company Limited
http://www.laurentianbank.com/
P.O. Box N4883
Nassau, N.P., The Bahamas
Tel: 242-326-5935
Fax: 242-326-5871
Managing Director: Mr. E. Andre Doyon

Lloyds Bank International Private Banking
http://www.lloydstsb.com/
P.O. Box N4843
Nassau, N.P., The Bahamas
Tel: 242-322-8711
Fax: 242-322-8719
Telex: 20107 BOLAM
Assistant Manager, Trust Department: Mr. Sam P. Haven

Mees Pierson Limited
http://www.meespiersonci.com/
P.O. Box SS5539
Nassau, N.P., The Bahamas
Tel: 242-393-8777
Fax: 242-393-0582
Managing Director: Mr. Geoffrey Dyson

Montaque Securities International Limited
http://www.montaquesecurities.com/
Saffrey Square
Bay Street & Bank Lane, 1st Floor
P.O. Box N-7474
Nassau, The Bahamas
Tel: (242) 356-6133
Fax: (242) 356-6144
President & Managing Director: Owen S. M. Bethel

Morgan Trust Company of The Bahamas
http://www.morimor.com/
P.O. Box N4899
Nassau, N.P., The Bahamas
Tel: 242-326-5519
Fax: 242-326-5520

Managing Director: Mr. Andrew G. Massie

Offshore Trust Banking Corporation Limited

West Bay Road, P.O. Box N-7179
Nassau, Bahamas
Tel: 809 322 4585
Telex: 20111

Rawson Trust Company Limited
P.O. Box N4465
Nassau, N.P., The Bahamas
Tel: 242-322-7461
Fax: 242-326-6177
Manager, Accounts: Mrs. B. M. Rolle

Royal Bank of Cananda
http://www.rbcprivatebanking.com/tier3_bahamas.html

Royal Bank of Scotland (NASSAU) Limited
http://www.royalbankscot.co.uk/
Box N-3045, 50 Shirley Street
Nassau, Bahamas
Tel: 809 322 4643
Fax: 809 326 7558
Email: *19163267558@faxsave.com*

Sand Ander Investment Bank Limited
P.O. Box N1682
Nassau, N.P., The Bahamas
Tel: 242-322-3588
Fax: 242-322-3585
Manager: Mrs. R. L. Symonette

The Private Trust Corporation Limited
http://www.privatetrustco.com/

The Chase Manhattan Private Bank
http://www.chase.com/
P.O. Box N1576
Nassau, N.P., The Bahamas
Tel: 242-323-6811
Fax: 242-326-8814
Unit Trust Department: Mrs. Eunice E. Smith Manager

The Citibank Private Bank
http://www.citibank.com/
P.O. Box N1576
Nassau, N.P., The Bahamas
Tel: 242-323-3521
Fax: 242-325-6147
Managing Director: Mr. David N. Tremblay

Thorand Trust & Management Limited
P.O. Box N3242
Nassau, N.P., The Bahamas
Tel: 242-393-8622
Fax: 242-393-3772
Managing Director: Mr. Robert V. Lotmore

Westpac Bank & Trust (Bahamas) Limited
http://www.westpac.com.au%20/
P.O. Box N8332
Nassau, N.P., The Bahamas
Tel: 242-328-8064
Fax: 242-326-0067
Managing Director: Mrs. Jacqueline M. Bain

Appendix 5

St Lucian Banks

Bank Of Novia Scotia The.
6 WM Peter Blvd,
Box 301, Castries,
St. Lucia
758-456-2100

Bank Of Novia Scotia The.
Cnr Chausee Rd & High St,
Castries,
St. Lucia
758-452-3797

Bank Of Novia Scotia The.
New Dock Rd,
Box 223, Vieux Fort,
St. Lucia
758-454-6314

Bank Of Novia Scotia The.
Rodney Bay,
Gross Islet,
St. Lucia
758-452-8805

Barclays Bank Plc.
Bridge St,
Box 335,
Castries,
St. Lucia
758-456-1000

Barclays Bank Plc.
Customer Services,
Castries,
St. Lucia
758-456-1125

Barclays Bank Plc.
Operations Department,

Castries,
St. Lucia
758-456-1118

Barclays Bank Plc.
Manager Operations,
Castries,
St. Lucia
758-456-1104

Barclays Bank Plc.
Barclays Bank Hotline,
Castries,
St. Lucia
758-451-8009

Barclays Bank Plc.
Foreign Business,
Castries,
St. Lucia
758-456-1142

Barclays Bank Plc.
Business Centre,
Castries, St. Lucia
758-456-1108

Barclays Bank Plc.
Senior Corporate Manager,
Castries, St. Lucia
758-456-1102

Barclays Bank Plc.
Manager Corporate Centre,
Castries,
St. Lucia
758-456-1103

Barclays Bank Plc.
Small Business Manager,
Castries, St. Lucia
758-456-1106

Barclays Bank Plc.

Business Banker,
Castries, St. Lucia
758-456-1233

Barclays Bank Plc.
Area Manager,
Castries, St. Lucia
758-456-1101

Barclays Bank Plc.
Merchant Services,
Castries, St. Lucia
758-452-2642

Barclays Bank Plc.
Manager Personal Banking,
Castries,
St. Lucia
758-452-4115

Barclays Bank Plc.
Personal Bankers,
Castries,
St. Lucia
758-456-1158

Barclays Bank Plc.
Vieux Fort,
St. Lucia
758-454-6255

Barclays Bank Plc.
Manager,
St. Lucia
758-454-6914

Barclays Bank Plc.
Rodney Bay Marina,
Gross Islet,
St. Lucia
758-452-9384

Barclays Bank Plc.
Insurance Broking,

Barfincor,
St. Lucia
758-453-2015

Barclays Bank Plc.
L' Anse Rd,
Castries,
St. Lucia
758-452-4999

Barclays Bank Plc.
Appartment,
Castries,
St. Lucia
758-452-3347

Barclays Bank Plc.
Sports Club,
Castries,
St. Lucia
758-451-8259

Caribbean Banking Corporation Ltd.
Micoud St, Box 1531,
Castries,
St. Lucia
758-452-2265

Caribbean Banking Corporation Ltd.
Gablewoods Mall,
Vieux Fort,
St. Lucia
758-451-7469

Caribbean Banking Corporation Ltd.
Gablewoods Mall South,
Vieux Fort,
St. Lucia
758-4547264

Caribbean Banking Corporation Ltd.
Black Bay,
Vieux Fort,
St. Lucia

758-454-7264

Cibc Caribbean Ltd.
Wm Peter Bvld,
Box 350,
Castries,
St. Lucia
758-456-2422

Cibc Caribbean Ltd.
Fredrick Clark St,
Vieux Fort,
St. Lucia
758-454-6262

Eastern Caribbean Central Bank.
Financial Centre,
Bridge St, Box 295,
Castries,
St. Lucia
758-452-7449

First Citizens Bank ,
http://www.firstcitizenstt.com/
St. Lucia
(868) 623-2576

National Commercial Bank Of St Lucia Ltd.
Financial Centre Building
1 Bridge St
Box 1860
Castries
St. Lucia
758-456-6000

National Commercial Bank Of St Lucia Ltd.
Bridge St Branch
Box 1862
Castries
St. Lucia
758-456-6000

National Commercial Bank Of St Lucia Ltd.
Waterfront Branch

Box 1031
Castries
St. Lucia
758-456-6000

National Commercial Bank Of St Lucia Ltd.
Vieux Fort Branch
Box 261
Vieux Fort
St. Lucia
758-454-6327

National Commercial Bank Of St Lucia Ltd.
Soufriere Branch
Box 243
Soufriere
St. Lucia
758-459-7450

National Commercial Bank Of St Lucia Ltd.
Gros Islet Branch
Box 2046
Gros Islet
St. Lucia
758-450-8002

National Commercial Bank Of St Lucia Ltd.
Bureau De Change
Hewanorra Int Airport
Vieux Fort
St. Lucia
758-454-7780

Royal Bank Of Canada.
Wm Peter Bvld
Box 280
Castries
St. Lucia
758-452-2245

Royal Bank Of Canada.
Audit Dept
Box 280
Castries

St. Lucia
758-451-9463

Royal Bank Of Canada.
Rodney Bay Marina
Gros Islet
St. Lucia
758-452-9921

Royal Bank Of Canada.
New Dock Rd
Vieux Fort
St. Lucia
758-454-5804

Royal Bank Of Canada.
Business Banking Centre
Castries
St. Lucia
758-450-3951

St Lucia Co-operative Ltd.
21 Bridge St
Box 168
Castries
St. Lucia
758-452-2880

St Lucia Co-operative Ltd.
G F L Charles Airport
Castries
St. Lucia
758-451-8482

St Lucia Co-operative Ltd.
JQ'S Mall
Rodney Bay
St. Lucia
758-452-8882

St Lucia Co-operative Ltd.
Commercial St
Box 342
Vieux Fort

St. Lucia
758-454-6213

St Lucia Co-operative Ltd.
17 Bridge St
Box 168
Castries
St. Lucia
758-455-7000

St Lucia Co-operative Ltd.
George F L Charles Airport
Box 168
Castries
St. Lucia
758-451-8482

Appendix 6

Map Of Europe

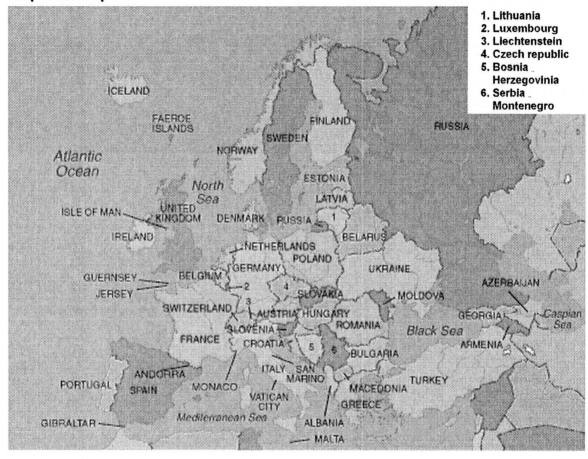

1. Lithuania
2. Luxembourg
3. Liechtenstein
4. Czech republic
5. Bosnia Herzegovinia
6. Serbia Montenegro

Appendix 7

UK Banks

Internet and Telephone Banking Current Accounts

Cahoot Abbey National
http://www.cahoot.co.uk/

Barclays internet banking
http://ibanking.barclays.co.uk/

Co-op Internet bank Smile
http://www.smile.co.uk

EGG
http://www.egg.com

Intelligent finance
http://www.if.com

Lloyds TSB
http://www.lloydstsb.com/services/internet/

Bank of Scotland
http://www.bosinternet.com/

First-e
http://www.first-e.com

Virgin
http://www.virgin-direct.co.uk

Internet savings bank
http://www.imbd.com

Woolwich
http://www.openplan.co.uk

High Street Banks and Building Societies With High Street Branches Throughout the UK for Saving and Banking

Abbey National High Street Bank
http://www.abbeynational.co.uk /

Barclays High Street

http://www.barclays.co.uk /

Cheltenham & Gloucester
http://www.cheltglos.co.uk

Alliance and Leicester
http://www.alliance-leicester.co.uk

Bristol & West
http://www.bristol-west.co.uk

Bradford & Bingley
http://www.bradford-bingley.co.uk

Britannia
http://www.britannia.co.uk/

Co-Op
http://www.co-operativebank.co.uk

Halifax
http://www.halifax.co.uk

HFC
http://www.hfcbank.co.uk

HSBC Midland Highstreet Bank
http://www.hsbc.com

Lloyds TSB
http://www.lloydstsb.co.uk

Nationwide
http://www.nationwide.co.uk

Natwest branches
http://www.natwest.co.uk

Royal bank of Scotland
http://www.rbs.co.uk

Portman
http://www.portman.co.uk/

Woolwich building society
http://www.woolwich.co.uk

Yorkshire
http://www.ybs.co.uk

Other Banks and Building Societies

Bank of England
http://www.bankofengland.co.uk

Bank of Ireland
http://www.bank-of-ireland.co.uk

Bank of Scotland
http://www.bankofscotland.co.uk

Bank of Wales
http://www.bankofwales.co.uk

Barnsley
http://www.barnsley-bs

Beverly
http://www.beverleybs

Birmingham
http://www.birminghammidshires.co.uk

Cambridge
http://www.cambridge-building-society

Capital Bank
http://www.capitalbank.co.uk

Cash Centres Ltd
http://www.cashcentres.co.uk

Cater Allen
http://www.caterallen.co.uk

Catholic
http://www.catholicbs.co.uk

Century
http://www.century-building-society

Charterhouse
http://www.charterhouse.co.uk

Chelsea
http://www.thechelsea.co.uk

Chesham
http://www.cheshambsoc.co.uk

Chesham
http://www.cheshambsoc.co.uk/

Cheshire
http://www.cheshirebs.co.uk/

Citybank
http://www.citibank.co.uk

Clay Cross
http://www.claycrossbs.co.uk/

Coinco International
http://www.coinco.co.uk

Coutts
http://www.coutts.com

Darlington
http://www.darlington.co.uk/

Derbyshire
http://www.thederbyshire.co.uk/

Dudley
http://www.dudleybuildingsociety.co.uk/

Dunfermline
http://www.dunfermline-bs.co.uk/

Earl Shilton
http://www.esbs.co.uk/

Ecology
http://www.ecology.co.uk/

ECU Group
http://www.ecu.co.uk/

Express Finance
http://www.express-finance.co.uk

First Trust Bank
http://www.ftbni.co.uk

Flemming
http://www.flemming.co.uk/premier

Furness
http://www.furnessbs.co.uk/

Gainsborough
http://www.gbbs.demon.co.uk/

Hambros
http://www.hambrosbank.com

Hamilton
http://www.hdb.co.uk

Hanley Economic
http://www.thehanley.co.uk/

Harpenden
http://www.harpendenbs.co.uk/

Hays
http://www.hays-banking.co.uk

Hinckley and Rugby
http://www.hrbs.co.uk/

ICC Bank
http://www.icc.ie

Ilkeston Permanent

http://www.ipbs.co.uk/

Ipswich
http://www.ipswich-bs.co.uk/

Kent Reliance
http://www.krbs.co.uk/

Lambeth
http://www.lambeth.co.uk/

Leeds & Holbeck
http://www.leeds-holbeck.co.uk/

Leek
http://www.leek-united.co.uk/

Legal & General
http://www.landg.com

Lombard
http://www.lombard.co.uk/banking

Loughborough
http://www.theloughborough.co.uk

Manchester
http://www.themanchester.co.uk/

Mansfield
http://www.mansfieldbs.co.uk/

Market Harborough
http://www.mhbs.co.uk

Market Harborough
http://www.mhbs.co.uk/

Marsden
http://www.marsdenbs.co.uk/

Melton Mowbray
http://www.mmbs.co.uk/

Mercantile
http://www.mercantile-bs.co.uk/

Newbury
http://www.newbury.co.uk/

Newcastle
http://www.newcastle.co.uk/

Northern
http://www.nbonline.co.uk

Norwich & Peterborough
http://www.npbs.co.uk

Nottingham
http://www.nottingham-bs.co.uk/

Personal Loan Corporation
http://www.loancorp.co.uk

Principality
http://www.principality.co.uk/

Progressive
http://www.theprogressive.com/

Prudential
http://www.pru.co.uk

Saffron Waldon Herts &amp
http://www.swhebs.co.uk/

Salomon Brothers
http://www.sbil.co.uk

Scarborough
http://www.scarboroughbs.co.uk/

Scottish
http://www.scottishbldgsoc.co.uk/

Shepshed
http://www.theshepshed.co.uk/

Skipton
http://www.skipton.co.uk

Spanish/Gibraltar
http://www.npbs-gibraltar.co.uk/

Stafford Railway
http://www.srbs.co.uk/

Staffordshire
http://www.staffordshirebuildingsociety.co.uk

Staffordshire
http://www.staffordshirebuildingsociety.co.uk/

Standard Bank
http://www.sbl.co.uk

Standard Chartered
http://www.stanchart.com

Standard Life
http://www.standardlifebank.com

Stroud & Swindon
http://www.stroudandswindon.co.uk

Swansea
http://www.swansea-bs.co.uk/

Teachers
http://www.teachersbs.co.uk

Tridos
http://www.tridos.co.uk

Appendix 8

Swiss Banks

A & A Actienbank **Zürich**
ABB Export Bank **Zürich**
ABN AMRO Bank (Schweiz) **Zürich**
ABN AMRO Bank N.V., Amsterdam **Zürich**
AIG Private Bank Ltd. **Zürich**
ANZ Grindlays Bank plc **Genève 1**
AP Anlage & Privatbank AG **Bäch**
Aargauische Kantonalbank **Aarau**
Adler & Co. AG **Zürich**
Alpha Rheintal Bank **Berneck**
Alternative Bank ABS **Olten**
Amas Bank (Switzerland) Ltd. **Genève**
American Express Bank (Switz.) **Genève 3**
Amtsersparniskasse Oberhasli **Meiringen (BE)**
Amtsersparniskasse Schwarzenbu **Schwarzenburg (BE)**
Amtsersparniskasse Thun **Thun (BE)**
Anker Bank **Zürich**
Appenzeller Kantonalbank **Appenzell**
Arab Bank (Switzerland) Ltd. **Zürich**
Armand von Ernst & Cie. AG **Bern 1**
Artesia (Suisse) SA **Genève 11**
Arzi Bank AG **Zürich**
Atlantic Vermögensverwaltungsbank **Zürich**
BB Bank Belp **Belp (BE)**
BBVA Privanza Bank (Switzerland) Ltd. **Zürich**
BDL Banco di Lugano **Lugano**
BEKB ¦ BCBE **Bern**
BFC Banque Financière de la Cité **Genève 11**
BGG Banque Genevoise de Gestion **Genève 3**
BHF-Bank (Schweiz) AG **Zürich**
BLP Banque de Portefeuilles **Lausanne**
BNP Paribas (Suisse) SA **Geneva 11**
BS Bank Schaffhausen **Hallau**
BSI SA **Lugano**
BZ Bank Aktiengesellschaft **Wilen b. Wollerau**
Banca Arner SA **Lugano**
Banca Commerciale Italiana (Switzerland) **Zürich**

Banca Commerciale Lugano **Lugano**
Banca Euromobiliare (Suisse) SA **Lugano**
Banca Monte Paschi (Suisse) SA **Genève 4**
Banca Popolare di Sondrio (Suisse) SA **Lugano**
Banca Privata Edmond de Rothschild Lugano SA **Lugano**
Banca Unione di Credito **Lugano**
Banca del Ceresio SA **Lugano**
Banca del Gottardo **Lugano**
Banca del Sempione **Lugano**
Banca dello Stato del Cantone Ticino **Bellinzona**
Banca di Credito e Commercio (BANKREDIT) **Lugano**
Banco Espirito Santo SA **Lausanne**
Banco Mercantil (Schweiz) AG **Zürich**
Banco Santander Central Hispano (Suiza) SA **Genève 1**
Bank Adamas AG **Zürich**
Bank Austria Creditanstalt (Schweiz) AG **Zürich**
Bank Bütschwil **Bütschwil (SG)**
Bank CIAL (Schweiz) **Basel**
Bank Coop **Basel**
Bank EEK **Bern 7**
Bank Ehinger & Cie. **Basel**
Bank Eschenback **Eschenbach SG**
Bank Hapoalim (Schweiz) AG **Zürich**
Bank Hofmann AG **Zürich**
Bank Hugo Kahn & Co. AG **Zürich**
Bank J. Vontobel & Co. AG **Zürich**
Bank Jacob Safra (Schweiz) AG **Zürich**
Bank Julius Bär & Co. AG **Zürich-Mülligen**
Bank Leerau **Kirchleerau-Moosle**
Bank Leu AG **Zürich**
Bank Leumi le-Israel (Schweiz) **Zürich**
Bank Linth **Uznach**
Bank Morgan Stanley AG **Zürich**
Bank Sal. Oppenheim Jr. & Cie. **Zürich**
Bank Sarasin & Cie. **Basel**
Bank Sparhafen Zürich **Zürich**
Bank Thorbecke AG **St. Gallen**
Bank Wartau-Sevelen **Azmoos**
Bank am Bellevue **Zürich**
Bank for International Settlements **Basel**
Bank für Handel & Effekten **Zürich**

Bank im Thal **Balsthal**

Bank in Gossau **Gossau SG**

Bank in Huttwil **Huttwil**

Bank in Langnau AG **Langnau im Emmental**

Bank in Zuzwil **Zuzwil SG**

Bank of America, National Association **Geneva 3**

Bank of New York - Inter-maritime Bank **Genève 11**

Bank of Tokyo-Mitsubishi (Schweiz) AG **Zürich**

Bank von Ernst & Cie AG **Zürich**

Banque Algérienne du Commerce Extérieur SA **Zürich**

Banque Audi (Suisse) SA **Genève 12**

Banque Banorient (Suisse) **Genève 3**

Banque Baring Brothers (Suisse) SA **Genève 3**

Banque Bonhôte & Cie SA **Neuchâtel**

Banque Bruxelles Lambert (Suisse) SA **Genève 3**

Banque CAI Caisse Alfa Banques **Genève 2**

Banque Cantonale Neuchâteloise Neuchâtel

Banque Cantonale Vaudoise Lausanne

Banque Cantonale de Fribourg Fribourg

Banque Cantonale de Genève Genève 2

Banque Cantonale du Jura Porrentruy

Banque Cantonale du Valais Sion

Banque Degroof Luxembourg SA Genève 1

Banque Diamantaire Anversoise (Suisse) SA Genève 3

Banque Edouard Constant SA Genève 3

Banque Franck SA Genève 3

Banque Française de l'Orient (Suisse) SA Genève 11

Banque Galland & Cie. SA Lausanne

Banque Général du Luxembourg (Suisse) SA Zürich

Banque Internationale de Commerce -- BRED Genève

Banque Ippa & Associés, Luxembourg Lausanne

Banque Jenni & Cie. SA Basel

Banque Jurassienne d'Epargne et de Crédit Bassecourt

Banque Labouchere SA Genève

Banque MeesPierson Gonet SA Nyon

Banque Multi Commerciale Genève 11

Banque Nationale de Paris (Suisse) SA Basel

Banque Notz Stucki SA Genève 11

Banque Pasche SA Genève 11

Banque Piguet & Cie. SA Yverdon

Banque Privée Edmond de Rothschild SA Genève 11

Banque SCS Alliance SA Genève 3

Banque Syz & Co. SA Genève 11

Banque Tardy, de Watteville & Cie. SA Genève 4
Banque Thaler Genève
Banque Unexim (Suisse) SA Genève 11
Banque Vontobel Genève SA Genève 4
Banque Worms (Genève) SA Genève 11
Banque de Camondo (Suisse) SA Genève 11
Banque de Commerce et de Placements SA Genève 1
Banque de Dépôts et de Gestion Lausanne
Banque de Gestion Financière BAGEFI Zürich
Banque de Patrimoines Privés Genève BPG SA Genève 25
Bantleon Bank AG Zug
Barclays Bank (Suisse) SA Genève 3
Basellandschaftliche Kantonalbank Liestal
Basler Kantonalbank Basel
Banque Cantonale de Bâle Genève 3
Baumann & Cie. Basel
Bayerische Landesbank (Schweiz) AG Zürich
Berenberg Bank (Schweiz) AG Zürich
Bezirks-Sparkasse Dielsdorf Dielsdorf
Bezirkskasse Laufen Laufen
Bezirkssparkasse Uster Uster
Biene - Bank im Rheintal Altstätten SG
Bordier & Cie. Genève 11
Burgerliche Ersparniskasse Bern Bern
C.I.M. Banque Genève 1
CBG Banca Privata Lugano SA Lugano
CBG Compagnie Bancaire Genève Genève 11
Caisse d'Epargne Le Crêt Le Crêt-p-Semsales
Caisse d'Epargne d'Aubonne Aubonne
Caisse d'Epargne de Nyon Nyon
Caisse d'Epargne de Prez, Corserey et Noréaz Prez-vers-Noréaz
Caisse d'Epargne de Siviriez Siviriez
Caisse d'Epargne de Vuisternenr-devant-Romont Vuisternens-Romont
Caisse d'Epargne de la Ville de Fribourg Fribourg
Caisse d'Epargne du District de Cossonay Cossonay-Ville
Caisse d'Epargne du District de Courtelary Courtelary
Caisse d'Epargne du District de Vevey Vevey
Caisse d'Epargne et de Crédit Mutuel de Chermignon Chermignon
Caisse d'Epargne et de Prevoyancce d'Yverdon-les-Bains SA Yverdon
Caisse d'Epargne et de Prévoyance de Lausanne Lausanne
Canto Consulting Baar
Cantrade Privatbank AG Zürich
Citibank (Switzerland) Zürich
Citibank N.A. Zürich

City Bank Zürich
Clariden Bank Zürich
Commerzbank (Schweiz) AG Zürich
Compagnie Bancaire Espirito Santo SA Lausanne
Cornèr Banca SA Lugano
Cosba private banking AG Zürich
Coutts & Co. AG Zürich
Credit Suisse Zürich SKA
Credit Suisse First Boston Genève 70
Crédit Agricole Indosuez (Suisse) SA Genève 3
Crédit Commercial de France (Suisse) SA Genève 3
Crédit Lyonnais (Suisse) SA Genève 11
Crédit Mutuel de la Vallée SA Le Sentier
DC Bank, Deposito-Cassa der Stadt Bern Bern 7
Dai-Ichi Kangyo Bank (Schweiz) AG Zürich
Deka (Swiss) Privatbank AG Zürich
Deutsche Bank (Schweiz) AG Zürich
Deutsche Bank (Suisse) SA Genève 1
Dexia Privatbank (Schweiz) Zürich
Direkt Anlage Bank (Schweiz) AG Bäch
Discount Bank and Trust Company Genève 11
Dominick Company AG Zürich
Dresdner Bank (Schweiz) AG Zürich
Dreyfus Söhne & Cie. AG Basel
E. Gutzwiller & Cie. Banquiers Basel
EB Entlebucher Bank Schüpfheim
EFG Bank European Financial Group Genève 2
EFG Private Bank SA Zürich
Erspariskasse Brienz Brienz BE
Ersparnisanstalt Oberuzwil Oberuzwil
Ersparnisanstalt Unterwasser Unterwasser
Ersparnisanstalt der Stadt St.Gallen St. Gallen
Ersparnisgesellschaft Küttigen Küttigen
Ersparniskasse Affoltern i.E. Affoltern i.E.
Ersparniskasse Dürrenroth Dürrenroth
Ersparniskasse Erlinsbach Erlinsbach
Ersparniskasse Murten Murten
Ersparniskasse Rüeggisberg Rüeggisberg
Ersparniskasse Schaffhausen Schaffhausen
Ersparniskasse Speicher Speicher
Ersparniskasse Wyssachen-Eriswil Wyssachen
Ersparniskasse des Amtsbezirks Interlaken Interlaken
Eurasco Bank AG Zürich
F. van Lanschot Bankiers (Schweiz) AG Zürich

FCE Bank plc Zürich
FIBI Bank (Schweiz) AG Zürich
FTI Banque Fiduciary Trust Genève 15
Ferrier Lullin & Cie SA Genève 3
Finansbank (Suisse) SA Genève 12
Finter Bank Zürich Zürich
Freie Gemeinschaftsbank BCL Basel
GE Capital Bank Brugg
GRB Glarner Regionalbank Schwanden GL
GZ-Bank (Schweiz) AG Zürich
Gewerbebank Männedorf Männedorf
Glarner Kantonalbank Glarus
Goldman Sachs & Co. Bank Zürich
Gonet & Cie. Genève 11
Graubündner Kantonalbank Chur
HSBC Bank Middle East Genève 11
HSBC Guyerzeller Bank AG Zürich
HSBC Republic Bank (Suisse) SA Genève 1
HYPOSWISS, Schweizerische Hypotheken- und Handelsbank Zürich
Habib Bank AG Zurich Zürich
Habibsons Bank Limited, London Zürich
Handelsfinanz-CCF Bank Genève 11
Helaba (Schweiz) Landesbank Hessen-Thüringen AG Zürich
Hentsch Henchoz & Cie. Lausanne
Hottinger & Cie Zürich
Hypothekarbank Lenzburg Lenzburg
IBI Bank AG Zürich
IBZ Investment Bank Zurich Zürich
ING Bank NV, Amsterdam Genève 11
ING Baring Private Bank (Schweiz) Zürich
IRB Interregiobank Reinach
Instinet (Schweiz) AG Zürich
Investec Bank (Switzerland) AG Zürich
Isbank GmbH, Frankfurt am MainZweigniederlassung Zürich Zürich
J.P. Morgan (Suisse) SA Genève 1
Jyske Bank (Schweiz) Zürich
KGS Sensebank Heitenried
Kanz Bank Genève 3
Kredietbank (Suisse) Lugano SA Lugano
Kredietbank (Suisse) SA Genève 11
LGT Bank in Liechtenstein AG Zürich
La Roche & Co Banquiers Basel
Landolt & Cie, Banquiers Lausanne
Lavoro Bank AG Zürich

Leihkasse Stammheim Oberstammheim

Liechtensteinische Landesbank (Schweiz) AG Zürich

Lienhardt & Partner Privatbank Zürich AG Zürich

Lloyds TSB Bank plc Genève 11

Lombard Odier Darier Hentsch & Cie. Geneva 11

Luzerner Kantonalbank Luzern

Luzerner Regiobank AG Luzern

M.M. Warburg Bank (Schweiz) AG Zürich

MFC Merchant Bank SA Genève 3

MIGROSBANK Zürich

Maerki, Baumann & Co. AG Zürich

Marcuard Cook & Cie. S.A. Genève 1

MediBank Zug

Merrill Lynch Bank (Suisse) SA Genève 3

Merrill Lynch Capital Markets AG Zürich

Mirabaud & Cie. Genève 11

Mitsubishi Tokyo Weath Management (Switzerland) Ltd. Genève

Mizuho Bank (Schweiz) AG Zürich

Morgan Guaranty Trust Company of New York Zürich

Morval & Cie SA, Banque Genève 12

Mourgue d'Algue & Cie. Genève 3

National Bank of Kuwait (Suisse) S.A. Genève 1

Neue Aargauer Bank Brugg AG

Nidwalder Kantonalbank Stans

Nomura Bank (Schweiz) AG Zürich

Nordea Bank S.A. Luxemburg, Zweigniederlassung Zürich Zürich

Nordfinanz Bank Zürich Zürich

OZ Bankers AG Pfäffikon

Obersimmentalische Volksbank Zweisimmen

Obwaldner Kantonalbank Sarnen

PBS Privat Bank Schweiz AG Zürich

PG Partner Bank AG Zürich

PKB Privatbank AG Lugano

Pictet & Cie. Genève 11

Privatbank Bellerive AG Zürich

Privatbank IHAG Zürich AG Zürich

Privatbank Vermag AG Chur

Privatbank Von Graffenried AG Bern 7

RBA Zentralbank Bern

Rabo Robeco Bank (Schweiz) AG Zürich

Rahn & Bodmer Zürich

Redsafe Bank Zürich

Regiobank Solothurn Solothurn

Reichmuth & Co. Luzern 7

Reisebank AG Basel
Robert Fleming (Switzerland) AG Zürich
Rothschild Bank AG Zürich
Royal Bank of Canada (Suisse) Genève 11
Russische Kommerzial Bank AG Zürich
Rüd, Blass & Cie AG Zürich
SB Saanen Bank Saanen
SEB Private Bank Genève
SG Rüegg Bank AG Zürich
SIS AGSegaIntersettle Olten
Sanwa Bank (Schweiz) AG Zürich
Schaffhauser Kantonalbank Schaffhausen
SchmidtBank (Schweiz) AG Zürich
Schroder & Co. Bank AG Zürich
Schweizer Verband der Raiffeisenbanken St. Gallen
Schweizerische Hypotheken- und Handelsbank Zürich
Schweizerische Nationalbank Bern
Schweizerische Schiffshypothekenbank Basel
Schwyzer Kantonalbank Schwyz
Scobag AG Basel
Skandia Bank (Switzerland) SA Zürich
Società Bancaria Ticinese Bellinzona
Société Générale, Succursale de Zürich Zürich
Solothurner Bank SoBa Solothurn
Spar + Leihkasse Frutigen Frutigen
Spar + Leihkasse Gürbetal Mühlethurnen
Spar- und Leihkasse Balgach Balgach
Spar- und Leihkasse Bucheggberg Lüterswil
Spar- und Leihkasse Ebnat-Kappel Ebnat-Kappel
Spar- und Leihkasse Kaltbrunn Kaltbrunn
Spar- und Leihkasse Kirchberg (SG) Kirchberg SG
Spar- und Leihkasse Leuk und Umgebung Leuk Stadt
Spar- und Leihkasse Madiswil Madiswil
Spar- und Leihkasse Melchnau Melchnau
Spar- und Leihkasse Münsingen Münsingen
Spar- und Leihkasse Rebstein Rebstein
Spar- und Leihkasse Riggisberg Riggisberg
Spar- und Leihkasse Steffisburg Steffisburg
Spar- und Leihkasse Sumiswald Sumiswald
Spar- und Leihkasse Thayngen Thayngen
Spar- und Leihkasse Wynigen Wynigen
Sparcassa 1816 Wädenswil
Spargenossenschaft Mosnang Mosnang
Sparkasse Engelberg Engelberg

Sparkasse Horgen Horgen
Sparkasse Küsnacht ZH Küsnacht ZH
Sparkasse Oberriet Oberriet SG
Sparkasse Oftringen Oftringen
Sparkasse Schwyz Schwyz
Sparkasse Thalwil Thalwil
Sparkasse Trogen Trogen
Sparkasse Wiesendangen Wiesendangen
Sparkasse Zürcher Oberland Wetzikon ZH
Sparkasse des Sensebezirks Tafers
St.Gallische Creditanstalt St. Gallen
St.Gallische Kantonalbank St. Gallen
Swissfirst Bank AG Zürich
Swissnetbank.com AG Zürich
Swissquote Bank Gland
Synthesis Bank Genève 3
Tempus Privatbank AG Zürich
The Chase Manhattan Private Bank (Switzerland) Genève 3
Thurgauer Kantonalbank Weinfelden
Tokai Bank (Schweiz) AG Zürich
Trafina Privatbank AG Basel
Triba Partner Bank Triengen
UBS AG Zürich
UBS Card Center AG Glattbrugg
UEB United European Bank Genève 1
UniCredit (Suisse) Bank SA Lugano
Unibank SA Luxemburg, Zweigniederlassung Zürich Zürich
Union Bancaire Privée Genève 1
United Bank AG Zürich
United Mizrahi Bank (Schweiz) AG Zürich
Urner Kantonalbank Altdorf UR
VP Bank (Schweiz) AG Zürich
Valiant Bank Bern
Valiant Privatbank AG Bern
Volksbank Bodensee AG St. Margrethen
Vorarlberger Landes- und Hypothekenbank AG St. Gallen
WIR Bank Basel
Wegelin & Co. Privatbankiers St. Gallen
Westdeutsche Landesbank (Schweiz) AG Zürich
ZLB Zürcher Landbank Elgg
Zuger Kantonalbank Zug
Zürcher Kantonalbank Zürich-Mülligen
Zürich Invest Bank AG Effretikon

Appendix 9

Map Of Oceania

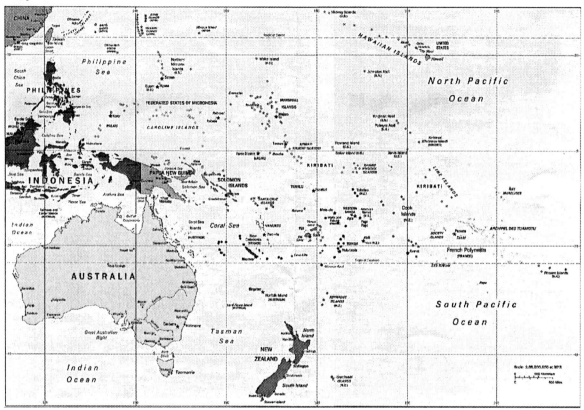

Notes

Other Works By Samuel Blankson

How to Destroy Your Debts

Printed: 165 pages, 6.0 x 9.0 in, Perfect-bound
Download: PDF (1739 kb)
ISBN: 1-4116-2374-6
Copyright Year: © 2005 by Samuel Blankson
Language: English
Publisher: Lulu.com

If you are like me, you hate being in debt! Every month you watch, your money run out before the end of the month. You scrape around for fuel and grocery money, and then finally you hit the credit cards, hoping they hold sufficient funds. If you want to get out of this cycle of worry over debt, this book may be your answer. I say, "May," because although this book will definitely give you techniques for controlling, managing, and even getting out of debt altogether, it will not do the work for you. That will be up to you. This book will reveal how to destroy your debts, including your mortgage. It will also make clear to you how you can increase your income, and have confidence in your financial future. Your journey to financial freedom begins here.

The Practical Guide to Total Financial Freedom: Volume 1

Printed: 124 pages, 8.5 x 11.0 in, Perfect-bound
Download: PDF (7761 kb)
ISBN: 1-4116-2058-5
Copyright Year: © 2005 by Samuel Blankson
Language: English
Publisher: Lulu.com

The first part of a five volume series on creating Total Financial Freedom. In this volume, you will learn the foundations of wealth building, and how to secure your family and your wealth against disasters and losses. This series offers practical, effective, and easy to follow advice for securely and quickly building wealth. If you are thinking of buying this book, you probably want to be free. Free from the rat race, free from the boss, free from the wage trap, and free from the mediocrity and hopelessness of poverty and lack of options. Until now, you may have had no other way of achieving this within the next half a decade. This book will change all that forever. This book, unlike many self-help books out there, will actually tell you what to do in order to achieve Total Financial Freedom. You will find out exactly how I went about achieving Total Financial Freedom. If you read, learn, and apply the lessons in this book, you too will achieve Total Financial Freedom.

The Practical Guide to Total Financial Freedom: Volume 2

Printed: 173 pages, 8.5 x 11.0 in, Perfect-bound
Download: PDF (31040 kb)
ISBN: 1-4116-2057-7
Copyright Year: © 2005 by Samuel Blankson
Language: English
Publisher: Lulu.com

The second part of a five volume series on creating Total Financial Freedom. In this volume, you will learn how to invest in Bonds, Stocks and Shares, and Funds. This series offers practical, effective, and easy to follow advice for securely and quickly building wealth. If you are thinking of buying this book, you probably want to be free. Free from the rat race, free from the boss, free from the wage trap, and free from the mediocrity and hopelessness of poverty and lack of options. Until now, you may have had no other way of achieving this within the next half a decade. This book will change all that forever. This book, unlike many self-help books out there, will actually tell you what to do in order to achieve Total Financial Freedom. You will find out exactly how I went about achieving Total Financial Freedom. If you read, learn, and apply the lessons in this book, you too will achieve Total Financial Freedom.

The Practical Guide to Total Financial Freedom: Volume 3

Printed: 143 pages, 8.5 x 11.0 in, Perfect-bound
Download: PDF (1716 kb)
ISBN: 1-4116-2056-9
Copyright Year: © 2005 by Samuel Blankson
Language: English
Publisher: Lulu.com

The third part of a five volume series on creating Total Financial Freedom. In this volume, you will learn how to invest in En Primeur Wine, Real Estate, Businesses, Life Insurances, Art, and Offshore investment opportunities. This series offers practical, effective, and easy to follow advice for securely and quickly building wealth. If you are thinking of buying this book, you probably want to be free. Free from the rat race, free from the boss, free from the wage trap, and free from the mediocrity and hopelessness of poverty and lack of options. Until now, you may have had no other way of achieving this within the next half a decade. This book will change all that forever. This book, unlike many self-help books out there, will actually tell you what to do in order to achieve Total Financial Freedom. You will find out exactly how I went about achieving Total Financial Freedom. If you read, learn, and apply the lessons in this book, you too will achieve Total Financial Freedom.

The Practical Guide to Total Financial Freedom: Volume 4

Printed: 134 pages, 8.5 x 11.0 in, Perfect-bound
Download: PDF (3961 kb)
ISBN: 1-4116-2055-0
Copyright Year: © 2005 by Samuel Blankson
Language: English
Publisher: Lulu.com

The fourth part of a five volume series on creating Total Financial Freedom. In this volume, you will learn how to trade and invest in Momentum products. These instruments are high-risk products that offer high returns, but also the possibilities of high losses. You will learn how to limit those losses by reducing the risk using effective and practical methods. Options, Futures, High Yield Investment Programs, and Gambling are some of the exciting topics covered in detail. This series offers practical, effective, and easy to follow advice for securely and quickly building wealth. This book, unlike many self-help books out there, will actually tell you what to do in order to achieve Total Financial Freedom. You will find out exactly how I went about achieving Total Financial Freedom. If you read, learn, and apply the lessons in this book, you too will achieve Total Financial Freedom.

The Practical Guide to Total Financial Freedom: Volume 5

Printed: 322 pages, 8.5 x 11.0 in, Perfect-bound
Download: PDF (7143 kb)
ISBN: 1-4116-2054-2
Copyright Year: © 2005 by Samuel Blankson
Language: English
Publisher: Lulu.com

The last part of a five volume series on creating Total Financial Freedom. In this volume, you will learn how to lower your taxes, avoid paying unfair and unnecessary taxes, and how to move offshore and pay no taxes at all. This series offers practical, effective, and easy to follow advice for securely and quickly building wealth. If you are thinking of buying this book, you probably want to be free. Free from the rat race, free from the boss, free from the wage trap, and free from the mediocrity and hopelessness of poverty and lack of options. Until now, you may have had no other way of achieving this within the next half a decade. This book will change all that forever. This book, unlike many self-help books out there, will actually tell you what to do in order to achieve Total Financial Freedom. You will find out exactly how I went about achieving Total Financial Freedom. If you read, learn, and apply the lessons in this book, you too will achieve Total Financial Freedom.

Living the Ultimate Truth, 2nd Edition

Printed: 166 pages, 6.0 x 9.0 in, Perfect-bound
Download: PDF (855 kb)
ISBN: 1-4116-2375-4
Copyright Year: © 2005 by Samuel Blankson
Language: English
Publisher: Lulu.com

Today most people live a poor example of a balanced life. The centuries of wisdom passed down from the great leaders of our past seem lost amid lives centred on minutia and selfishness. Today we care more about what we wear and where we are seen, than we do about discovering and Living the Ultimate Truth. Throughout the world, there is an imbalance in people's spirituality, consciousness, and inner harmony. This has taken a great toll on our environment, our health, and our happiness. Many are wondering around like lost sheep, seeking a shepherd in all the wrong places. Many false prophets have promised quick fixes to these problems, but if these solutions are not firmly rooted in The Creator, love, integrity and inner harmony, they are doomed to fail. This book is a reminder of all those virtues and universal principles that we need, to return to a balanced, harmonious, and happy life. You will learn to love yourself, love others, and finally find that inner peace you seek through spiritual growth.

Developing Personal Integrity, 2nd Edition

Printed: 118 pages, 6.0 x 9.0 in, Perfect-bound
Download: PDF (627 kb)
ISBN: 1-4116-2376-2
Copyright Year: © 2005 by Samuel Blankson
Language: English
Publisher: Lulu.com

In the field of human character development, integrity is the last frontier. Many people use the word, but few really know what real integrity is. This book breaks down the fundamental components of personal integrity and offers a path to attaining it. Like success or happiness, integrity is a journey not a destination. We can only measure how far on the path we are through the observation of our inner voice, the voice of our conscience, and through deep contemplation and reflection. This journey of personal excellence is not an easy one, and as a friend once said, "When peeling this onion, sometimes you cry." Nevertheless, in all great endeavours, the harder the struggle, the greater the victory will be.

The Guide to Real Estate Investing

Printed: 117 pages, 6.0 x 9.0 in, Perfect-bound
Download: PDF (723 kb)
ISBN: 1-4116-2383-5
Copyright Year: © 2005 by Samuel Blankson
Language: English
Publisher: Lulu.com

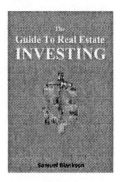

If you have ever wanted to know how to make money from real estate, but could never find one source that listed and explained all the different options available to you, then your search is over. This book covers over 20 different ways of investing in real estate. You will find the author's style easy to understand and very practical. The section on self-build is so in-depth, that after reading it you will actually know how to build a house, and the section on REITs, Indexes, and REIT Options will leave your mind boggling at the potential profits available to you. This book also covers the conversional and popular methods of real estate investing as well. Therefore, whether you want to learn to develop real estate projects, build your own home, or simply rent a room in your house, this book will help you maximise your success and avoid the pitfalls.

Making Money with Funds

Printed: 79 pages, 6.0 x 9.0 in., Perfect-bound
Download: PDF (8769 kb)
ISBN: 1-4116-2671-0
Copyright Year: © 2005 by Samuel Blankson
Language: English
Publisher: Lulu.com

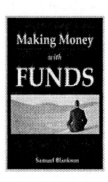

Today the world fund market is a multi trillion-dollar industry. There are many types of funds and as many reasons for choosing them. In this book, you will learn how Funds work, and how you, can make money with them.

How to make a fortune on the Stock Markets

Printed: 190 pages, 8.5 x 11.0 in, Perfect-bound
Download: PDF (8769 kb)
ISBN: 1-4116-2379-7
Copyright Year: © 2005 by Samuel Blankson
Language: English
Publisher: Lulu.com

This book contains simple but effective techniques for achieving regular and consistent profits from stock trading. Unlike other books on the topic, it is not full of theory and projections, but practical advice learned the hard way, by trading personal hard-earned cash daily in the world's stock exchanges. Moreover, unlike other books on the subject, it is not about how to be a stock trader and trade other people's money, but on how to grow your own funds to a level where you will never have to work for anyone else again. This book contains real techniques used by the author to amass a fortune significant enough to have made him Financially Free. Now you too can use these simple but highly effective techniques to achieve the same results. Therefore, whether you are a professional trader or a total beginner, this book will show you how to achieve Financial Freedom through trading Stocks and Shares.

How to make a fortune with Options trading

Printed: 59 pages, 8.5 x 11.0 in, Perfect-bound
Download: PDF (1808 kb)
ISBN: 1-4116-2378-9
Copyright Year: © 2005 by Samuel Blankson
Language: English
Publisher: Lulu.com

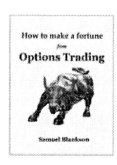

This is a practical book on winning in the Options trading market. Whether you are a sophisticated investor or a complete novice, this book is for you. The author takes complex ideas, and explains them in a way that is both practical and easily understood by anyone. Having used these techniques to achieve financial freedom, Mr Blankson now shares with you how he did it. There is no waffling here, just plain speaking and powerful techniques that anyone can apply.

Tax Avoidance A practical guide for UK residents

Printed: 104 pages, 6.0 x 9.0 in, Perfect-bound
Download: PDF (355 kb)
ISBN: 1-4116-2380-0
Copyright Year: © 2005 by Samuel Blankson
Language: English
Publisher: Lulu.com

UK residents pay some of the highest taxes in the world. Most of these taxes are hidden through VAT and service charges. This guide clearly explains what taxes you are paying, and which ones you can and should avoid paying through claiming your allowed deductions and allowances. Prudent tax efficient estate planning is explained in detail, and hundreds of tax saving ideas are shared within these pages. Whether you are a qualified accountant or a non-professional, you will find this little guide an invaluable source of tax saving ideas and strategies.

The Ultimate Guide to Offshore Tax Havens

Printed: 418 pages, 8.5 x 11.0 in, Perfect-bound
Download: PDF (12602 kb)
ISBN: 1-4116-2384-3
Copyright Year: © 2005 by Samuel Blankson
Language: English
Publisher: Lulu.com

This book is a detailed listing of all the known and not so commonly known Tax Havens, their benefits, and their suitability for relocation by the low tax seeker. If you are looking for ways to cut your taxes, there is no better way than to relocate to a low or no tax haven. The South East Asian Tsunamis and earthquakes have shown us that it is prudent to select the haven you will reside in carefully. Low taxes cannot be your only gauge for this task. This book will help you make that decision.

A must read for all who aspire to changing their lifestyles by relocating offshore. The havens are listed in geographical order, starting with the USA and ending with the South Pacific Islands.

Attitude

Printed: 418 pages, 6.0 x 9.0 in, Perfect-bound
Download: PDF (13700 kb)
ISBN: 1-4116-2382-7
Copyright Year: © 2005 by Samuel Blankson
Language: English
Publisher: Lulu.com

Attitude, so often misunderstood, yet so vital for success in every aspect of our lives. A positive attitude will guarantee happiness in your life, promotion and growth in your career or job, peace and joy in your family life, and in addition, a positive attitude has been scientifically proven to help extend your life expectancy. In this book, this essential success attribute is explained in detail. You will learn how to safeguard against positive attitude erosion, and learn how to build a positive mental attitude to help you achieve measurable success in every aspect of your life.

How to win at Greyhound betting

Printed: 68 pages, 8.5 x 11.0 in, Perfect-bound
Download: PDF (639 kb)
ISBN: 1-4116-2377-0
Copyright Year: © 2005 by Samuel Blankson
Language: English
Publisher: Lulu.com

Today, sports betting is a big industry for the bookmakers and organisers. Of all the people who benefit from sports racing, the "punters" (or in this case, you), are the last on the list of people who consistently gain. In fact, the greyhounds probably gain more from these races than most punters. Why is that? Well, there are many reasons, but most of them centre on these two things: lack of a proven system, and greed. This book closely examines these two points, and offers techniques and systems for achieving consistent wins in greyhound betting.

The Ultimate Greyhound Betting System

Download: MS Excel (233 kb)
Copyright Year: © 2005 by Samuel Blankson
Language: English
Publisher: Lulu.com

If you think there is no trustworthy betting system out there, then prepare to be proven wrong. This is the betting system described in the series *The Practical Guide to Total Financial Freedom,* and the book *How to win at Greyhound betting.* This semi-automatic system allows its user to achieve a minimum of 30% profits per week by following a proven statistical and rule based system betting on UK Greyhound races. The system only requires you to supply the race results and place the bets with your bookmaker. Armed with this incredible system, you will be able to beat the odds, and win one over the bookmakers.

How to Win at Online Roulette

Printed: 81 pages, 6.0 x 9.0 in, Perfect-bound
ISBN: 1-4116-2570-6
Copyright Year: © 2005 by Samuel Blankson
Language: English
Publisher: Lulu.com

This is a guide to consistently winning at online Roulette. It is a simple and to the point writing about an amazing system for gaining an advantage at online Casinos. This book will show you how to make £1000 per day or more from online Roulette.

Sixty Original Song Lyrics

Printed: 200 pages, 6.0 x 9.0 in, Perfect-bound
Download: PDF (1072 kb)
ISBN: 1-4116-2059-3
Copyright Year: © 2004 by Samuel Blankson
Language: English
Publisher: Lulu.com

This is a compilation of original song lyrics by Samuel Blankson. This book contains 60 of the songs he wrote in between 2000 – 2002. Having had some of these lyrics made into songs for an album (see *www.practicalbooks.org*), and several of them now on compilations, Samuel now shares these 60 song lyrics with you.

Images of Kilimanjaro

Printed: 26 pages, 11 x 8.5 in, Coil-bound
Start Date: January 1st, 2006
Duration: 12 months
Copyright Year: © 2004 by Samuel Blankson
Language: English
Publisher: Lulu.com

Kilimanjaro, the tallest freestanding mountain in the world, is captured here for you to feast your eyes on each month through 2006. Kilimanjaro is a source of life for Tanzania and Kenya locals, who live on its life giving rains and water. I had the honour of climbing this majestic mountain, and captured the essence of its allure and mystery through these pictures.

Images of Kilimanjaro

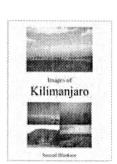

Printed: 53 pages, 8.5 x 11.0 in, Perfect-bound
Download: PDF (2573 kb)
ISBN: 1-4116-2016-X
Copyright Year: © 2004
Language: English
Publisher: Lulu.com

This is a book of pictures taken from Kilimanjaro. This is an accompanying book to the Calendar of the same name.

Uju

Download: MPG (6523 kb)
UPC: 4-3157-3526-2
Copyright Year: © 2004 by Samuel and Uju Blankson
Language: English
Publisher: Lulu.com

A six track EP with soulful R&B tracks with a pop flavour. This EP is bound to have you humming along addictively. For more info about the artist Uju, visit *www.uju-music.com* and look out for her forthcoming album.

The Bass by Samuel Blankson

Download: MPG (4811 kb)
Copyright Year: © 2004 by Samuel and Uju Blankson
Language: English
Publisher: Lulu.com

A sexy, R&B track with wicked beats and a deep baseline. With a melody and chorus that will stay with you for a long time, this addictive and catchy tune deserves your download (see *www.practicalbooks.org*).

Investing in En Primeur Wine

Printed: 88 pages, 6.0 x 9.0 in, Perfect-bound
Download: PDF (1,095 kb)
ISBN: 1-4116-2867-5
Copyright Year: © 2005
Language: English
Publisher: Lulu.com

Wine investing is not new, it has been going on for centuries. In more recent years (the last two centuries), government tax laws on alcoholic drinks have made buying wine a little more prohibitive to the investor who wants to keep them at home in his/her private cellar. Nevertheless, as usual, the market has found a way around this problem.

You can avoid taxes and V.A.T. (Value Added Tax) by buying fine wine on Bond (also called wine Futures or En Primeur). This book covers a simple and effective way in which anybody coming into the fine wine investing market place can safely securely and successfully select, and invest in En Primeur Wine.

Eight Steps to Success

Printed: 105 pages, 6.0 x 9.0 in, Perfect-bound
Download: PDF (1,095 kb)
ISBN: 1-4116-2738-5
Copyright Year: © 2005
Language: English
Publisher: Lulu.com

We would all like to live a successful life, a life where our relationships and finances are a source of happiness and joy. This life is attainable by following timeless success principles. These principles have been forgotten by our fast food, fast-paced, reality TV society.

This book defines, explains, and shows you how to apply these principles and skills in your life to attain happiness, contentment, peace, joy, and prosperity. The eight fundamental virtues and skills required to succeed long-term in any endeavour, are explained in detail and in a style that everyone can understand and immediately apply.

The Eight Steps to Success is an inspirational book that will help you understand, acquire, hone, and apply the principles of success.

Taking Action

Printed: 105 pages, 6.0 x 9.0 in, Perfect-bound
Download: PDF (1,095 kb)
ISBN: 1-4116-2735-0
Copyright Year: © 2005
Language: English
Publisher: Lulu.com

This is a book about taking action. For some, taking action means something you will do, might do, should do, have done, or never will do. This book will show you how to change your understanding of taking action to mean something you are doing NOW! When you change this focus in your life, you will release great powers. This book will show you how to tap into this phenomenal power and change your life.

About The Author

An entrepreneur at heart, Samuel Blankson blends art, creativity, passion, business acumen, and financial expertise with careful planning and execution in the achievement of measurable results. He is an avid reader, writer, researcher, and securities trader.

He is an advocate of self-empowerment and an individual's ability to control their destiny through the achievement of personal freedom from economic, financial, spiritual, social, mental, and interrelationship restrictions. Samuel is constantly working to push the boundaries of personal achievements to their limits, recognising that these limits are only self-imposed.

Samuel has authored over twenty books (*How to Destroy Your Debts*, *Living the Ultimate Truth*, *Developing Personal Integrity*, *The Practical Guide to Total Financial Freedom* volumes 1, 2, 3, 4 and 5, and *Attitude* are some of these works). He has written over 100 songs, sixty of which are featured in *Sixty Original Song Lyrics*. He writes poetry, creates artwork, and works daily to express his creativity in many ways.

Having successfully run several businesses, Samuel diversified into securities trading over a decade ago, with great success. After learning from the masters of the time, Samuel progressed to develop his own methods and systems for successful trading. Today, he trades many financial instruments and has developed ways of successfully generating profits from his many investments.

A firm believer in knowledge sharing, Samuel travels the globe, teaching and sharing his personal knowledge with groups of friends, associates, and anyone who seeks to improve their life. This is the spirit of Samuel Blankson, a God centred philanthropist, overcomer, and high achiever.

Printed in the United States
58501LVS00006B/78

9 781411 623842